COMMON CORE MATHEMATICS

A Story of Units

Grade 3, Module 5: Fractions as Numbers on the Number Line

consider the source

ℬ JOSSEY-BASS™
A Wiley Brand

WELCOME

Dear Teacher,

Thank you for your interest in Common Core's curriculum in mathematics. Common Core is a non-profit organization based in Washington, DC dedicated to helping K-12 public schoolteachers use the power of high-quality content to improve instruction.[1] We are led by a board of master teachers, scholars, and current and former school, district, and state education leaders. Common Core has responded to the Common Core State Standards' (CCSS) call for "content-rich curriculum"[2] by creating new, CCSS-based curriculum materials in mathematics, English Language Arts, history, and (soon) the arts. All of our materials are written by teachers who are among the nation's foremost experts on the new standards.

In 2012 Common Core won three contracts from the New York State Education Department to create a PreKindergarten–12th grade mathematics curriculum for the teachers of that state, and to conduct associated professional development. The book you hold contains a portion of that work. In order to respond to demand in New York and elsewhere, modules of the curriculum will continue to be published, on a rolling basis, as they are completed. This curriculum is based on New York's version of the CCSS (the CCLS, or Common Core Learning Standards). Common Core will be releasing an enhanced version of the curriculum this summer on our website, commoncore.org. That version also will be published by Jossey-Bass, a Wiley brand.

Common Core's curriculum materials are not merely aligned to the new standards, they take the CCSS as their very foundation. Our work in math takes its shape from the expectations embedded in the new standards—including the instructional shifts and mathematical progressions, and the new expectations for student fluency, deep conceptual understanding, and application to real-life context. Similarly, our ELA and history curricula are deeply informed by the CCSS's new emphasis on close reading, increased use of informational text, and evidence-based writing.

Our curriculum is distinguished not only by its adherence to the CCSS. The math curriculum is based on a theory of teaching math that is proven to work. That theory posits that mathematical knowledge is most coherently and

1. Despite the coincidence of name, Common Core and the Common Core State Standards are not affiliated. Common Core was established in 2007, prior to the start of the Common Core State Standards Initiative, which was led by the National Governors Association and the Council for Chief State School Officers.
2. *Common Core State Standards for English Language Arts & Literacy in History/Social Studies, Science, and Technical Subjects* (Washington, DC: Common Core State Standards Initiative), 6.

effectively conveyed when it is taught in a sequence that follows the "story" of mathematics itself. This is why we call the elementary portion of this curriculum "A Story of Units," to be followed by "A Story of Ratios" in middle school, and "A Story of Functions" in high school. Mathematical concepts flow logically, from one to the next, in this curriculum. The sequencing has been joined with methods of instruction that have been proven to work, in this nation and abroad. These methods drive student understanding beyond process, to deep mastery of mathematical concepts. The goal of the curriculum is to produce students who are not merely literate, but fluent, in mathematics.

It is important to note that, as extensive as these curriculum materials are, they are not meant to be prescriptive. Rather, they are intended to provide a basis for teachers to hone their own craft through study, collaboration, training, and the application of their own expertise as professionals. At Common Core we believe deeply in the ability of teachers and in their central and irreplaceable role in shaping the classroom experience. We strive only to support and facilitate their important work.

The teachers and scholars who wrote these materials are listed beginning on the next page. Their deep knowledge of mathematics, of the CCSS, and of what works in classrooms defined this work in every respect. I would like to thank Louisiana State University professor of mathematics Scott Baldridge for the intellectual leadership he provides to this project. Teacher, trainer, and writer Robin Ramos is the most inspired math educator I've ever encountered. It is Robin and Scott's aspirations for what mathematics education in America *should* look like that is spelled out in these pages.

Finally, this work owes a debt to project director Nell McAnelly that is so deep I'm confident it never can be repaid. Nell, who leads LSU's Gordon A. Cain Center for STEM Literacy, oversees all aspects of our work for NYSED. She has spent days, nights, weekends, and many cancelled vacations toiling in her efforts to make it possible for this talented group of teacher-writers to produce their best work against impossible deadlines. I'm confident that in the years to come Scott, Robin, and Nell will be among those who will deserve to be credited with putting math instruction in our nation back on track.

Thank you for taking an interest in our work. Please join us at www.commoncore.org.

Lynne Munson
President and Executive Director
Common Core
Washington, DC
October 25, 2013

Common Core's K-5 Math Staff

Scott Baldridge, Lead Mathematician and Writer
Robin Ramos, Lead Writer, PreKindergarten-5
Jill Diniz, Lead Writer, 6-12
Ben McCarty, Mathematician

Nell McAnelly, Project Director
Tiah Alphonso, Associate Director
Jennifer Loftin, Associate Director
Catriona Anderson, Curriculum Manager, PreKindergarten-5

Sherri Adler, PreKindergarten
Debbie Andorka-Aceves, PreKindergarten

Kate McGill Austin, Kindergarten
Nancy Diorio, Kindergarten
Lacy Endo-Peery, Kindergarten
Melanie Gutierrez, Kindergarten
Nuhad Jamal, Kindergarten
Cecilia Rudzitis, Kindergarten
Shelly Snow, Kindergarten

Beth Barnes, First Grade
Lily Cavanaugh, First Grade
Ana Estela, First Grade
Kelley Isinger, First Grade
Kelly Spinks, First Grade
Marianne Strayton, First Grade
Hae Jung Yang, First Grade

Wendy Keehfus-Jones, Second Grade
Susan Midlarsky, Second Grade
Jenny Petrosino, Second Grade
Colleen Sheeron, Second Grade
Nancy Sommer, Second Grade
Lisa Watts-Lawton, Second Grade
MaryJo Wieland, Second Grade
Jessa Woods, Second Grade

Eric Angel, Third Grade
Greg Gorman, Third Grade
Susan Lee, Third Grade
Cristina Metcalf, Third Grade
Ann Rose Santoro, Third Grade
Kevin Tougher, Third Grade
Victoria Peacock, Third Grade
Saffron VanGalder, Third Grade

Katrina Abdussalaam, Fourth Grade
Kelly Alsup, Fourth Grade
Patti Dieck, Fourth Grade
Mary Jones, Fourth Grade
Soojin Lu, Fourth Grade
Tricia Salerno, Fourth Grade
Gail Smith, Fourth Grade
Eric Welch, Fourth Grade
Sam Wertheim, Fourth Grade
Erin Wheeler, Fourth Grade

Leslie Arceneaux, Fifth Grade
Adam Baker, Fifth Grade
Janice Fan, Fifth Grade
Peggy Golden, Fifth Grade
Halle Kananak, Fifth Grade
Shauntina Kerrison, Fifth Grade
Pat Mohr, Fifth Grade
Chris Sarlo, Fifth Grade

Additional Writers

Bill Davidson, Fluency Specialist
Robin Hecht, UDL Specialist
Simon Pfeil, Mathematician

Document Management Team

Tam Le, Document Manager
Jennifer Merchan, Copy Editor

Common Core

3 GRADE

Mathematics Curriculum

Table of Contents

GRADE 3 • MODULE 5

Fractions as Numbers on the Number Line

Grade 3 • Module 5

Fractions as Numbers on the Number Line

OVERVIEW

In this 35-day Grade 3 module, students extend and deepen Grade 2 practice with equal shares to understanding fractions as equal partitions of a whole (**2.G.3**). Their knowledge becomes more formal as they work with area models and the number line.

Topic A opens Module 5 with students actively partitioning different models of wholes into equal parts (e.g., concrete models, fraction strips, and drawn pictorial area models on paper). They identify and count equal parts as *1 half, 1 fourth, 1 third, 1 sixth,* and *1 eighth* in unit form before an introduction to the unit fraction $1/b$ (**3.NF.1**). In Topic B, students compare unit fractions and learn to build non-unit fractions with unit fractions as basic building blocks (**3.NF.3d**). This parallels the understanding that the number 1 is the basic building block of whole numbers. In Topic C, students practice comparing unit fractions with fraction strips, specifying the whole and labeling fractions in relation to the number of equal parts in that whole (**3.NF.3d**).

Students transfer their work to the number line in Topic D. They begin by using the interval from 0 to 1 as the whole. Continuing beyond the first interval, they partition, place, count, and compare fractions on the number line (**3.NF.2a, 3.NF.2b, 3.NF.3d**). In Topic E, they notice that some fractions with different units are placed at the exact same point on the number line, and therefore are equal (**3.NF.3a**). For example, 1/2, 2/4, 3/6, and 4/8 are equivalent fractions (**3.NF.3b**). Students recognize that whole numbers can be written as fractions, as exemplified on the number lines below (**3.NF.3c**).

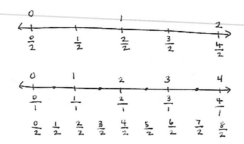

Topic F concludes the module with comparing fractions that have the same numerator. As they compare fractions by reasoning about their size, students understand that fractions with the same numerator and a larger denominator are actually smaller pieces of the whole (**3.NF.3d**). Topic F leaves students with a new method for precisely partitioning a number line into unit fractions of any size without using a ruler.

Distribution of Instructional Minutes

This diagram represents a suggested distribution of instructional minutes based on the emphasis of particular lesson components in different lessons throughout the module.

- ■ Fluency Practice
- ☐ Concept Development
- ▨ Application Problems
- ■ Student Debrief

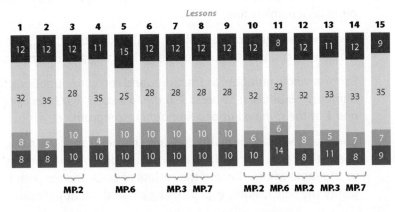

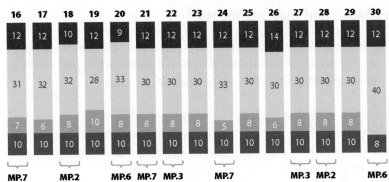

MP = Mathematical Practice

Focus Grade Level Standards

Develop understanding of fractions as numbers.

3.NF.1 Understand a fraction 1/b as the quantity formed by 1 part when a whole is partitioned into b equal parts; understand a fraction a/b as the quantity formed by a parts of size 1/b.

3.NF.2 Understand a fraction as a number on the number line; represent fractions on a number line diagram.

     a. Represent a fraction 1/b on a number line diagram by defining the interval from 0 to 1 as the whole and partitioning it into b equal parts. Recognize that each part has size 1/b and that the endpoint of the part based at 0 locates the number 1/b on the number line.

     b. Represent a fraction a/b on a number line diagram by marking off a lengths 1/b from 0. Recognize that the resulting interval has size a/b and that its endpoint locates the number a/b on the number line.

3.NF.3 Explain equivalence of fractions in special cases, and compare fractions by reasoning about their size.

    a.   Understand two fractions as equivalent (equal) if they are the same size, or the same point on a number line.

    b.   Recognize and generate simple equivalent fractions, e.g., 1/2 = 2/4, 4/6 = 2/3). Explain why the fractions are equivalent, e.g., by using a visual fraction model.

    c.   Express whole numbers as fractions, and recognize fractions that are equivalent to whole numbers. *Examples: Express 3 in the form of 3 = 3/1; recognize that 6/1 = 6; locate 4/4 and 1 at the same point of a number line diagram.*

    d.   Compare two fractions with the same numerator or the same denominator by reasoning about their size. Recognize that comparisons are valid only when the two fractions refer to the same whole. Record the results of comparisons with the symbols >, =, or <, and justify the conclusions, e.g., by using a visual fraction model.

Reason with shapes and their attributes.[1]

3.G.2   Partition shapes into parts with equal areas. Express the area of each part as a unit fraction of the whole. *For example, partition a shape into 4 parts with equal area and describe the area of each part as 1/4 of the area of the shape.*

Foundational Standards

2.G.2   Partition a rectangle into rows and columns of same-size squares and count to find the total number of them.

2.G.3   Partition circles and rectangles into two, three, or four equal shares, describe the shares using the words *halves, thirds, half of, a third of*, etc., and describe the whole as two halves, three thirds, four fourths. Recognize that equal shares of identical wholes need not have the same shape.

2.MD.3   Estimate lengths using units of inches, feet, centimeters, and meters.

---

[1] 3.G.1 is taught in Module 7.

	Module 5:	Fractions as Numbers on the Number Line
	Date:	11/19/13

Focus Standards for Mathematical Practice

MP.2   **Reason abstractly and quantitatively.** Students represent fractions concretely, pictorially, and abstractly and move back and forth between representations. Students also represent word problems involving fractions pictorially and then express the answer in the context of the problem.

MP.3   **Construct viable arguments and critique the reasoning of others.** Students reason about the area of a shaded region to decide what fraction of the whole it represents.

MP.6   **Attend to precision.** Students specify the whole amount when referring to a unit fraction and explain what is meant by *equal parts* in their own words.

MP.7   **Look for and make use of structure.** Students understand and use the unit fraction as the basic building block or structure of all fractions on the number line.

Overview of Module Topics and Lesson Objectives

Standards		Topics and Objectives	Days
3.G.2 3.NF.1	A	**Partitioning a Whole into Equal Parts** Lesson 1: Specify and partition a whole into equal parts, identifying and counting unit fractions using concrete models. Lesson 2: Specify and partition a whole into equal parts, identifying and counting unit fractions by folding fraction strips. Lesson 3: Specify and partition a whole into equal parts, identifying and counting unit fractions by drawing pictorial area models. Lesson 4: Represent and identify fractional parts of different wholes.	4
3.NF.1 3.NF.3c 3.G.2	B	**Unit Fractions and their Relation to the Whole** Lesson 5: Partition a whole into equal parts and define the equal parts to identify the unit fraction numerically. Lesson 6: Build non-unit fractions less than one whole from unit fractions. Lesson 7: Identify and represent shaded and non-shaded parts of one whole as fractions. Lesson 8: Represent parts of one whole as fractions with number bonds. Lesson 9: Build and write fractions greater than one whole using unit fractions.	5
3.NF.3d 3.NF.1 3.NF.3a 3.NF.3b 3.NF.3c 3.G.2	C	**Comparing Unit Fractions and Specifying the Whole** Lesson 10: Compare unit fractions by reasoning about their size using fraction strips. Lesson 11: Compare unit fractions with different sized models representing the whole. Lesson 12: Specify the corresponding whole when presented with one equal part. Lesson 13: Identify a shaded fractional part in different ways depending on the designation of the whole.	4
		Mid-Module Assessment: Topics A–C (assessment 1 day, return 1 day, remediation or further applications 1 day)	3

Standards		Topics and Objectives	Days
3.NF.2a **3.NF.2b** **3.NF.3c** **3.NF.3d** 3.MD.4	D	**Fractions on the Number Line** Lesson 14: Place unit fractions on a number line with endpoints 0 and 1. Lesson 15: Place any fraction on a number line with endpoints 0 and 1. Lesson 16: Place whole number fractions and unit fractions between whole numbers on the number line. Lesson 17: Practice placing various fractions on the number line. Lesson 18: Compare fractions and whole numbers on the number line by reasoning about their distance from 0. Lesson 19: Understand distance and position on the number line as strategies for comparing fractions. (Optional.)	6
3.NF.3a **3.NF.3b** **3.NF.3c**	E	**Equivalent Fractions** Lesson 20: Recognize and show that equivalent fractions have the same size, though not necessarily the same shape. Lesson 21: Recognize and show that equivalent fractions refer to the same point on the number line. Lessons 22–23: Generate simple equivalent fractions by using visual fraction models and the number line. Lesson 24: Express whole numbers as fractions and recognize equivalence with different units. Lesson 25: Express whole number fractions on the number line when the unit interval is 1. Lesson 26: Decompose whole number fractions greater than 1 using whole number equivalence with various models. Lesson 27: Explain equivalence by manipulating units and reasoning about their size.	8
3.NF.3d	F	**Comparison, Order, and Size of Fractions** Lesson 28: Compare fractions with the same numerator pictorially. Lesson 29: Compare fractions with the same numerator using <, >, or = and use a model to reason about their size. Lesson 30: Partition various wholes precisely into equal parts using a number line method.	3
		End-of-Module Assessment: Topics A–F (assessment 1 day, return 1 day, remediation or further applications 1 day)	3

Standards	Topics and Objectives	Days
	Total Number of Instructional Days	**35**

Terminology

New or Recently Introduced Terms

- Unit fraction (fractions with numerator 1)
- Non-unit fraction (fractions with numerators other than 1)
- Fractional unit (half, third, fourth, etc.)
- Equal parts (parts with equal measurements)
- Unit interval (the interval from 0 to 1, measured by length)
- Equivalent fraction (2 fractions that name the same size)
- Copies (refers to the number of unit fractions in 1 whole)

Familiar Terms and Symbols[2]

- Number line
- Arrays
- Halves, thirds, fourths, sixths, eighths (1/2, 1/3, 1/4, 1/6, 1/8)
- Half of, one third of, one fourth of, etc. (1/2, 1/3, 1/4, 1/6, 1/8)
- =, <, > (equal, less than, greater than)
- Equal shares (pieces of a whole that are the same size)
- Whole (e.g., 2 halves, 3 thirds, etc.)
- Fraction (e.g., 1/3, 2/3, 3/3, 4/3)
- Partition (divide a whole into equal parts)

Suggested Tools and Representations

- Number line
- Tape diagram
- Arrays
- Concrete area models (e.g., water, string, clay)
- Pictorial area model (e.g., drawing of a circle or square)
- Fraction strips (made from paper, used to fold and model parts of a whole)
- Beaker
- 12 oz clear plastic cups

---

[2] These are terms and symbols students have used or seen previously.

- Food coloring (to color water)
- Rulers
- 12" × 1" strips of yellow construction paper
- 2" × 6" strips of brown construction paper
- $4\frac{1}{4}$" × 1" paper strips
- 4" × 4" orange squares
- Partition shapes into fractional parts
- Rectangular and circle shaped paper
- 1 m length of yarn
- 200 g ball of clay or playdough
   Sets of <, >, = cards

Scaffolds[3]

The scaffolds integrated into *A Story of Units* give alternatives for how students access information as well as express and demonstrate their learning. Strategically placed margin notes are provided within each lesson elaborating on the use of specific scaffolds at applicable times. They address many needs presented by English language learners, students with disabilities, students performing above grade level, and students performing below grade level. Many of the suggestions are organized by Universal Design for Learning (UDL) principles and are applicable to more than one population. To read more about the approach to differentiated instruction in *A Story of Units,* please refer to "How to Implement *A Story of Units.*"

Assessment Summary

Type	Administered	Format	Standards Addressed
Mid-Module Assessment Task	After Topic C	Constructed response with rubric	3.G.2 3.NF.1 3.NF.3c 3.NF.3d
End-of-Module Assessment Task	After Topic F	Constructed response with rubric	3.NF.2a 3.NF.2b 3.NF.3a 3.NF.3b 3.NF.3c 3.NF.3d

---

[3] Students with disabilities may require Braille, large print, audio, or special digital files. Please visit the website, www.p12.nysed.gov/specialed/aim, for specific information on how to obtain student materials that satisfy the National Instructional Materials Accessibility Standard (NIMAS) format.

Module 5:   Fractions as Numbers on the Number Line
Date: 11/19/13

ix

Topic A

Partition a Whole into Equal Parts

3.G.2, 3.NF.1

Focus Standard:	3.G.2	Partition shapes into parts with equal areas. Express the area of each part as a unit fraction of the whole. *For example, partition a shape into 4 parts with equal area and describe the area of each part as 1/4 of the area of the shape.*
Instructional Days:	4	
Coherence -Links from:	G2–M7	Time, Shapes, and Fractions as Equal Parts of Shapes
-Links to:	G4–M5	Fraction Equivalence, Ordering, and Operations

In Topic A, students partition a whole using a ruler to precisely measure equal parts. They then use a cup to measure equal parts of water. From there, students are invited to fold fraction strips, and estimate to draw pictorial models. The topic culminates in an exploration wherein they model a designated fraction with a meter string, 12 ounces of water, 200 grams of clay, a 4" × 4" square, a 12" × 1" strip, and a 6" × 2" strip. Students then tour the fraction displays created by their peers and analyze their observations. They specify that the whole has a certain number of equal parts.

A Teaching Sequence Towards Mastery of Partitioning a Whole into Equal Parts
Objective 1: Specify and partition a whole into equal parts, identifying and counting unit fractions using concrete models.   **(Lesson 1)**
Objective 2: Specify and partition a whole into equal parts, identifying and counting unit fractions by folding fraction strips.   **(Lesson 2)**
Objective 3: Specify and partition a whole into equal parts, identifying and counting unit fraction by drawing pictorial area models.   **(Lesson 3)**
Objective 4: Represent and identify fractional parts of different wholes.   **(Lesson 4)**

Lesson 1

Objective: Specify and partition a whole into equal parts, identifying and counting unit fractions using concrete models.

Suggested Lesson Structure

■ Fluency Practice   (12 minutes)
■ Application Problem   (8 minutes)
■ Concept Development   (32 minutes)
■ Student Debrief   (8 minutes)
  Total Time   **(60 minutes)**

Fluency Practice (12 minutes)

- Skip Counting by Four and Eight **3.OA.4**   (6 minutes)
- Multiplication by Four and Eight **3.OA.4**   (6 minutes)

Skip Counting by Four and Eight (6 minutes)

Materials: (S) Personal white boards (use if students struggle to answer verbally)

By Fours:

Skip count forward and backward by fours two times with a pause between each effort so students see themselves improve on the second try. After doing the fours twice, have students underline the multiples of 8. (e.g., 0, 4, 8, 12, 16, 20, 24, 28, 32, 36, 40, 36, 32, 28, 24, 20, 16, 12, 8, 4, 0)

By Eights:

Skip count forward and backward by eights two times with a pause between each effort to analyze weak points.

2 x 4 = 8	2 x 8 = 16
3 x 4 = 12	3 x 8 = 24
4 x 4 = 16	4 x 8 = 32

Multiplication by Four and Eight (6 minutes)

Choose your mode of delivery (e.g., oral work, personal white board, etc.). Have students pair facts of 4 and 8 and uncover the doubling.

Lesson 1:	Specify and partition a whole into equal parts, identifying and counting unit fractions using concrete models.	5.A.2
Date:	11/19/13	

Application Problem (8 minutes)

Measure the length of your paper or math textbook using a ruler. Your teacher will tell you whether to measure in inches or centimeters. (Assign partners different units.) After students complete the measurement on their own and compare their answer to their partner's, have them consider the following questions.

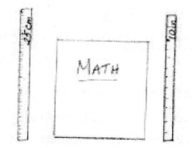

- Which is a larger unit, an inch or a centimeter?

- Therefore, which would yield a greater number when measuring the book, inches or centimeters?

- Measure at least 2 different items with your partner, again using different units. What do you notice?

- Change units with your partner. Measure different items again.

Concept Development (32 minutes)

Materials: (T) 1 clear plastic cup full of colored water, 2 other empty identical clear plastic cups, two 12" by 1" strips of yellow construction paper (S) Two 12" by 1" strips of yellow construction paper for each student, 12 inch rulers for each student

T: Measure your yellow strip of paper using inches. How long is it?

S: 12 inches.

T: Make a small mark at 6 inches at both the top and bottom of the strip. Connect the two points with a straight line.

T: (After students do so.) How many equal parts or units have I split the paper into now?

S: Two.

T: What fraction of the whole strip is one of the parts?

S: 1 half.

T: Point and count the halves with me.

S: 1 half, 2 halves. (Point to each half of the strip as students count "one half, two halves.")

T: Discuss with your partner how we know these parts are equal.

S: When I fold the strip along the line, the two sides match perfectly. → Because I measured and saw that each part was 6 inches long. → The whole strip is 12 inches long. 12 divided by 2 is six. → 6 times 2 or 6 plus 6 is 12, so they are equal in length.

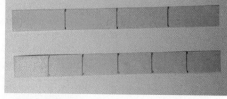

Lesson 1:   Specify and partition a whole into equal parts, identifying and counting unit fractions using concrete models.

Date: 11/19/13

5.A.3

Continue with fourths on the same strip followed by thirds and sixths on the second strip.

Fourths:

Repeat the same line of questioning as with measuring halves.

> T: Make a small mark at 3 inches and 9 inches at the top and bottom of your strip. Connect the two points with a straight line. How many equal parts do you have now?
>
> S: Four.
>
> T: Count the fourths.
>
> S: 1 fourth, 2 fourths, 3 fourths, 4 fourths.
>
> T: Discuss with your partner how you know that these parts are equal.

Thirds:

Again repeat the same line of questioning. Have the students mark off 4 inches and 8 inches at the top and bottom of their strips. Ask them to identify the fraction. Ask them how they know the parts are equal and then have them count the equal parts, "1 third, 2 thirds, 3 thirds".

Sixths:

Have the students mark off points at 2 inches, 6 inches and 10 inches. Repeat the same process as with halves, fourths, and thirds. Ask students to think about the relationship of the halves to the fourths and the thirds to the sixths.

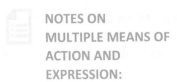

NOTES ON MULTIPLE MEANS OF ACTION AND EXPRESSION:

Some students may benefit from a review of how to use a ruler to measure. You might suggest the following:

1. Identify the zero mark on the ruler.

2. Line up the zero mark with the left end of the yellow paper strip.

3. Push down on the ruler as you make your mark.

Additionally, students who would like more of a challenge can think about how to find eighths.

> T: Just as we measured a whole strip of paper with a ruler to make halves, let's now measure precisely to make 2 equal parts of a whole amount of liquid.
>
> ▪ Present two identical glasses as below.

- ▪ The glass to the right has a mark about 1 fourth the way up the cup.
- ▪ Fill the cup to that mark as in the second image.
- ▪ Pour that amount of liquid into the cup on the left and mark off the top of that amount of liquid.

Lesson 1: Specify and partition a whole into equal parts, identifying and counting unit fractions using concrete models.

Date: 11/19/13

5.A.4

- Repeat the process. Fill the right hand cup again to the mark and pour it into the left hand cup.
- Mark off the top of that amount of liquid. The cup now shows precisely the markings for half the amount of water and the whole amount of water. Have the students share to discuss how they can be sure the middle mark shows half the liquid. Compare the yellow strip showing a whole partitioned into 2 equal parts and the blue liquid partitioned into 2 equal parts. Have the students discuss how they are the same and different.

Problem Set (10 minutes)

Students should do their personal best to complete the Problem Set within the allotted 10 minutes. Some problems do not specify a method for solving. This is an intentional reduction of scaffolding that invokes MP.5, Use Appropriate Tools Strategically. Students should solve these problems using the RDW approach used for Application Problems.

For some classes, it may be appropriate to modify the assignment by specifying which problems students should work on first. With this option, let the careful sequencing of the Problem Set guide your selections so that problems continue to be scaffolded. Balance word problems with other problem types to ensure a range of practice. Assign incomplete problems for homework or at another time during the day.

Student Debrief (8 minutes)

Lesson Objective: Specify and partition a whole into equal parts, identifying and counting unit fractions using concrete methods.

The Student Debrief is intended to invite reflection and active processing of the total lesson experience.

Invite students to review their solutions for the Problem Set. They should check work by comparing answers with a partner before going over answers as a class. Look for misconceptions or misunderstandings that can be

Name _____ Gina _____   Date _____

1. A beaker is considered full when the liquid reaches the fill line shown near the top. Estimate the amount of water in the beaker by shading the drawing as indicated. The first one is done for you.

1 half   1 fourth   1 third

2. Juanita cut her string cheese into equal pieces as shown in the rectangles below. In the blanks below, name the fraction of the string cheese represented by the shaded part.

I third

I sixth

I fourth

4. In the space below, draw a small rectangle. Split it into 2 equal parts. How many lines did you draw to make four equal parts? 1
→ I half
- Draw another small rectangle. Split it into 3 equal parts. How many lines did you draw to make 3 equal parts? 2
→ I third
- Draw another small rectangle. Split it into 4 equal parts. How many lines did you draw to make 4 equal parts? 3
→ I fourth

5. Each rectangle represents 1 sheet of paper. Estimate to show how you would cut the paper into fractional units as indicated below.

sevenths   ninths

- What do you notice? How many lines do you think you would draw to make a rectangle with 20 equal parts? 19

6. Rochelle has a strip of wood 12 inches long. She cuts it into pieces that are each 6 inches in length. What fraction of the wood is one piece? Use your yellow strip from the lesson to help you. Draw a picture to show the piece of wood and how Rochelle cut it.

cut
I half   I half

addressed in the Debrief. Guide students in a conversation to debrief the Problem Set and process the lesson.

You may choose to use any combination of the questions below to lead the discussion.

- Encourage students to use the words, "equal parts, fraction, the whole, half, fourths, thirds, sixths."
- The whole, the yellow strip never changes. What happened to the size of the equal parts when it was divided into more parts?
- In Problem 1, which was the harder fraction for you to draw well?
- Using our method with the cups, how could we make a cup that showed thirds?
- In Problem 2, what do you notice about the thirds and the sixths? When we made our measurements on the yellow strips, what did you remember about the measurement of 1 third of the strip and 1 sixth of the strip?
- In Problem 3, did you start drawing fourths by making a half? Can you do the same to draw eighths?
- Walk through the process explicitly of estimating to draw a half, then a half of a half to make fourths, etc.
- In Problem 4, describe to your partner how you can use an estimate of thirds to draw sixths.
- In Problems 5 and 6, let's look at two different solution strategies and compare them.

Exit Ticket (3 minutes)

After the Student Debrief, instruct students to complete the Exit Ticket. A review of their work will help you assess the students' understanding of the concepts that were presented in the lesson today and plan more effectively for future lessons. You may read the questions aloud to the students.

COMMON CORE

Lesson 1:   Specify and partition a whole into equal parts, identifying and
counting unit fractions using concrete models.

Date: 11/19/13

5.A.6

Name _____   Date _____

1. A beaker is considered full when the liquid reaches the fill line shown near the top. Estimate the amount of water in the beaker by shading the drawing as indicated. The first one is done for you.

   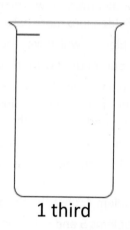

1 half   1 fourth   1 third

2. Juanita cut her string cheese into equal pieces as shown in the rectangles below. In the blanks below, name the fraction of the string cheese represented by the shaded part.

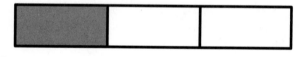   _____

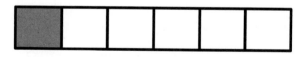   _____

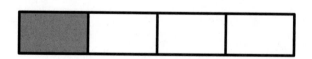   _____

COMMON CORE

Lesson 1:   Specify and partition a whole into equal parts, identifying and
              counting unit fractions using concrete models.

Date: 11/19/13

5.A.7

3. In the space below, draw a small rectangle. Estimate to split it into 2 equal parts. How many lines did you draw to make 2 equal parts? What is the name of each fractional unit?

    ▪ Draw another small rectangle. Estimate to split it into 3 equal parts. How many lines did you draw to make 3 equal parts? What is the name of each fractional unit?

    ▪ Draw another small rectangle. Estimate to split it into 4 equal parts. How many lines did you draw to make 4 equal parts? What is the name of each fractional unit?

4. Each rectangle represents 1 sheet of paper. Estimate to show how you would cut the paper into fractional units as indicated below.

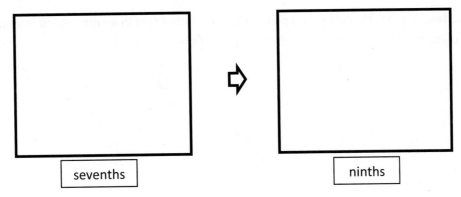

sevenths   ninths

    ▪ What do you notice? How many lines do you think you would draw to make a rectangle with 20 equal parts?

5. Rochelle has a strip of wood 12 inches long. She cuts it into pieces that are each 6 inches in length. What fraction of the wood is one piece? Use your yellow strip from the lesson to help you. Draw a picture to show the piece of wood and how Rochelle cut it.

COMMON CORE | Lesson 1:   Specify and partition a whole into equal parts, identifying and   5.A.8
                   | counting unit fractions using concrete models.
                   | Date: 11/19/13

Name _____   Date _____

1. Name the fraction that is shaded

_____

2. Estimate to partition the rectangle into thirds

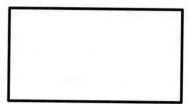

3. A plumber has 12 feet of pipe. He cuts it into pieces that are each 3 feet in length. What fraction of the pipe would one piece represent? (Use your yellow strip from the lesson to help you.)

COMMON CORE

Lesson 1:   Specify and partition a whole into equal parts, identifying and counting unit fractions using concrete models.

Date: 11/19/13

5.A.9

Name _____   Date _____

1. A beaker is considered full, when the liquid reaches the fill line shown near the top. Estimate the amount of water in the beaker by shading the drawing as indicated. The first one is done for you.

1 half

1 fifth

1 sixth

2. Danielle cut her candy bar into equal pieces as shown in the rectangles below. In the blanks below, name the fraction of candy bar represented by the shaded part.

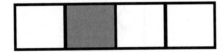

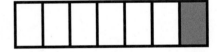

_____   _____   _____

3. Each circle represents 1 whole pie. Estimate to show how you would cut the pie into fractional units as indicated below.

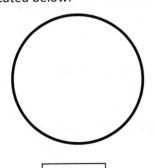

halves

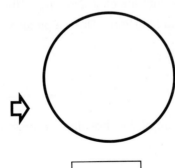

thirds

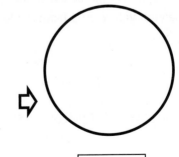

sixths

COMMON CORE

Lesson 1:   Specify and partition a whole into equal parts, identifying and counting unit fractions using concrete models.

Date: 11/19/13

5.A.10

4. Each rectangle represents 1 sheet of paper. Estimate to draw lines to show how you would cut the paper into fractional units as indicated below.

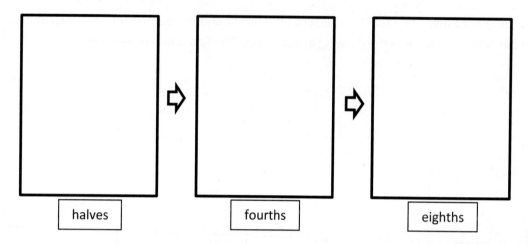

| halves | fourths | eighths |

5. Each rectangle represents 1 sheet of paper. Estimate to draw lines to show how you would cut the paper into fractional units as indicated below.

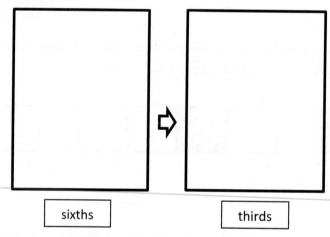

| sixths | thirds |

6. Yuri has a rope 12m long. He cuts it into pieces that are each 2m long. What fraction of the rope is one piece? (Use your yellow strip from the lesson to help you.) Draw a picture.

7. Dawn bought 12 grams of chocolate. She ate half of the chocolate. How many grams of chocolate did she eat?

COMMON CORE

Lesson 1:

Date:

Specify and partition a whole into equal parts, identifying and counting unit fractions using concrete models.

11/19/13

5.A.11

Lesson 2

Objective: Specify and partition a whole into equal parts, identifying and counting unit fractions by folding fraction strips.

Suggested Lesson Structure

■ Fluency Practice   (12 minutes)
■ Application Problem   (5 minutes)
■ Concept Development   (35 minutes)
■ Student Debrief   (8 minutes)

Total Time   **(60 minutes)**

Fluency Practice (12 minutes)

- Skip Counting by Three and Six **3.OA.4**   (6 minutes)
- Multiplication by Three and Six **3.OA.4**   (6 minutes)

Skip Counting by Three and Six (6 minutes)

Materials: (S) Use personal white boards (if students struggle to answer verbally)

By Threes:

Skip count forward and backward by threes two times with a pause between each effort so that students see themselves improve on the second try. After doing the threes twice, have students underline the multiples of 6. (e.g., <u>0</u>, 3, <u>6</u>, 9, <u>12</u>, 15, <u>18</u>, 21, <u>24</u>, 27, <u>30</u>, 27, <u>24</u>, 21, <u>18</u>, 15, <u>12</u>, 9, <u>6</u>, 3, <u>0</u>)

By Sixes:

Skip count forward and backward by sixes two times with a pause between each effort to analyze weak points.

Multiplication by Three and Six (6 minutes)

Materials: (T) Choose your mode of delivery (e.g., oral work, personal white boards)

Students pair facts of 3 and 6 and uncover the doubling.

2 x 3 = 6	2 x 6 = 12
3 x 3 = 9	3 x 6 = 18
4 x 3 = 12	4 x 6 = 24

Lesson 2:   Specify and partition a whole into equal parts, identifying and
counting unit fractions by folding fraction strips.

Date: 11/19/13

5.A.12

Application Problem (5 minutes)

Anu needs to cut a piece of paper into 6 equal parts. Draw at least three pictures to show how Anu can cut her paper so that all the parts are equal. (Early finishers can do the same thing with halves, fourths or eighths.)

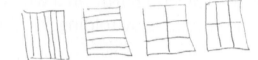

Concept Development (35 minutes)

Materials: (S) About 8 paper strips sized 4¼" x 1" per student (vertically cut an 8 ½" x 11" paper down the middle), pencil, and crayon

Have students take one strip and fold it to make halves. (They might fold it one of two ways. This is correct but for the purpose of this lesson it is best to fold as pictured below.)

T: How many equal parts do you have in the whole?

S: Two.

T: What fraction of the whole is 1 part?

S: 1 half.

T: Draw a line to show where you folded your paper. Write the name of the unit onto each equal part.

Use the following sentence frames with the students chorally.

1.   There are _____ equal parts in all.
2.   One equal part is called _____.

Students should fold and label strips showing fourths and eighths to start, followed by thirds and sixths, and fifths and tenths. Some students may create more strips than others.

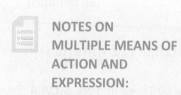

NOTES ON
MULTIPLE MEANS OF
ACTION AND
EXPRESSION:

For *English Language Learners* and others sentence frames support English language acquisition. Students are able to form complete sentences while providing details about the fraction they are analyzing.

For students above grade level, ask students to predict a method for partitioning the whole into ninths (after partitioning thirds for example).

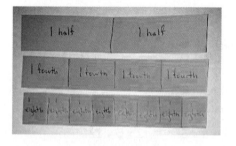

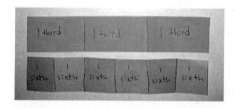

Circulate as you watch for students who are not folding in equal parts. Encourage students to try specific strategies for folding equal parts. A word wall would be helpful to support correct spelling of the units, especially eighths.

Lesson 2:   Specify and partition a whole into equal parts, identifying and
              counting unit fractions by folding fraction strips.
Date: 11/19/13   5.A.13

Before beginning the activity sheet when the students have all created their fraction strips, ask a series of questions such as the following:

- Look at your set of fraction strips. Suppose they are pieces of delicious pasta. Raise the strip in the air that best shows how to cut one piece of pasta in two equal parts with your fork.
- Look at your fraction strips. Suppose they are lengths of ribbon. Raise the strip in the air that best shows how to divide the ribbon into 3 equal parts.
- Look at your fraction strips. Suppose they are candy bars. Which best shows how to share your candy bar fairly with one person? Which shows how to share your half fairly with three people?

Problem Set (10 minutes)

Students should do their personal best to complete the Problem Set within the allotted 10 minutes. For some classes, it may be appropriate to modify the assignment by specifying which problems they work on first. Some problems do not specify a method for solving. Students solve these problems using the RDW approach used for Application Problems.

Student Debrief (8 minutes)

Lesson Objective: Specify and partition a whole into equal parts, identifying and counting unit fractions by folding fraction strips.

The Student Debrief is intended to invite reflection and active processing of the total lesson experience.

Invite students to review their solutions for the Problem Set. They should check work by comparing answers with a partner before going over answers as a class. Look for misconceptions or misunderstandings that can be addressed in the Debrief. Guide students in a conversation to debrief the Problem Set and process the lesson.

You may choose to use any combination of the questions below to lead the discussion.

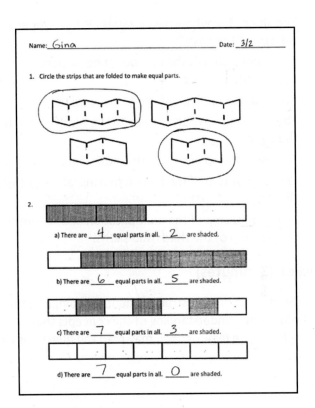

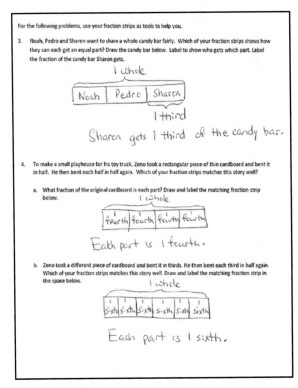

Lesson 2: Specify and partition a whole into equal parts, identifying and counting unit fractions by folding fraction strips.
Date: 11/19/13

5.A.14

- The size of the whole never varies. What happens to the size of the parts?
- The relationship of the number of equal parts to the name of the fraction.
- Methods for folding different fractional parts.
- The relationship of the halves to the fourths then to the eighths.
- The relationship of the thirds to the sixths.
- The relationship of the halves, fourths, and eighths to the thirds and sixths.
- The relationship of the multiplication and "count by" activity beginning the lesson in fluency to the relationship of the thirds and sixths.

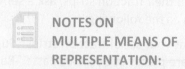

NOTES ON MULTIPLE MEANS OF REPRESENTATION:

Act out both word problems on the Problem Set using concrete materials which will aid students in better understanding.

Exit Ticket (3 minutes)

After the Student Debrief, instruct students to complete the Exit Ticket. A review of their work will help you assess the students' understanding of the concepts that were presented in the lesson today and plan more effectively for future lessons. You may read the questions aloud to the students.

Lesson 2:	Specify and partition a whole into equal parts, identifying and counting unit fractions by folding fraction strips.
Date:	11/19/13

5.A.15

Name _____   Date _____

1. Circle the strips that are folded to make equal parts.

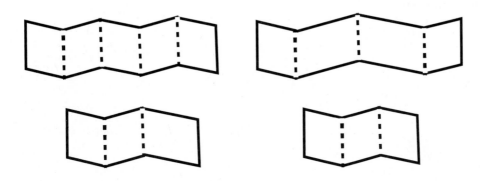

2.

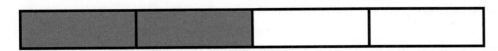

   a. There are _____ equal parts in all. _____ are shaded.

   b. There are _____ equal parts in all. _____ are shaded.

   c. There are _____ equal parts in all. _____ are shaded.

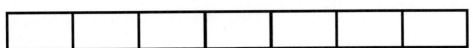

   d. There are _____ equal parts in all. _____ are shaded.

COMMON CORE

Lesson 2: Specify and partition a whole into equal parts, identifying and
counting unit fractions by folding fraction strips.
Date: 11/19/13

5.A.16

For the following problems, use your fraction strips as tools to help you.

3. Noah, Pedro, and Sharon want to share a whole candy bar fairly. Which of your fraction strips shows how they can each get an equal part? Draw the candy bar below. Label to show who gets which part. Label the fraction of the candy bar Sharon gets.

4. To make a small playhouse for his toy truck, Zeno took a rectangular piece of thin cardboard and bent it in half. He then bent each half in half again. Which of your fraction strips matches this story well?

    a. What fraction of the original cardboard is each part? Draw and label the matching fraction strip below.

    b. Zeno took a different piece of cardboard and bent it in thirds. He then bent each third in half again. Which of your fraction strips matches this story well? Draw and label the matching fraction strip in the space below.

COMMON CORE | Lesson 2:   Specify and partition a whole into equal parts, identifying and
                     counting unit fractions by folding fraction strips.   5.A.17
                   | Date: 11/19/13

© 2013 Common Core, Inc. All rights reserved. commoncore.org

Name _____   Date _____

1. Circle the model that shows one third.

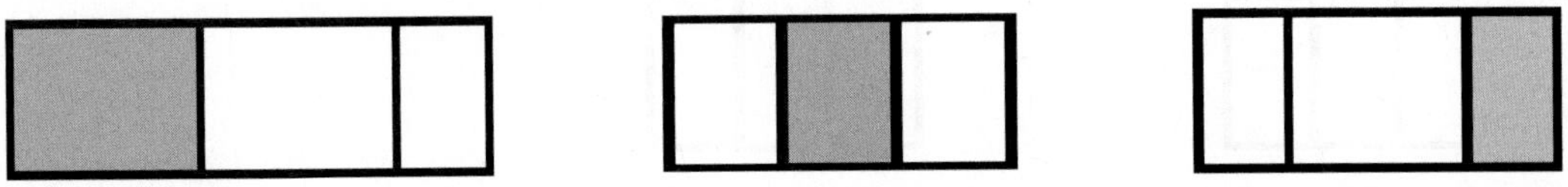

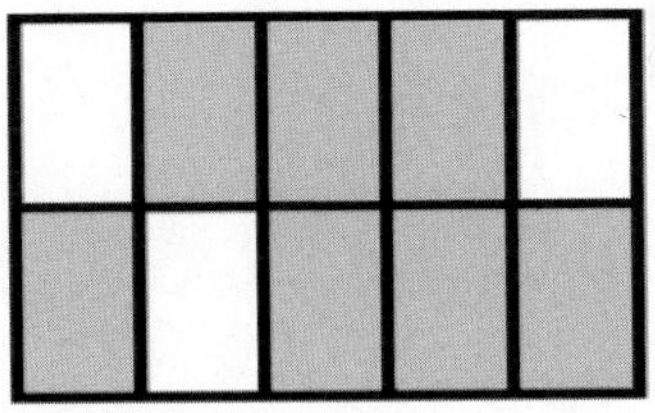

3. 2.

There are _____ equal parts in all. _____ are shaded.

2. Michael bakes a piece of garlic bread for dinner. He shares it equally with his three sisters. Show how Michael and his three sisters can each get an equal share of the garlic bread.

COMMON CORE

Lesson 2:   Specify and partition a whole into equal parts, identifying and counting unit fractions by folding fraction strips.

Date: 11/19/13

5.A.18

Name _____   Date _____

1. Circle the strips that are cut into equal parts.

2.

   a. There are _____ equal parts in all. _____ are shaded.

   b. There are _____ equal parts in all. _____ are shaded.

   c. There are _____ equal parts in all. _____ are shaded.

   d. There are _____ equal parts in all. _____ are shaded.

3. Dylan plans to eat $\frac{1}{5}$ of his candy bar. His 4 friends want him to share the rest equally. Show how Dylan and his friends can each get an equal share of the candy bar.

4. Nasir baked a pie and cut it in fourths. He then took each of the pieces and cut them in half.

   a. What fraction of the original pie does each piece represent?

   b. Nasir ate one piece of pie on Wednesday and two pieces on Tuesday. What fraction of the original pie was not eaten?

Lesson 2:	Specify and partition a whole into equal parts, identifying and counting unit fractions by folding fraction strips.
Date:	11/19/13

5.A.20

Lesson 3

Objective: Specify and partition a whole into equal parts, identifying and counting unit fractions by drawing pictorial area models.

Suggested Lesson Structure

■ Fluency Practice   (12 minutes)
■ Application Problem   (10 minutes)
■ Concept Development   (28 minutes)
■ Student Debrief   (10minutes)
  Total Time   **(60 minutes)**

Fluency Practice (12 minutes)

- Multiply by Six **3.OA.4**   (10 minutes)
- Skip Counting **3.OA.4**   (2 minutes)

Multiply by Six (10 minutes)

Materials: (S) Multiply by Six Sprint

Skip Counting (2 minutes)

Skip count forward and backward by sevens, eights, and nines without exceeding ten multiples of each number.

> **NOTES ON SPRINT AND SKIP COUNTING:**
>
> Modify the routine to be finished with both drills within 12 minutes.
>
> Consider counting by sevens, eights, or nines during the exercise stage of the Sprint routine.

Application Problem (10 minutes)

MP.2

Marcos has a 1-liter container of milk he is going to share with his mother, father, and sister at dinner. Draw a picture to show how Marcos must share the container of milk so that all 4 of them get the same amount of milk. What fraction of the milk does each person get?

COMMON CORE | Lesson 3:   Specify and partition a whole into equal parts, identifying and
                  | counting unit fractions by drawing pictorial area models.   5.A.21
                  | Date: 11/19/13

© 2013 Common Core, Inc. All rights reserved. **commoncore.org**

Concept Development (28 minutes)

Materials: (T) Rectangular and circle-shaped papers (S)
Personal white boards, marker for each student

NOTES ON
MULTIPLE MEANS OF
ENGAGEMENT:

Increase your wait time for responses
from ELLs and record student
responses of the unit fraction and
shaded amount on the board beside
the model.

T: I have a rectangle. I want to split it into 4 equal units.

Fold the paper so that the parts are not the same size. Then
open it up to draw the lines where it was folded, and show the
class. Invite the students to notice the inequality of the parts.

T: Let me try again. (Fold it equally into 4 equal parts.)

T: How many total units did I split the whole into?

S: 4.

T: What is each fractional unit called?

S: 1 fourth or 1 quarter.

T: I'm going to shade in 3 copies of 1 fourth. (Shade in 3 units.) What fraction is shaded?

S: 3 fourths are shaded.

T: Let's count them.

S: 1 fourth, 2 fourths, 3 fourths.

T: I have a circle. I want to split it into 2 equal parts.

Fold the paper so that the parts are not the same size. Then open it up to draw the lines where it was folded,
and show the class. Again, invite the students to notice and analyze the inequality of the parts.

T: Let me try again. (Fold it into 2 equal parts.)

T: How many total units did I split the whole into?

S: 2.

T: Good. What's the fractional unit called?

S: 1 half.

T: I'm going to shade in 1 unit. (Shade in 1 unit.) What fraction is shaded?

S: 1 half is shaded.

Having established the meaning of equal parts, proceed to briskly analyze the following shapes possibly using
the brief sequence of questions mapped out with Shape 1:

Shape 1:

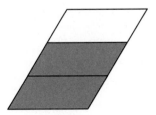

Lesson 3:	Specify and partition a whole into equal parts, identifying and counting unit fractions by drawing pictorial area models.	5.A.22
Date:	11/19/13	

T: How many fractional units are there in all?
S: 3.
T: What's each unit called?
S: 1 third.
T: How many units are shaded?
S: 2 thirds.
T: Count them.
S: 1 third, 2 thirds.

Shape 2:

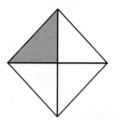

NOTES ON
MULTIPLE MEANS OF
ACTION AND
EXPRESSION:

Some students may benefit from
manipulating concrete models
simultaneously as they work on the
pictorial level.

Shape 3:

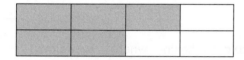

NOTES ON
MULTIPLE MEANS OF
ENGAGEMENT:

Open-ended activities, such as
partitioning a whole into student-
chosen fractional units, challenge
above grade level students.

Shape 4:

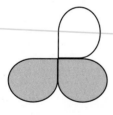

Repeat the steps and procedures with other shapes. Use more or fewer examples as needed.

T: Now take out your white board, and we'll try to draw a few shapes and split them equally into smaller units.
T: Draw a rectangle and show a third. (Circulate while students draw.)
T: How many units do we have altogether?
S: 3.
T: Shade in 1 unit. (Circulate while students draw.) What fraction is shaded?

Lesson 3:	Specify and partition a whole into equal parts, identifying and counting unit fractions by drawing pictorial area models.
Date:	11/19/13

5.A.23

S: 1 third.

Select a couple student drawings to show the class.

Repeat sequence to have students show 2 sixths of a square, 3 fourths of a line segment, and other examples as needed.

Problem Set (10 minutes)

Students should do their personal best to complete the Problem Set within the allotted 10 minutes. For some classes, it may be appropriate to modify the assignment by specifying which problems they work on first. Some problems do not specify a method for solving. Students solve these problems using the RDW approach used for Application Problems.

Student Debrief (10 minutes)

Lesson Objective: Specify and partition a whole into equal parts, identifying and counting unit fractions by drawing pictorial area models.

The Student Debrief is intended to invite reflection and active processing of the total lesson experience.

Invite students to review their solutions for the Problem Set. They should check work by comparing answers with a partner before going over answers as a class. Look for misconceptions or misunderstandings that can be addressed in the Debrief. Guide students in a conversation to debrief the Problem Set and process the lesson.

You may choose to use any combination of the questions below to lead the discussion.

- What is the same and different about these two problems?
- What is the same and different about fair shares of a jug of milk and fair shares of a candy bar? (Though a fraction of a jug of milk and a fraction of a candy bar is clearly different, we might draw each of them by drawing a rectangle.)
- How can drawing fourths help you to draw fifths well?

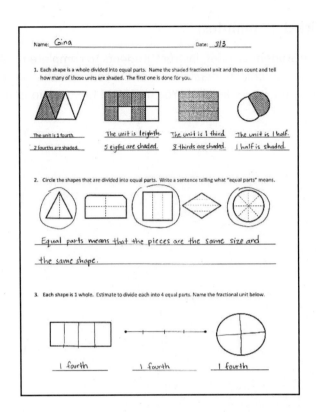

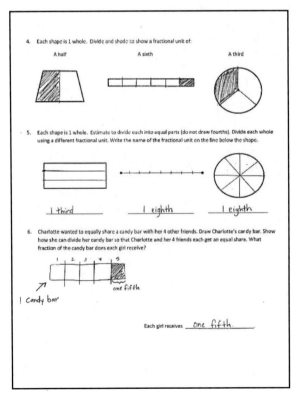

Lesson 3:   Specify and partition a whole into equal parts, identifying and counting unit fractions by drawing pictorial area models.
Date: 11/19/13

5.A.24

Exit Ticket (3 minutes)

After the Student Debrief, instruct students to complete the Exit Ticket. A review of their work will help you assess the students' understanding of the concepts that were presented in the lesson today and plan more effectively for future lessons. You may read the questions aloud to the students.

Lesson 3:

Date:

Specify and partition a whole into equal parts, identifying and counting unit fractions by drawing pictorial area models.

11/19/13

5.A.25

A

Correct _____

Multiply.

1	1 x 6 =		23	10 x 6 =	
2	6 x 1 =		24	9 x 6 =	
3	2 x 6 =		25	4 x 6 =	
4	6 x 2 =		26	8 x 6 =	
5	3 x 6 =		27	6 x 3 =	
6	6 x 3 =		28	7 x 6 =	
7	4 x 6 =		29	6 x 6 =	
8	6 x 4 =		30	6 x 10 =	
9	5 x 6 =		31	6 x 5 =	
10	6 x 5 =		32	6 x 4 =	
11	6 x 6 =		33	6 x 1 =	
12	7 x 6 =		34	6 x 9 =	
13	6 x 7 =		35	6 x 6 =	
14	8 x 6 =		36	6 x 3 =	
15	6 x 8 =		37	6 x 2 =	
16	9 x 6 =		38	6 x 7 =	
17	6 x 9 =		39	6 x 8 =	
18	10 x 6 =		40	11 x 6 =	
19	6 x 10 =		41	6 x 11 =	
20	6 x 3 =		42	12 x 6 =	
21	1 x 6 =		43	6 x 12 =	
22	2 x 6 =		44	13 x 6 =	

Lesson 3: Specify and partition a whole into equal parts, identifying and counting unit fractions by drawing pictorial area models.

Date: 11/19/13

5.A.26

B   Improvement _____   # Correct _____

Multiply.

1	6 x 1 =		23	9 x 6 =	
2	1 x 6 =		24	3 x 6 =	
3	6 x 2 =		25	8 x 6 =	
4	2 x 6 =		26	4 x 6 =	
5	6 x 3 =		27	7 x 6 =	
6	3 x 6 =		28	5 x 6 =	
7	6 x 4 =		29	6 x 6 =	
8	4 x 6 =		30	6 x 5 =	
9	6 x 5 =		31	6 x 10 =	
10	5 x 6 =		32	6 x 1 =	
11	6 x 6 =		33	6 x 6 =	
12	6 x 7 =		34	6 x 4 =	
13	7 x 6 =		35	6 x 9 =	
14	6 x 8 =		36	6 x 2 =	
15	8 x 6 =		37	6 x 7 =	
16	6 x 9 =		38	6 x 3 =	
17	9 x 6 =		39	6 x 8 =	
18	6 x 10 =		40	11 x 6 =	
19	10 x 6 =		41	6 x 11 =	
20	1 x 6 =		42	12 x 6 =	
21	10 x 6 =		43	6 x 12 =	
22	2 x 6 =		44	13 x 6 =	

Lesson 3:   Specify and partition a whole into equal parts, identifying and counting unit fractions by drawing pictorial area models.

Date: 11/19/13

5.A.27

Name _____ Date _____

1. Each shape is a whole divided into equal parts. Name the fractional unit and then count and tell how many of those units are shaded. The first one is done for you.

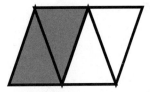 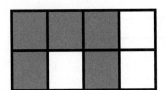 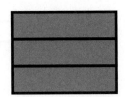

The unit is 1 fourth.   _____   _____   _____

2 fourths are shaded.   _____   _____   _____

2. Circle the shapes that are divided into equal parts. Write a sentence telling what "equal parts" means.

  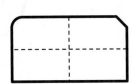 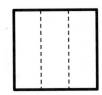 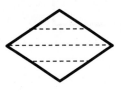 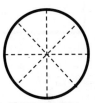

_____

_____

3. Each shape is 1 whole. Estimate to divide each into 4 equal parts. Name the fractional unit below.

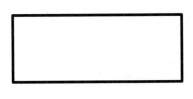  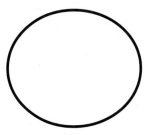

_____   _____   _____

COMMON CORE | Lesson 3: | Specify and partition a whole into equal parts, identifying and counting unit fractions by drawing pictorial area models. | **5.A.28**

Date: | 11/19/13

4. Each shape is 1 whole. Divide and shade to show a fractional unit of:

    A half   A sixth   A third

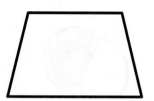 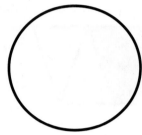

5. Each shape is 1 whole. Estimate to divide each into equal parts (Do not draw fourths.). Divide each
    whole using a different fractional unit. Write the name of the fractional unit on the line below the shape.

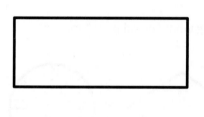  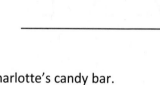

    _____   _____   _____

6. Charlotte wanted to equally share a candy bar with her 4 other friends. Draw Charlotte's candy bar.
    Show how she can divide her candy bar so that Charlotte and her 4 friends each get an equal share. What
    fraction of the candy bar does each girl receive?

                                                        Each girl receives _____.

COMMON CORE   Lesson 3:   Specify and partition a whole into equal parts, identifying and
                                   counting unit fractions by drawing pictorial area models.   5.A.29
                  Date: 11/19/13

Name _____   Date _____

1. 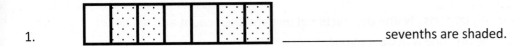   _____ sevenths are shaded.

2. Circle the shapes that are divided into equal parts.

3. Steven wants to equally share his pizza with his 3 sisters. What fraction of the pizza do he and each sister receive?

He and each sister receive _____.

COMMON CORE   Lesson 3:   Specify and partition a whole into equal parts, identifying and counting unit fractions by drawing pictorial area models.   5.A.30

Date: 11/19/13

Name _____   Date _____

1. Each shape is a whole divided into equal parts. Name the fractional unit and then count and tell how many of those units are shaded. The first one is done for you.

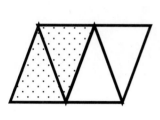 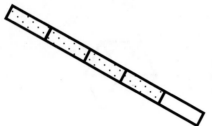 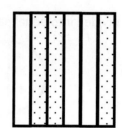 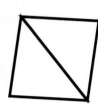

_The unit is 1 fourth._____   _____   _____   _____

_2 fourths are shaded._____   _____   _____   _____

2. Each shape is 1 whole. Estimate to divide each into equal parts. Divide each whole using a different fractional unit. Write the name of the fractional unit on the line below the shape.

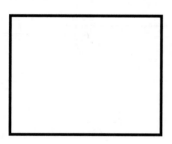      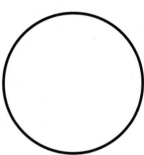

_____   _____   _____

3. An artist wants to draw a calendar on one sheet of paper to show each month of the year. Draw the artist's calendar. Show how he can divide his calendar so that each month is given the same space. What fraction of the calendar bar does each month receive?

Each month receives _____.

COMMON CORE

Lesson 3:   Specify and partition a whole into equal parts, identifying and counting unit fractions by drawing pictorial area models.
Date: 11/19/13

5.A.31

Lesson 4

Objective: Represent and identify fractional parts of different wholes.

Suggested Lesson Structure

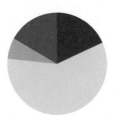

■ Fluency Practice	(11 minutes)
▨ Application Problem	(4 minutes)
▨ Concept Development	(35 minutes)
■ Student Debrief	(10 minutes)
Total Time	**(60 minutes)**

Fluency Practice (11 minutes)

- Dividing by Six Sprint **3.OA.4**   (9 minutes)
- Skip Counting **3.OA.4**   (2 minutes)

Dividing by Six Sprint (9 minutes)

Materials: (S) Dividing by Six Sprint

Skip Counting (2 minutes)

Skip count forward and backward by sixes, eights, and/or nines without exceeding ten multiples of each number.

NOTES ON MULTIPLE MEANS OF ACTION AND EXPRESSION:

If students struggle with higher multiples, have them work with the first 3 or 4 multiples of each number (e.g., 8, 16, 24, 32, 24, 16, 8, 0).

Stop before students become frustrated. End with success.

Application Problems (4 minutes)

Mr. Ramos sliced an orange into 8 equal pieces. He ate 1 slice. Draw a picture to represent the 8 slices of an orange. Shade in the slice Mr. Ramos ate. What fraction of the orange did Mr. Ramos eat? What fraction did he not eat?

Remember that students should always answer a problem with a complete statement.

What he ate.
1 eighth

Mr Ramos ate 1 eighth.
He did not eat 7 eighths.

Concept Development (35 minutes)

Exploration: Designate the following stations for 3 students per station (More than 3 not suggested.).

Lesson 4:   Represent and identify fractional parts of different wholes.
Date: 11/19/13

5.A.32

Station A: Halves

Station B: Fourths

Station C: Eighths

Station D: Thirds

Station E: Sixths

Station F: Ninths

Station G: Fifths

Station H: Tenths

NOTES ON MULTIPLE MEANS OF ENGAGEMENT:

Organize students below grade level at the stations with the easier fractional units and students above grade level stations with the most challenging fractional units.

Equip each station with the following suggested materials:

- 1 meter length of yarn
- 1 rectangular piece of yellow construction paper (1" by 12")
- 1 piece of brown construction paper (candy bar) (2" by 6")
- 1 square piece of orange construction paper (4"by 4")
- A number of 12 ounce cups corresponding to the denominator of the station's fractional unit and 12 ounces of water in a separate larger cup.
- A 200 ggram ball of clay or play dough (The key is to have precisely the same amount at each station.)

(Optional stations for sevenths and/or twelfths.)

The students are to represent their fraction using the materials at their station.

Note:

- Each item at their station represents one whole.
- They are to show the whole partitioned into equal parts as designated by their station.
- The entire quantity of each item must be used. So, for example, if showing thirds, all the clay must be used to do so, all the water must be used.
- The clay is to be partitioned by subdividing it into smaller equal pieces formed into equal sized balls. Demonstrate for the students.

To get them going, give as little direction as possible but enough for your particular class. Ask for clarification of the task by the students.

Note: It is suggested to work without scissors or cutting. Paper and yarn are folded. Clay is formed into smaller balls. Pencil can be used on the paper to designate equal parts rather than folding.

Give the students 15 minutes to create their display. Next, conduct a "museum walk" where they tour the work of the other stations.

NOTES ON MULTIPLE MEANS OF ACTION AND EXPRESSION:

As the students move around the room during the "museum walk", have students gently and respectfully pick up the materials to encourage better analysis. This will encourage more talk, too.

| Lesson 4: | Represent and identify fractional parts of different wholes. |
| Date: | 11/19/13 |

5.A.33

Before the "museum walk" review the following charted analysis points. If analysis dwindles during the tour, circulate and refer them back to the chart.

- Identify the fractional unit.
- Think about how that unit relates to your own and to other units.
- Think about how the units relate to each other at that station.
- Compare the yarn to the yellow strip.
- Compare the yellow strip to the brown paper or candy bar.
- Compare the water to the clay.

Problem Set (10 minutes)

Students should do their personal best to complete the Problem Set within the allotted 10 minutes. For some classes, it may be appropriate to modify the assignment by specifying which problems they work on first. Some problems do not specify a method for solving. Students solve these problems using the RDW approach used for Application Problems.

Student Debrief (10 minutes)

Lesson Objective: Represent and identify fractional parts of different wholes.

The Student Debrief is intended to invite reflection and active processing of the total lesson experience.

Invite students to review their solutions for the Problem Set. They should check work by comparing answers with a partner before going over answers as a class. Look for misconceptions or misunderstandings that can be addressed in the Debrief. Guide students in a conversation to debrief the Problem Set and process the lesson.

You may choose to use any combination of the questions below to lead the discussion.

- What were the different wholes we saw at each station that were the same?
- What different fractional units did you see as you went from station to station?
- What did you notice about different fractional units at the stations?

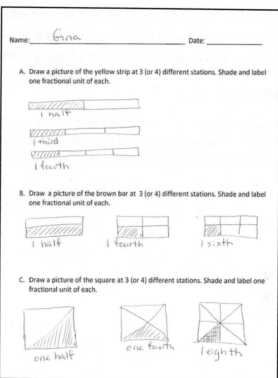

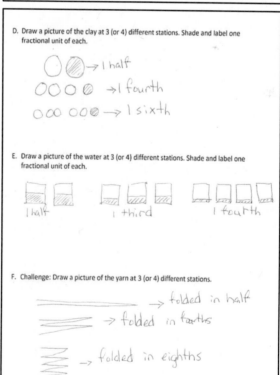

COMMON
CORE

Lesson 4:
Date:

Represent and identify fractional parts of different wholes.
11/19/13

5.A.34

- Which fractional units had the most and the smallest equal parts?
- Which fractional units had the least and the largest equal parts?
- What surprised you when you were looking at the different fractional units?

Exit Ticket (3 minutes)

After the Student Debrief, instruct students to complete the Exit Ticket. A review of their work will help you assess the students' understanding of the concepts that were presented in the lesson today and plan more effectively for future lessons. You may read the questions aloud to the students.

Lesson 4:   Represent and identify fractional parts of different wholes.
Date: 11/19/13

5.A.35

A   # Correct _____

Multiply or divide.

#	Problem		#	Problem	
1	2 x 6 =		23	__ x 6 = 60	
2	3 x 6 =		24	__ x 6 =12	
3	4 x 6 =		25	__x 6 = 18	
4	5 x 6 =		26	60 ÷ 6 =	
5	1 x 6 =		27	30 ÷ 6 =	
6	12 ÷ 6 =		28	6 ÷ 6 =	
7	18 ÷ 6 =		29	12 ÷ 6 =	
8	30 ÷ 6 =		30	18 ÷ 6 =	
9	6 ÷ 6 =		31	__ x 6 = 36	
10	24 ÷ 6 =		32	__ x 6 = 42	
11	6 x 6 =		33	__ x 6 = 54	
12	7 x 6 =		34	__ x 6 = 48	
13	8 x 6 =		35	42 ÷ 6 =	
14	9 x 6 =		36	54 ÷ 6 =	
15	10 x 6 =		37	36 ÷ 6 =	
16	48 ÷ 6 =		38	48 ÷ 6 =	
17	42 ÷ 6 =		39	11 x 6 =	
18	54 ÷ 6 =		40	66 ÷ 6 =	
19	36 ÷ 6 =		41	12 x 6 =	
20	60 ÷ 6 =		42	72 ÷ 6 =	
21	__x 6 = 30		43	14 x 6 =	
22	__x6 = 6		44	84 ÷ 6 =	

B　　　　　　　　　Improvement _____　　　　# Correct _____

Multiply or divide.

1	1 x 6 =		23	__ x 6 = 12	
2	2 x 6 =		24	__ x 6 = 60	
3	3 x 6 =		25	__ x 6 = 18	
4	4 x 6 =		26	12 ÷ 6 =	
5	5 x 6 =		27	6 ÷ 6 =	
6	18 ÷ 6 =		28	60 ÷ 6 =	
7	12 ÷ 6 =		29	30 ÷ 6 =	
8	24 ÷ 6 =		30	18 ÷ 6 =	
9	6 ÷ 6 =		31	__ x 6 = 18	
10	30 ÷ 6 =		32	__ x 6 = 24	
11	10 x 6 =		33	__ x 6 = 54	
12	6 x 6 =		34	__ x 6 = 42	
13	7 x 6 =		35	48 ÷ 6 =	
14	8 x 6 =		36	54 ÷ 6 =	
15	9 x 6 =		37	36 ÷ 6 =	
16	42 ÷ 6 =		38	42 ÷ 6 =	
17	36 ÷ 6 =		39	11 x 6 =	
18	48 ÷ 6 =		40	66 ÷ 6 =	
19	60 ÷ 6 =		41	12 x 6 =	
20	54 ÷ 6 =		42	72 ÷ 6 =	
21	__ x 6 = 6		43	13 x 6 =	
22	__ x 6 = 30		44	78 ÷ 6 =	

COMMON CORE　Lesson 4:　Represent and identify fractional parts of different wholes.
Date:　11/19/13

5.A.37

Name _____   Date _____

A. Draw a picture of the yellow strip at 3 (or 4) different stations. Shade and label one fractional unit of each.

B. Draw a picture of the brown bar at 3 (or 4) different stations. Shade and label one fractional unit of each.

C. Draw a picture of the square at 3 (or 4) different stations. Shade and label one fractional unit of each.

D. Draw a picture of the clay at 3 (or 4) different stations. Shade and label one fractional unit of each.

E. Draw a picture of the water at 3 (or 4) different stations. Shade and label one fractional unit of each.

F. Challenge: Draw a picture of the yarn at 3 (or 4) different stations.

Name _____   Date _____

Each shape is 1 whole. Estimate to equally partition the image to show the fractional unit of:

1. $\frac{1}{4}$

2. $\frac{1}{5}$ _____

3. The shape represents 1 whole. Write the fractional unit of the shaded part.

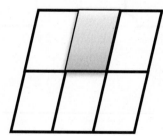   The shaded part is _____

COMMON CORE

Lesson 4:   Represent and identify fractional parts of different wholes.
Date: 11/19/13

5.A.40

Name _____ Date _____

Each shape is 1 whole. Estimate to equally partition the following images to show the fractional unit of:

1. $\dfrac{1}{2}$

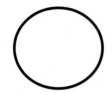

     A   B   C   D

2. $\dfrac{1}{4}$

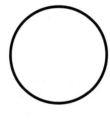

     A   B   C   D

3. $\dfrac{1}{3}$

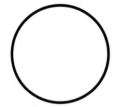

     A   B   C   D

4. Each of the shapes represent 1 whole. Match each shape to its unit fraction.

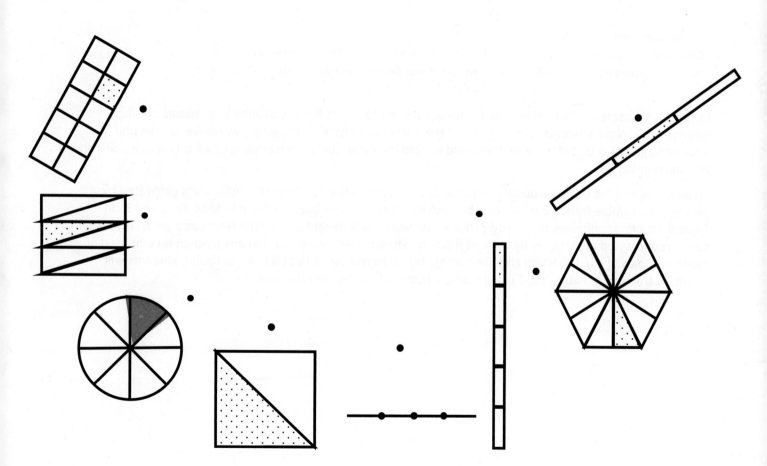

Topic B

Unit Fractions and their Relation to the Whole

3.NF.1, 3.NF.3c, 3.G.2

Focus Standard:	3.NF.1	Understand a fraction 1/*b* as the quantity formed by 1 part when a whole is partitioned into *b* equal parts; understand a fraction *a/b* as the quantity formed by *a* parts of size 1/*b*.
Instructional Days:	5	
Coherence -Links from:	G2–M7	Time, Shapes, and Fractions as Equal Parts of Shapes
-Links to:	G4–M5	Fraction Equivalence, Ordering, and Operations

In Topic A students divided a given whole into equal parts to create fractional units (e.g., halves, thirds, fourths, etc.). Now, students associate one of the fractional units with a number, which we call the unit fraction (e.g., 1/2, 1/3, 1/4, etc.), as they build toward their eventual understanding of a fraction as a point on the real number line.

An advantage of the term *fractional unit* is that it distinguishes the nature of the equal parts generated by partitioning a whole from the whole number division students have been studying in Modules 1 and 3. In Topic B, to avoid confusion, the term *fractional unit* will largely be replaced by the term *equal part*. The equal part is represented numerically by the *unit fraction*. Students will recognize that any fraction is composed of multiple copies of a unit fraction and use number bonds to represent this fact. In particular, students will construct fractions greater than 1 using multiple copies of a given unit fraction.

A Teaching Sequence Towards Mastery of Unit Fractions and their Relation to the Whole

Objective 1: Partition a whole into equal parts and define the equal parts to identify the unit fraction numerically.
(Lesson 5)

Objective 2: Build non-unit fractions less than one whole from unit fractions.
(Lesson 6)

Objective 3: Identify and represent shaded and non-shaded parts of one whole as fractions.
(Lesson 7)

Objective 4: Represent parts of one whole as fractions with number bonds.
(Lesson 8)

Objective 5: Build and write fractions greater than one whole using unit fractions.
(Lesson 9)

Lesson 5

Objective: Partition a whole into equal parts and define the equal parts to identify the unit fraction numerically.

Suggested Lesson Structure

■ Fluency Practice   (15 minutes)
▨ Application Problem   (10 minutes)
▨ Concept Development   (25 minutes)
■ Student Debrief   (10 minutes)
    Total Time   **(60 minutes)**

Fluency Practice (15 minutes)

- Count by Eight **3.OA.7**   (5 minutes)
- Write the Fractional Unit **3.NF.1**   (5 minutes)
- Partition Shapes **3.NF.1**   (5 minutes)

Count by Eight (5 minutes)

Materials: (S) Personal white boards

Step 1: Students count by eight as high as they can for 90 seconds. 0, 8, 16, 24, 32, 40, 48, 56.

Step 2: Correct by reading the multiples. Students practice for an additional minute after correction.

Step 3: Students count by eight once again. Quickly celebrate improvement.

Write the Fractional Unit (5 minutes)

Materials: (S) Personal white boards

T: (Draw a shape with 3 units, 2 shaded in.) Write the fractional unit on your personal white board.

S: (Write: thirds)

T: Blank thirds are shaded. Write the number that goes in the blank.

S: (Write: 2)

Continue with possible sequence: 3 fourths, 2 fifths, 5 sixths, 7 tenths, 5 eighths, etc.

Partition Shapes (5 minutes)

Materials: (S) Personal white boards

Lesson 5:	Partition a whole into equal parts and define the equal parts to identify the unit fraction numerically.
Date:	11/19/13

5.B.3

T: Draw a square.

S: (Students draw.)

T: (Write: $\frac{1}{2}$.) Estimate to equally partition the square into halves.

S: (Students partition.)

Continue with possible sequence: line $\frac{1}{5}$, circle $\frac{1}{4}$, circle $\frac{1}{8}$, bar $\frac{1}{10}$, and bar $\frac{1}{6}$.

Application Problem (10 minutes)

Ms. Browne cut a 6 meter rope into 3 equal size pieces to make jump ropes. Mr. Ware cut a 5 meter rope into 3 equal size pieces to make jump ropes. Which class has longer jump ropes? (Bonus: How long are the jump ropes in Ms. Browne's class?)

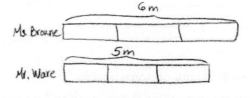

Ms. Browne's class gets longer jump ropes because the original rope was longer.

Bonus: 2m because I can count by 2 until I get to 6 m.

Concept Development (25 minutes)

Materials: (S) Personal white boards

T: Whisper the name of this shape.

S: Circle.

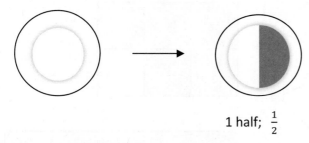

1 half; $\frac{1}{2}$

T: Watch as I cut the whole. How many equal parts are there?

S: 2 equal parts.

T: What's the name of each unit?

S: 1 half.

T: (Shade one unit.) What fraction is shaded?

S: 1 half.

T: 1 half is the unit form. This is how we write it numerically: $\frac{1}{2}$. (Write both forms under the circle.) Both of these refer to the same thing: 1 out of 2 equal units.

NOTES ON MULTIPLE MEANS OF REPRESENTATION:

As you introduce two new terms— "unit form" and "numerical form", check for student understanding. English Language Learners may choose to discuss definitions of these terms in their first language with you or peers.

Lesson 5:   Partition a whole into equal parts and define the equal parts to identify the unit fraction numerically.

Date: 11/19/13

5.B.4

T: What's the name of this shape?

S: It's a square.

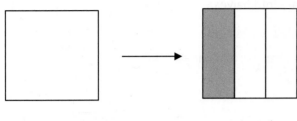

1 third; $\frac{1}{3}$

NOTES ON
MULTIPLE MEANS OF
ENGAGEMENT:

Students above grade level may enjoy identifying fractions with an added challenge of each shape representing a *fraction* rather than the whole. For example, ask:

"If shape 2 is 1 third, name the shaded region (e.g., $\frac{3}{12}$ or $\frac{1}{4}$)."

T: Draw it on your personal board.

T: Estimate to partition the square into 3 equal parts.

S: (Students partition.)

T: What's the name of each unit?

S: 1 third.

T: Shade the unit. Then write the fraction in unit form and numerically on your board.

S: (Students shade and write 1 third and $\frac{1}{3}$.)

Continue the process with more shapes as needed. The following suggested shapes include examples of both shaded and non-shaded unit fractions. Alter language accordingly.

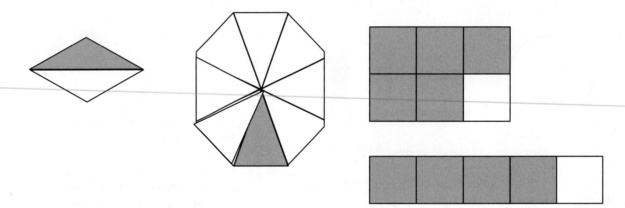

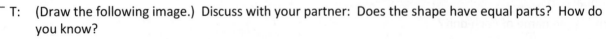

T: (Draw the following image.) Discuss with your partner: Does the shape have equal parts? How do you know?

MP.6

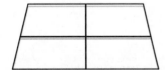

S: No. The parts are not the same size. → They're also

COMMON CORE

Lesson 5:   Partition a whole into equal parts and define the equal parts to identify the unit fraction numerically.

Date: 11/19/13

5.B.5

not exactly the same shape. → The parts are not equal because the bottom parts are bigger. The lines on the sides lean in at the top.

T: Most agree that the parts are not equal. Alex, can you share how you would partition the shape to make the parts equal?

`MP.6`

S: I can cut it into 2 equal parts. You have to cut it right down the middle going up and down. The lines aren't all the same length like in a square.

T: Turn and talk: If the parts are not equal, can we call these fourths? Why or why not?

NOTES ON MULTIPLE MEANS OF ENGAGEMENT:

Review personal goals with students. For example, if students below grade level have chosen to solve one word problem (per lesson) last week, encourage them to work towards completing two word problems by the end of this week.

Problem Set (10 minutes)

Students should do their personal best to complete the Problem Set within the allotted 10 minutes. For some classes, it may be appropriate to modify the assignment by specifying which problems they work on first. Some problems do not specify a method for solving. Students solve these problems using the RDW approach used for Application Problems.

Student Debrief (10 minutes)

Lesson Objective: Partition a whole into equal parts and define the equal parts to identify the unit fraction numerically.

The Student Debrief is intended to invite reflection and active processing of the total lesson experience.

Invite students to review their solutions for the Problem Set. They should check work by comparing answers with a partner before going over answers as a class. Look for misconceptions or misunderstandings that can be addressed in the Debrief. Guide students in a conversation to debrief the Problem Set and process the lesson.

You may choose to use any combination of the questions below to lead the discussion.

- Use the following possible introduction to start a discussion about Problem 4: Let's imagine we're at Andre's birthday party. Who would rather have an eighth of the cake? Who would rather have a tenth? Why? Suggested sentence frames: "I would rather have a _____ because _____.", and "I agree/disagree because _____."

Name: Gina   Date: 3/5

1. Fill in the chart. Then whisper the fractional unit.

	Total Number of Equal Parts	Total Number of Equal Parts Shaded	Unit Form	Fraction
a)	2	1	half	$\frac{1}{2}$
b)	3	1	third	$\frac{1}{3}$
c)	4	1	fourth	$\frac{1}{4}$
d)	5	1	fifth	$\frac{1}{5}$
e)	6	1	sixth	$\frac{1}{6}$
f)	8	1	eighth	$\frac{1}{8}$

COMMON CORE

Lesson 5:   Partition a whole into equal parts and define the equal parts to identify the unit fraction numerically.

Date: 11/19/13

5.B.6

- Guide students to start understanding that a greater number of parts results in smaller pieces.

Exit Ticket (3 minutes)

After the Student Debrief, instruct students to complete the Exit Ticket. A review of their work will help you assess the students' understanding of the concepts that were presented in the lesson today and plan more effectively for future lessons. You may read the questions aloud to the students.

COMMON CORE Lesson 5: Partition a whole into equal parts and define the equal parts to identify the unit fraction numerically.
Date: 11/19/13

5.B.7

Name _____   Date _____

1. Fill in the chart. Then whisper the fractional unit.

	Total Number of Equal Parts	Total Number of Equal Parts Shaded	Unit Form	Fraction
a.				
b.				
c.				
d.				
e.				
f.				

Lesson 5:   Partition a whole into equal parts and define the equal parts to
            identify the unit fraction numerically.
Date: 11/19/13

5.B.8

2.   Andre's mom baked his 2 favorite cakes for his birthday party. The cakes were the exact same size. Andre cut his first cake into 8 pieces for him and his 7 friends. The picture below shows how he cut it. Did Andre cut the cake into eighths? Explain your answer.

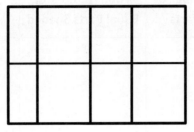

_____

_____

_____

3.   Two of Andre's friends came late to his party. They decide they will all share the second cake. Show how Andre can slice the second cake so that he and his nine friends can each get an equal amount with none leftover. What fraction of the second cake will they each receive?

4.   Andre thinks it's strange that $\frac{1}{10}$ of the cake would be less than $\frac{1}{8}$ of the cake, since ten is bigger than eight. To explain to Andre, draw 2 identical rectangles to stand for the cakes. Show 1 tenth shaded on one and 1 eighth shaded on the other. Label the unit fractions and show him which slice is bigger.

COMMON CORE | Lesson 5:   Partition a whole into equal parts and define the equal parts to identify the unit fraction numerically.   5.B.9

Date: 11/19/13

Name _____   Date _____

1. Fill in the chart.

	Total Number of Equal Parts	Total Number of Equal Parts Shaded	Unit Form	Fraction
a. 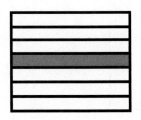				

2. Each image below is 1 whole. Write the fraction that is shaded.

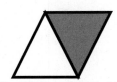
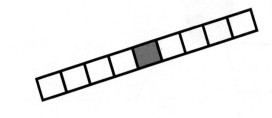

_____   _____   _____

3. Draw two rectangles. Partition one into 5 equal parts. Partition the other into 8 equal parts. Label the unit fractions and shade 1 equal part in each rectangle. Use your drawing to explain why $\frac{1}{5}$ is larger than $\frac{1}{8}$.

COMMON CORE   Lesson 5: Partition a whole into equal parts and define the equal parts to identify the unit fraction numerically.   5.B.10

Date: 11/19/13

Name _____ Date _____

1. Fill in the chart. Then whisper the fraction.

	Total Number of Equal Parts	Total Number of Equal Parts Shaded	Unit Form	Fraction
a. 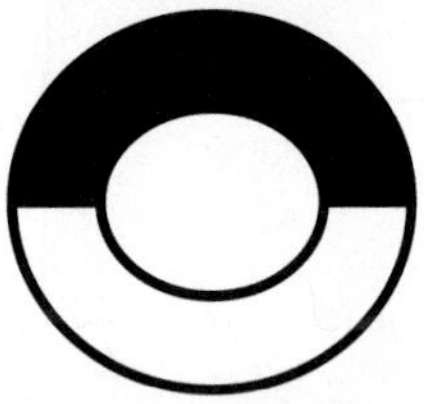				
b. 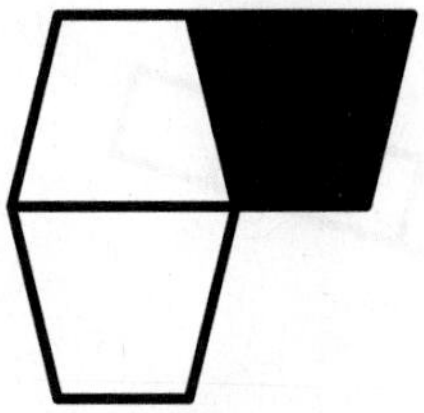				
c. 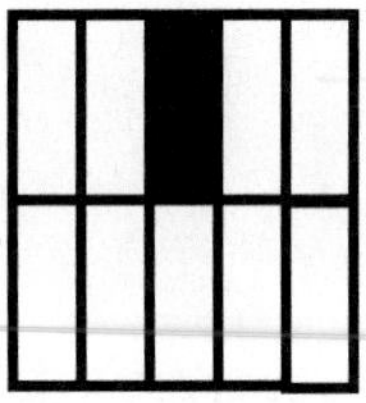				
d. 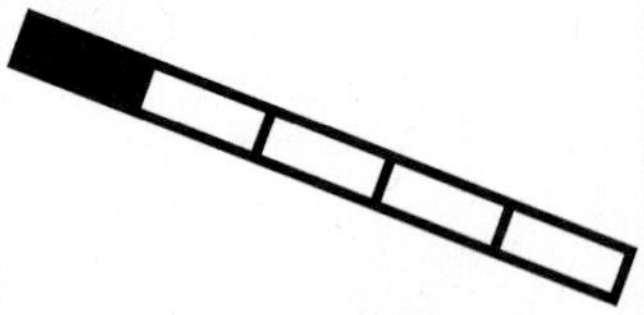				
e. 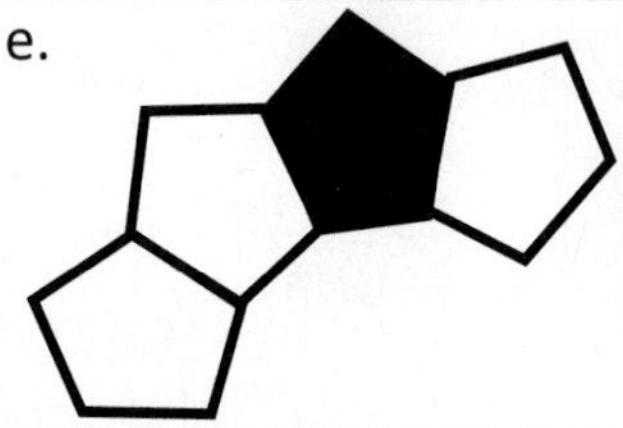				

Lesson 5: Partition a whole into equal parts and define the equal parts to identify the unit fraction numerically.

Date: 11/19/13

5.B.11

2. This figure is divided into six parts. Are they sixths? Explain your answer.

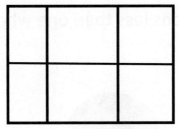

_____

_____

_____

3. Terry and his 3 friends baked a pizza during his sleepover. They want to share the pizza equally. Show how Terry can slice the pizza so that he and his 3 friends can each get an equal amount with none leftover.

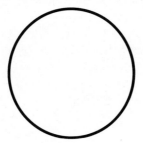

4. Draw two identical rectangles. Shade 1 seventh of one rectangle and 1 tenth of the other. Label the unit fractions. Use your rectangles to explain why $\frac{1}{7}$ is greater than $\frac{1}{10}$.

COMMON CORE   **Lesson 5:**   Partition a whole into equal parts and define the equal parts to   **5.B.12**
                    identify the unit fraction numerically.
                    Date: 11/19/13

Lesson 6

Objective: Build non-unit fractions less than one whole from unit fractions.

Suggested Lesson Structure

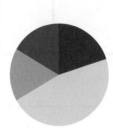

■ Fluency Practice   (12 minutes)
■ Application Problem   (10 minutes)
■ Concept Development   (28 minutes)
■ Student Debrief   (10 minutes)
   Total Time   **(60 minutes)**

Fluency Practice (12 minutes)

- Sprint Multiplication by Seven **3.OA.4**   (8 minutes)
- Write the Unit Fraction **3.G.2, 3.NF.1**   (2 minutes)
- Find the Whole **3.NF.3d**   (2 minutes)

Sprint Multiplication by Seven (8 minutes)

Materials: (S) Multiplication by Seven Sprint

Write the Unit Fraction (2 minutes)

Materials: (S) Personal white boards

T: (Draw a shape with $\frac{1}{2}$ shaded.) Write the unit fraction.

S: (Write: $\frac{1}{2}$.)

Continue with possible sequence: $\frac{1}{4}$, $\frac{1}{8}$, $\frac{1}{6}$, $\frac{1}{10}$, $\frac{1}{5}$

Find the Whole (2 minutes)

Materials: (T) Blank number bond

T: (Project number bond with parts $\frac{3}{5}$ and $\frac{2}{5}$.) Say the biggest part.

S: 3 fifths.

T: Say the smallest part.

Lesson 6:   Build non-unit fractions less than one whole from unit fractions.
Date: 11/19/13

5.B.13

S: 2 fifths.

T: How many fifths are in the whole?

S: 5 fifths.

T: (Write $\frac{5}{5}$ in the whole space.) Say the number sentence.

S: 3 fifths and 2 fifths equals 5 fifths.

Repeat with parts: $\frac{7}{10}$ and $\frac{3}{10}$, $\frac{5}{8}$ and $\frac{3}{8}$. Replace 8 eighths with one whole.

Application Problem (10 minutes)

Chloe's dad partitions his garden into 4 equal size sections to plant tomatoes, squash, peppers, and cucumbers. What fraction of the garden is available for growing tomatoes?

(Bonus: Chloe talked her dad into planting beans and lettuce too. He used equal size sections for all the vegetables. What fraction do the tomatoes have now?)

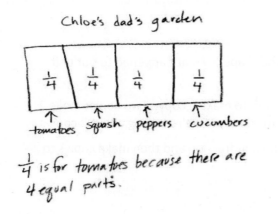

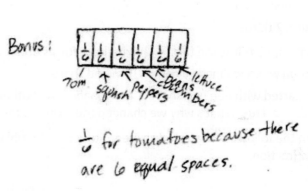

Concept Development (28 minutes)

Materials: (S) Personal white boards

T: Here is unit form. (Write: 1 half.)

T: Here is numerical form. (Write: $\frac{1}{2}$.)

T: What does the 2 mean?

S: 2 is the number of equal parts that the whole is cut into.

T: What does the 1 mean?

S: We are talking about 1 of the equal parts.

Shape 1:

T: (Show a circle partitioned into thirds.) This is 1 whole.

NOTES ON MULTIPLE MEANS OF REPRESENTATION:

Recording choral response on the board alongside the model supports English language acquisition.

Lesson 6:   Build non-unit fractions less than one whole from unit fractions.
Date: 11/19/13

5.B.14

2 thirds $\frac{2}{3}$

T: What unit is it partitioned into?

S: Thirds.

T: What is the unit fraction?

S: 1 third.

T: (Shade 1 third.) I'm going to make a copy of my shaded unit fraction. (Shade one more unit.) How many units are shaded now?

S: 2 thirds.

T: Let's count them.

S: 1 third, 2 thirds.

T: I can write 2 thirds like this: $\frac{2}{3}$. (Write both forms under the shape.) What happened to our unit fraction when we made a copy? Turn and share.

S: We started with one unit shaded, then shaded in another unit to make a copy. Two copies make 2 thirds. → True. That's why we changed the 1 on the top to a 2. Now we're talking about 2 copies.

Continue with the following suggested shapes. Students identify the unit fraction and then make copies to build the new fraction.

Shape 2:   **Shape 3:**

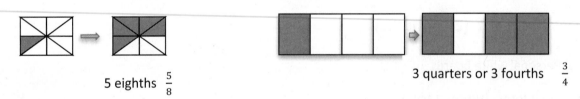

5 eighths $\frac{5}{8}$ 3 quarters or 3 fourths $\frac{3}{4}$

Students transition into guided practice using personal boards.

Directions:

1.   Draw a unit fraction (select examples).

2.   Make copies of the unit fraction to build a new fraction.

3.   Count the unit fractions.

4.   Identify the new fraction both in unit form and numerical form.

> **NOTES ON MULTIPLE MEANS OF REPRESENTATION:**
>
> To assist comprehension, develop multiple ways to ask the same question. For example, you might change the question, "What's happening to my parts?" to "How are my parts changing?" or "Do you notice an increase or decrease?" or "Is the amount growing or shrinking?"

> **NOTES ON MULTIPLE MEANS OF ENGAGEMENT:**
>
> Offer students working above grade level a Problem Set alternative of constructing written responses to open-ended questions, such as, "What do these wholes and fractions (pictured on the Problem Set) remind you of?"

Lesson 6:   Build non-unit fractions less than one whole from unit fractions.
Date: 11/19/13

5.B.15

Problem Set (10 minutes)

Students should do their personal best to complete the Problem Set within the allotted 10 minutes. For some classes, it may be appropriate to modify the assignment by specifying which problems they work on first. Some problems do not specify a method for solving. Students solve these problems using the RDW approach used for Application Problems.

Student Debrief (10 minutes)

Lesson Objective: Build non-unit fractions less than one whole from unit fractions.

The Student Debrief is intended to invite reflection and active processing of the total lesson experience.

Invite students to review their solutions for the Problem Set. They should check work by comparing answers with a partner before going over answers as a class. Look for misconceptions or misunderstandings that can be addressed in the Debrief. Guide students in a conversation to debrief the Problem Set and process the lesson.

You may choose to use any combination of the questions below to lead the discussion.

- Through discussion, guide students to articulate the idea that in order to show non unit fractions they are creating copies of the unit fractions. This is just as when counting to 3 we are making copies of 1 or when counting by 8 we are making copies of 8.

Exit Ticket (3 minutes)

After the Student Debrief, instruct students to complete the Exit Ticket. A review of their work will help you assess the students' understanding of the concepts that were presented in the lesson today and plan more effectively for future lessons. You may read the questions aloud to the students.

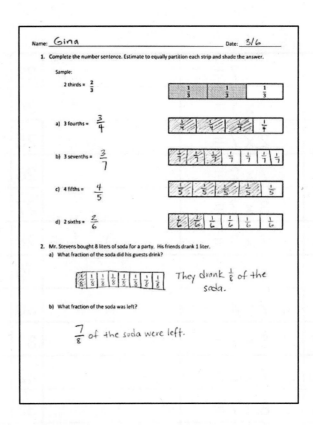

Lesson 6:   Build non-unit fractions less than one whole from unit fractions.
Date: 11/19/13

5.B.16

A

Correct _____

Multiply.

1	1 x 7 =		23	10 x 7 =	
2	7 x 1 =		24	9 x 7 =	
3	2 x 7 =		25	4 x 7 =	
4	7 x 2 =		26	8 x 7 =	
5	3 x 7 =		27	7 x 3 =	
6	7 x 3 =		28	7 x 7 =	
7	4 x 7 =		29	6 x 7 =	
8	7 x 4 =		30	7 x 10 =	
9	5 x 7 =		31	7 x 5 =	
10	7 x 5 =		32	7 x 6 =	
11	6 x 7 =		33	7 x 1 =	
12	7 x 6 =		34	7 x 9 =	
13	7 x 7 =		35	7 x 4 =	
14	8 x 7 =		36	7 x 3 =	
15	7 x 8 =		37	7 x 2 =	
16	9 x 7 =		38	7 x 7 =	
17	7 x 9 =		39	7 x 8 =	
18	10 x 7 =		40	11 x 7 =	
19	7 x 10 =		41	7 x 11 =	
20	7 x 3 =		42	12 x 7 =	
21	1 x 7 =		43	7 x 12 =	
22	2 x 7 =		44	13 x 7 =	

Lesson 6: Build non-unit fractions less than one whole from unit fractions.
Date: 11/19/13

5.B.17

B

Improvement _____   # Correct _____

Multiply.

1	7 x 1 =		23	9 x 7 =	
2	1 x 7 =		24	3 x 7 =	
3	7 x 2 =		25	8 x 7 =	
4	2 x 7 =		26	4 x 7 =	
5	7 x 3 =		27	7 x 7 =	
6	3 x 7 =		28	5 x 7 =	
7	7 x 4 =		29	6 x 7 =	
8	4 x 7 =		30	7 x 5 =	
9	7 x 5 =		31	7 x 10 =	
10	5 x 7 =		32	7 x 1 =	
11	7 x 6 =		33	7 x 6 =	
12	6 x 7 =		34	7 x 4 =	
13	7 x 7 =		35	7 x 9 =	
14	7 x 8 =		36	7 x 2 =	
15	8 x 7 =		37	7 x 7 =	
16	7 x 9 =		38	7 x 3 =	
17	9 x 7 =		39	7 x 8 =	
18	7 x 10 =		40	11 x 7 =	
19	10 x 7 =		41	7 x 11 =	
20	1 x 7 =		42	12 x 7 =	
21	10 x 7 =		43	7 x 12 =	
22	2 x 7 =		44	13 x 7 =	

Lesson 6: Build non-unit fractions less than one whole from unit fractions.
Date: 11/19/13

5.B.18

Name _____   Date _____

1. Complete the number sentence. Estimate to equally partition each strip and shade the answer.

    Sample:

    2 thirds = $\dfrac{2}{3}$

    a. 3 fourths =

    b. 3 sevenths =

    c. 4 fifths =

    d. 2 sixths =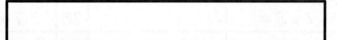

2. Mr. Stevens bought 8 liters of soda for a party. His friends drank 1 liter.

    a. What fraction of the soda did his guests drink?

    b. What fraction of the soda was left?

3. Fill in the chart. Whisper the total number of fractional units.

	Total Number of Equal Parts	Total Number of Shaded Equal Parts	Unit Fraction	Fraction Shaded
Sample:	4	3	$\frac{1}{4}$	$\frac{3}{4}$
a.				
b.				
c.				
d.				
e.				

Lesson 6: Build non-unit fractions less than one whole from unit fractions.
Date: 11/19/13

Name _____   Date _____

Estimate to equally partition the strip and shade the answer. Write the unit fraction inside each shaded unit.

2 fifths =

1.

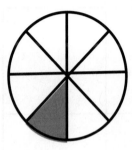

    a. What fraction of the circle is shaded?

    b. What fraction of the circle is not shaded?

2. Complete the chart.

	Total Number of Equal Parts	Total Number of Shaded Equal Parts	Unit Fraction	Fraction Shaded

Name _____   Date _____

1. Complete the number sentence. Estimate to equally partition each strip and shade the answer.

Sample:

3 fourths = $\dfrac{3}{4}$

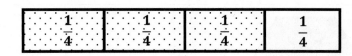

a. 2 thirds =

b. 5 sevenths =

c. 3 fifths =

d. 2 eighths =

2. Mr. Abney bought 6 kg of rice. He cooked 1 kg of it for dinner.

a. What fraction of the rice did he cook for dinner?

b. What fraction of the rice was left?

3. Fill in the chart.

	Total Number of Equal Parts	Total Number of Shaded Equal Parts	Unit Fraction	Fraction Shaded
Sample:	6	5	$\dfrac{1}{6}$	$\dfrac{5}{6}$
a.				
b.				
c.				
d.				

| Lesson 6:   Build non-unit fractions less than one whole from unit fractions.
Date: 11/19/13

5.B.23

Lesson 7

Objective: Identify and represent shaded and non-shaded parts of one whole as fractions.

Suggested Lesson Structure

■ Fluency Practice   (12 minutes)
■ Application Problem   (10 minutes)
■ Concept Development   (28 minutes)
■ Student Debrief   (10 minutes)
   Total Time   **(60 minutes)**

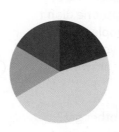

Fluency Practice (12 minutes)

- Count by Nine **3.OA.7**   (2 minutes)
- Sprint: Divide by Seven **3.OA.4**   (8 minutes)
- Skip-Count by Halves on the Clock **3.G.2, 3.NF.1**   (2 minutes)

Count by Nine (2 minutes)

Materials: (S) Personal white boards

Students count up to and down from 90 by nines on their personal white boards.

    T: Circle 27. How many nines did you count?
    S: 3 nines.
    T: What is 27 divided by 9?
    S: 3.

Repeat with other examples.

Sprint: Divide by Seven (8 minutes)

Materials: (S) Divide by Seven Sprint

Skip-Count by Halves on the Clock (2 minutes)

    T: (Hold or project a clock.) Let's skip-count by halves on the clock starting with 1.
    S: 1 o'clock, half past 1, 2, half past 2, 3, half past 3, 4, (Switch direction.) half past 3, 3, half past 2, 2,

---

Lesson 7:   Identify and represent shaded and non-shaded parts of one whole as
                fractions.
Date: 11/19/13

5.B.24

half past 1, 1.

Continue counting up and down.

Application Problem (10 minutes)

Robert was snacking on a small container of applesauce. He ate half of the container. His mother and sister were upset he didn't save much for them. So he split up the remaining applesauce into 2 bowls. Robert said, "I ate 1 half, and each of you got 1 half." Is Robert right? Draw a picture to prove your answer.

Bonus Questions:

- What fraction of the apple sauce did his mother get?
- Why can't the container be partitioned into 3 equal parts?
- What fraction of the applesauce did Robert's sister eat?

You can only have 2 halves in a whole. Robert is wrong!!! So 3 people cannot have $\frac{1}{2}$ each. His mom and sister got $\frac{1}{2}$ together!

Concept Development (28 minutes)

Materials: (T) Beaker, water (S) Paper, scissors, crayons, math journals

Show a beaker of liquid half full.

- T: Whisper the fraction of liquid that you see to your partner.
- S: 1 half.
- T: What about the part that is not full? Talk to your partner: Could that be a fraction, too? Why or why not?
- S: No, because there's nothing there. → I disagree. It's another part. It's just not full. → It's another half. Because half is filled, and so it has 1 more half to be all the way full.
- T: Even though parts might not be full or shaded, they are still part of the whole.
- T: Let's explore this idea more. I'll give you 1 sheet of paper. Partition it into any shape you choose. Just be sure of these 3 things:
  1. The parts must be equal.
  2. There are no less than 5, and no more than 20 parts in all.
  3. You use the entire sheet of paper.

NOTES ON MULTIPLE MEANS OF ACTION AND EXPRESSION:

Give explicit steps for problem solving to students below grade level. These steps can be organized as a checklist such as, "Underline important words, draw a model, label your model."

NOTES ON MULTIPLE MEANS OF REPRESENTATION:

These daily class discussions, as well as "Think-pair-share", support ELLs English language acquisition, offering them an opportunity to talk about their math ideas in English and to actively use the language of mathematics.

Lesson 7:	Identify and represent shaded and non-shaded parts of one whole as fractions.	5.B.25
Date:	11/19/13	

S: (Students estimate by folding to partition.)

T: Now use a crayon to shade the unit fraction.

S: (Students shade 1 part.)

T: Next we're going to cut our whole into parts. You'll reassemble your parts into a unique piece of art for our fraction museum. As you make your art, be sure that all parts are touching but not on top of or under each other.

S: (Students cut along the folds and reassemble pieces.)

T: As you tour our museum admiring the art, identify which unit fraction the artist chose and identify the fraction representing the un-shaded equal parts of the art. Write both fractions in your journal next to each other.

S: (Students walk around and collect data, to be used in the Debrief portion of the lesson.)

NOTES ON MULTIPLE MEANS OF ENGAGEMENT:

Offer students working above grade level a Problem Set alternative of constructing a word problem for one of the models (pictured in number 10). Constructively review errors with students who are accustomed to always scoring correctly or who may be perfectionists.

Problem Set (10 minutes)

Students should do their personal best to complete the Problem Set within the allotted 10 minutes. For some classes, it may be appropriate to modify the assignment by specifying which problems they work on first. Some problems do not specify a method for solving. Students solve these problems using the RDW approach used for Application Problems.

Student Debrief (10 minutes)

Lesson Objective: Identify and represent shaded and non-shaded parts of one whole as fractions.

The Student Debrief is intended to invite reflection and active processing of the total lesson experience.

Invite students to review their solutions for the Problem Set. They should check work by comparing answers with a partner before going over answers as a class. Look for misconceptions or misunderstandings that can be addressed in the Debrief. Guide students in a conversation to debrief the Problem Set and process the lesson.

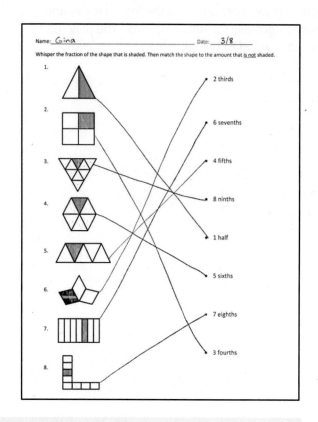

You may choose to use any combination of the questions below to lead the discussion.

MP.3

- ▪ Revisit students' art. Guide a discussion helping them recognize that everyone used the same whole but that each whole is composed of different unit fractions.

- ▪ Returning to the Problem Set, show examples of student work on question 4. Justin mowed 9 tenths of his lawn. What fraction of his lawn did he not mow? Isn't Justin's goal to mow the whole lawn? Guide the students to notice that the whole lawn can be depicted as the part he has mowed and the part he has not mowed. From that discussion, you might briefly return to the opening "shaded" and "un-shaded" figures and have students notice that the whole is able to be expressed as two parts, the shaded and un-shaded.

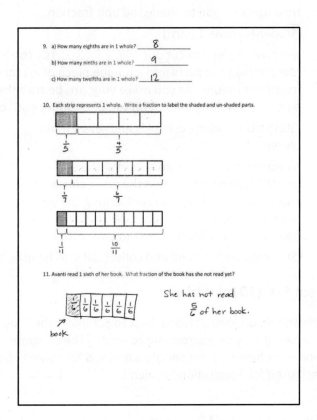

Exit Ticket (3 minutes)

After the Student Debrief, instruct students to complete the Exit Ticket. A review of their work will help you assess the students' understanding of the concepts that were presented in the lesson today and plan more effectively for future lessons. You may read the questions aloud to the students.

Lesson 7:	Identify and represent shaded and non-shaded parts of one whole as fractions.	5.B.27
Date:	11/19/13	

A

Multiply or divide.

Correct _____

1	$2 \times 7 =$		23	$\_\_ \times 7 = 70$	
2	$3 \times 7 =$		24	$\_\_ \times 7 = 14$	
3	$4 \times 7 =$		25	$\_\_ \times 7 = 21$	
4	$5 \times 7 =$		26	$70 \div 7 =$	
5	$1 \times 7 =$		27	$35 \div 7 =$	
6	$14 \div 7 =$		28	$7 \div 7 =$	
7	$21 \div 7 =$		29	$14 \div 7 =$	
8	$35 \div 7 =$		30	$21 \div 7 =$	
9	$7 \div 7 =$		31	$\_\_ \times 7 = 42$	
10	$28 \div 7 =$		32	$\_\_ \times 7 = 49$	
11	$6 \times 7 =$		33	$\_\_ \times 7 = 63$	
12	$7 \times 7 =$		34	$\_\_ \times 7 = 56$	
13	$8 \times 7 =$		35	$49 \div 7 =$	
14	$9 \times 7 =$		36	$63 \div 7 =$	
15	$10 \times 7 =$		37	$42 \div 7 =$	
16	$56 \div 7 =$		38	$56 \div 7 =$	
17	$49 \div 7 =$		39	$11 \times 7 =$	
18	$63 \div 7 =$		40	$77 \div 7 =$	
19	$42 \div 7 =$		41	$12 \times 7 =$	
20	$70 \div 7 =$		42	$84 \div 7 =$	
21	$\_\_ \times 7 = 35$		43	$14 \times 7 =$	
22	$\_\_ \times 7 = 7$		44	$98 \div 7 =$	

B

Improvement _____   # Correct _____

Multiply or divide.

1	1 x 7 =		23	__ x 7 = 14	
2	2 x 7 =		24	__ x 7 = 70	
3	3 x 7 =		25	__ x 7 = 21	
4	4 x 7 =		26	14 ÷ 7 =	
5	5 x 7 =		27	7 ÷ 7 =	
6	21 ÷ 7 =		28	70 ÷ 7 =	
7	14 ÷ 7 =		29	35 ÷ 7 =	
8	28 ÷ 7 =		30	21 ÷ 7 =	
9	7 ÷ 7 =		31	__ x 7 = 21	
10	35 ÷ 7 =		32	__ x 7 = 28	
11	10 x 7 =		33	__ x 7 = 63	
12	6 x 7 =		34	__ x 7 = 49	
13	7 x 7 =		35	56 ÷ 7 =	
14	8 x 7 =		36	63 ÷ 7 =	
15	9 x 7 =		37	42 ÷ 7 =	
16	49 ÷ 7 =		38	49 ÷ 7 =	
17	42 ÷ 7 =		39	11 x 7 =	
18	56 ÷ 7 =		40	77 ÷ 7 =	
19	70 ÷ 7 =		41	12 x 7 =	
20	63 ÷ 7 =		42	84 ÷ 7 =	
21	__ x 7 = 7		43	13 x 7 =	
22	__ x 7 = 35		44	91 ÷ 7 =	

COMMON CORE

Lesson 7:   Identify and represent shaded and non-shaded parts of one whole as fractions.

Date: 11/19/13

5.B.29

Name _____ Date _____

Whisper the fraction of the shape that is shaded. Then match the shape to the amount that <u>is not</u> shaded.

1.

- 2 thirds

2.

- 6 sevenths

3.

- 4 fifths

- 8 ninths

4.

- 1 half

5.

- 5 sixths

6.
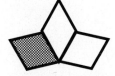

7.
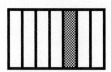

- 7 eighths

- 3 fourths

8.
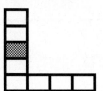

Lesson 7: Identify and represent shaded and non-shaded parts of one whole as fractions.

Date: 11/19/13

5.B.30

9.

    a.   How many eighths are in 1 whole? _____

    b.   How many ninths are in 1 whole? _____

    c.   How many twelfths are in 1 whole? _____

10. Each strip represents 1 whole. Write a fraction to label the shaded and un-shaded parts.

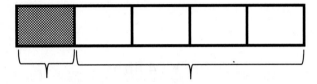

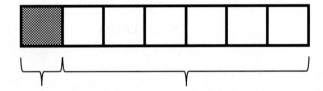

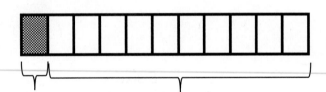

11. Avanti read 1 sixth of her book. What fraction of the book has she not read yet?

Name _____   Date _____

1. Write the fraction that is <u>not</u> shaded.

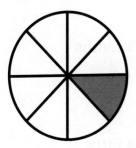

2. There are _____ sixths in 1 whole.

3. The fraction strip is 1 whole. Write fractions to label the shaded and un-shaded parts.

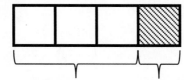

4. Justin mows part of his lawn. Then his lawnmower runs out of gas. He has not mowed $\frac{9}{10}$ of the lawn.
    What part of his lawn is mowed?

Lesson 7:	Identify and represent shaded and non-shaded parts of one whole as fractions.
Date:	11/19/13

Name _____   Date _____

Whisper the fraction of the shape that is shaded. Then match the shape to the amount that is not shaded.

1.

2.

3.

4.

5.

6.

7.

8.

- 9 tenths

- 4 fifths

- 10 elevenths

- 5 sixths

- 1 half

- 2 thirds

- 3 fourths

Lesson 7:   Identify and represent shaded and non-shaded parts of one whole as fractions.

Date: 11/19/13

5.B.33

9. Each strip represents 1 whole. Write a fraction to label the shaded and un-shaded parts.

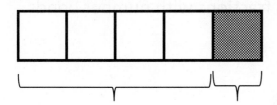

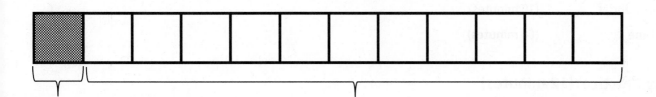

10. Carlia finished 1 fourth of her homework on Saturday. What fraction of her homework has she not finished? Draw and explain.

11. Jerome cooks 8 cups of oatmeal for his family. They eat 7 eighths of the oatmeal. What fraction of the oatmeal is uneaten? Draw and explain.

COMMON CORE

Lesson 7: Identify and represent shaded and non-shaded parts of one whole as fractions.
Date: 11/19/13

5.B.34

Lesson 8

Objective: Represent parts of one whole as fractions with number bonds.

Suggested Lesson Structure

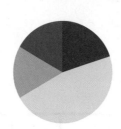

■ Fluency Practice	(12 minutes)	
■ Application Problem	(10 minutes)	
■ Concept Development	(28 minutes)	
■ Student Debrief	(10 minutes)	
Total Time	**(60 minutes)**	

Fluency Practice (12 minutes)

- Unit and Non-Unit Fractions of 1 Whole **3.NF.1**   (2 minutes)
- Sprint: Identify Fractions **3.G.2, 3.NF.2**   (10 minutes)

Unit and Non-Unit Fractions of 1 Whole (2 minutes)

Materials: (S) Personal white boards

    T: (Draw a shape partitioned in halves with 1 half shaded.) Write the fraction that is shaded.

    S: (Students write $\frac{1}{2}$.)

    T: Write the fraction that is not shaded.

    S: (Students write $\frac{1}{2}$.)

Continue with a possible sequence that includes the following shaded or non-shaded parts:

$\frac{2}{3}$ and $\frac{1}{3}$, $\frac{4}{5}$ and $\frac{1}{5}$, $\frac{9}{10}$ and $\frac{1}{10}$, $\frac{7}{8}$ and $\frac{1}{8}$.

Sprint: Identify Fractions (10 minutes)

Materials: (S) Identify Fractions Sprint

Important: Have the students keep Sprint B to use in the Concept Development lesson.

Application Problem (10 minutes)

Mr. Schwartz went to a coffee shop before school. He spent

Lesson 8:	Represent parts of one whole as fractions with number bonds.	5.B.35
Date:	11/19/13	

1 sixth of his money on a coffee and 1 sixth of his money on a bagel with cream cheese. How much of his money did Mr. Schwartz spend before school?

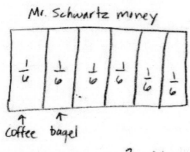

NOTES ON
MULTIPLE MEANS OF
ENGAGEMENT:

Challenge students working above grade level with extension questions, such as, "Did Mr. Schwartz spend more or less than 1 half of his money? How do you know?"

Concept Development (28 minutes)

Materials: (S) Personal white boards, Sprint B from the fluency

Problem 1: Decomposing 4 into ones

T: On your personal white board, write a number bond decomposing 4 into 4 ones.

S: (Students do so.)

T: Now, work with your partner to show a number bond decomposing 4 into 2 parts, one of which is composed of 3 ones.

S: (Students do so.)

T: It took 3 copies of one to make 3.

T: What are the two parts of your number bond? Please specify the unit.

S: 3 ones and 1 one.

T: Talk to your partner about the difference between these two number bonds.

S: The first bond has the ones all separated. → The second bond has 3 instead of 3 ones. → Both bonds are different ways of showing the same number, 4. → You could also show 4 as one part 2 and one part two. → The first bond has more parts than the second one.

NOTES ON
MULTIPLE MEANS OF
REPRESENTATION:

Emphasize key concepts and clarify unfamiliar words with gestures as you speak to ELLs. For example, when you say "decompose", hold your hands together then, with a downward motion, open them up to indicate a breaking apart, a separation, a splitting, a partitioning. This will clearly help English speakers, too, since this is probably a new word for them.

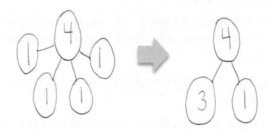

COMMON
CORE

Lesson 8:   Represent parts of one whole as fractions with number bonds.
Date: 11/19/13

5.B.36

Problem 2: Decomposing 1 into fourths

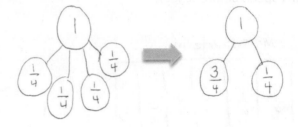

T: Write a number bond decomposing 1 into 4 unit fractions.

S: (Students do so.)

MP.7

T: Now, work with your partner to show a number bond decomposing 1 into 2 parts, one part of which is composed of 3 copies of the unit fraction.

T: What unit did we copy to make the number 3 fourths?

S: 1 fourth.

T: What are the two parts of your number bond? Please specify the unit.

S: 3 fourths and 1 fourth.

T: (Encourage students to compare the two number bonds just as they did with the number bond of 4.)

T: Look at your Sprint B. Discuss with your partner which of figures matches your number bond.

S: (#s 3, 6, 11, 18 – 25.)

Problem 3: Decomposing 1 into fifths (two non-unit fractions)

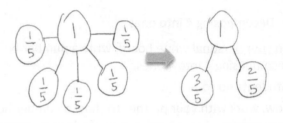

T: Write a number bond decomposing 1 into 5 unit fractions.

S: (Students do so.)

T: Now, work with your partner to show a number bond decomposing 1 into 2 parts, one part of which is 2 copies of 1 fifth.

S: What unit did we copy to make the number 2 fifths?

S: 1 fifth.

T: What are the two parts of your number bond? Please specify the unit.

S: 2 fifths and 3 fifths.

T: Look at your sprint side B. Discuss with your partner which of these wholes matches your number bond.

S: (#'s 30 -33)

T: Yes, 3 fourths can represent either the shaded or un-shaded part.

Having done these three problems, you might have the students use same process to model Questions 1, 12, 28, 39, and 44 from Sprint B. Ask them to find other models on the Sprint which are represented by the same bond.

 NOTES ON MULTIPLE MEANS OF ACTION AND EXPRESSION:

As you support a small group, go step by step. Avoid talking and doing at the same time. Draw a number bond in silence. Turn and face the group and ask them to explain to a partner what you just did. Then take the next action in silence. Ask them to explain your action again. This gives them the opportunity to analyze and reconstruct your actions so that they internalize a process they can use.

Lesson 8:   Represent parts of one whole as fractions with number bonds.
Date: 11/19/13

5.B.37

Problem Set (10 minutes)

Students should do their personal best to complete the Problem Set within the allotted 10 minutes. For some classes, it may be appropriate to modify the assignment by specifying which problems they work on first. Some problems do not specify a method for solving. Students solve these problems using the RDW approach used for Application Problems.

Student Debrief (10 minutes)

Lesson Objective: Represent parts of one whole as fractions with number bonds.

The Student Debrief is intended to invite reflection and active processing of the total lesson experience.

Invite students to review their solutions for the Problem Set. They should check work by comparing answers with a partner before going over answers as a class. Look for misconceptions or misunderstandings that can be addressed in the Debrief. Guide students in a conversation to debrief the Problem Set and process the lesson.

You may choose to use any combination of the questions below to lead the discussion.

- Share different representations for Problem 6 about the hamburger. Guide the students to see that the chef's refrigerated meat can be made into 3 more burgers and that each of those burgers is ¼ of the meat.

- As in Lesson 7's debrief, return to the shaded and un-shaded figures so that students articulate that 1 whole can ultimately be decomposed into unit fractions. The number bond is a perfect tool for seeing the transition from 1 whole to two parts to unit fractions. It is analogous as well to our beginning problem wherein we decomposed 4 into 4 ones.

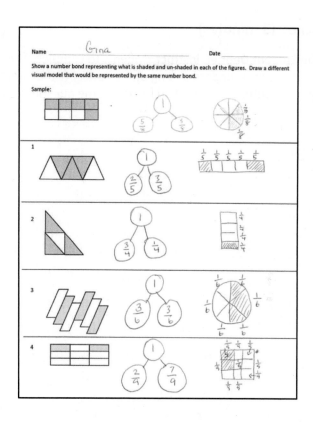

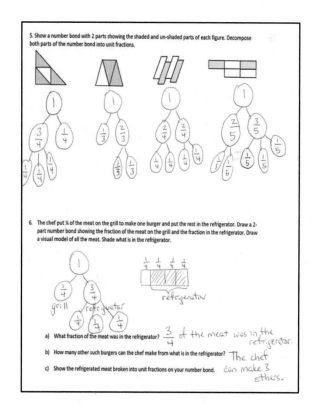

Lesson 8: Represent parts of one whole as fractions with number bonds.
Date: 11/19/13

5.B.38

Exit Ticket (3 minutes)

After the Student Debrief, instruct students to complete the Exit Ticket. A review of their work will help you assess the students' understanding of the concepts that were presented in the lesson today and plan more effectively for future lessons. You may read the questions aloud to the students

A

Correct _____

Write the fraction that is shaded.

1		/	23		/
2		/	24		/
3		/	25		/
4		/	26		/
5		/	27		/
6		/	28		/
7		/	29		/
8		/	30		/
9		/	31		/
10		/	32		/
11		/	33		/
12		/	34		/
13		/	35		/
14		/	36		/
15		/	37		/
16		/	38		/
17		/	39		/
18		/	40		/
19		/	41		/
20		/	42		/
21		/	43		/
22		/	44		/

Lesson 8:   Represent parts of one whole as fractions with number bonds.
Date: 11/19/13

5.B.40

B   Improvement _____   # Correct _____

Write the fraction that is shaded.

1	/	23	/
2	/	24	/
3	/	25	/
4	/	26	/
5	/	27	/
6	/	28	/
7	/	29	/
8	/	30	/
9	/	31	/
10	/	32	/
11	/	33	/
12	/	34	/
13	/	35	/
14	/	36	/
15	/	37	/
16	/	38	/
17	/	39	/
18	/	40	/
19	/	41	/
20	/	42	/
21	/	43	/
22	/	44	/

Lesson 8: Represent parts of one whole as fractions with number bonds.
Date: 11/19/13

5.B.4

Name _____ Date _____

Show a number bond representing what is shaded and unshaded in each of the figures. Draw a different visual model that would be represented by the same number bond.

Sample:

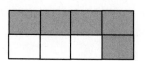 .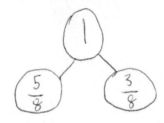

1.

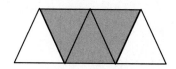

2.

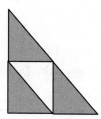

3.

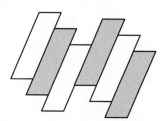

4.

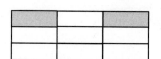

Lesson 8:   Represent parts of one whole as fractions with number bonds.
Date: 11/19/13

5.B.42

5. Draw a number bond with 2 parts showing the shaded and unshaded fractions of each figure. Decompose both parts of the number bond into unit fractions.

         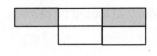

6. The chef put $\frac{1}{4}$ of the meat on the grill to make one burger and put the rest in the refrigerator. Draw a 2-part number bond showing the fraction of the meat on the grill and the fraction in the refrigerator. Draw a visual model of all the meat. Shade what is in the refrigerator.

   a. What fraction of the meat was in the refrigerator?

   b. How many other such burgers can the chef make from what is in the refrigerator?

   c. Show the refrigerated meat broken into unit fractions on your number bond.

Name _____   Date _____

1. Draw a number bond that shows the shaded and the unshaded parts of the shape below. Then show each part decomposed into unit fractions.

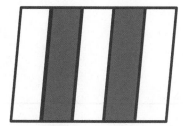

2. Complete the number bond. Draw a shape that has shaded and unshaded parts that match the completed number bond.

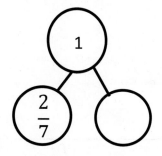

COMMON CORE

Lesson 8:   Represent parts of one whole as fractions with number bonds.
Date: 11/19/13

5.B.44

Name _____ Date _____

Show a number bond representing what is shaded and unshaded in each of the figures. Draw a different visual model that would be represented by the same number bond.

Sample:

1.

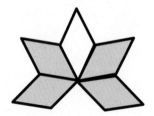

2.

3.

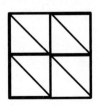

4.

5.B.46

5. Draw a number bond with 2 parts showing the shaded and unshaded fractions of each figure. Decompose both parts of the number bond into unit fractions.

  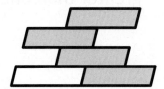 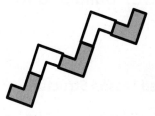

6. Johnny made a square peanut butter and jelly sandwich. He ate $\frac{1}{3}$ of it and left the rest on his plate. Draw a picture of Johnny's sandwich. Shade the part he left on his plate then draw a number bond that matches what you drew. What part of his sandwich did Johnny leave on his plate?

Lesson 8: Represent parts of one whole as fractions with number bonds.
Date: 11/19/13

5.B.46

Lesson 9

Objective: Build and write fractions greater than one whole using unit fractions.

Suggested Lesson Structure

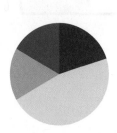

- ■ Fluency Practice   (12 minutes)
- ■ Application Problem   (10 minutes)
- ▢ Concept Development   (28 minutes)
- ■ Student Debrief   (10 minutes)

    Total Time   **(60 minutes)**

Fluency Practice (12 minutes)

- ▪ Multiply by Eight Sprint **3.OA.2**   (8 minutes)
- ▪ Find the Missing Part **3.NF.3d**   (2 minutes)
- ▪ Skip-Count by Halves on the Clock **3.G.2, 3.NF.1**   (2 minutes)

Multiply by Eight Sprint (8 minutes)

Materials: (S) Multiplication by Eight Sprint

Find the Missing Part (2 minutes)

Materials: (T) Blank number bond

T: (Project number bond with $\frac{3}{3}$ as the whole and $\frac{2}{3}$ as a part.) Say the whole.

S: 3 thirds.

T: Say the given part.

S: 2 thirds.

T: Say the missing part.

S: 1 third.

T: (Writes $\frac{1}{3}$ in the missing part space.)

Continue with whole and part sequence: $\frac{6}{6}$ and $\frac{1}{6}$, $\frac{8}{8}$ and $\frac{3}{8}$, 1 whole and $\frac{3}{10}$, 1 whole and $\frac{7}{12}$.

Lesson 9:   Build and write fractions greater than one whole using unit fractions.
Date: 11/19/13

5.B.47

Skip-Count by Halves on the Clock (2 minutes)

T: (Hold or project a clock.) Let's skip-count by halves on the clock starting with 5.

S: 5 o'clock, half past 5, 6, half past 6, 7.

T: Stop. Skip-count by halves backwards starting with 7.

S: Half past 6, 6, half past 5, 5, half past 4, 4, half past 3, 3.

Continue counting up and down.

Application Problem (10 minutes)

Julianne's friendship bracelet has 8 beads. When it broke, the beads fell off. She could only find 1 of the beads. To fix her bracelet, what fraction of the beads does she need to buy?

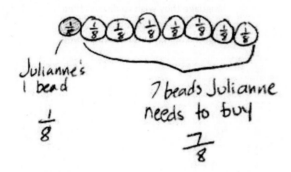

NOTES ON
MULTIPLE MEANS OF
ENGAGEMENT:

For students above grade level, extend the "application problem" with an open-ended prompt, such as, "If Julianne adds another bead of the same size and shape to her necklace, what fraction would the new bead represent? Why do you think so?"

Concept Development (28 minutes)

Materials: (S) Personal white boards, fraction strips

T: I brought 2 oranges for lunch today. I cut each one into fourths so that I could eat them easily. Draw a picture on your personal board to show how I cut my 2 oranges.

S: (Students draw.)

T: If 1 orange represents 1 whole, how many copies of 1 fourth are in 1 whole?

S: 4 copies.

T: Then what is our unit?

S: Fourths.

T: How many copies of 1 fourth in two whole oranges?

S: 8 copies.

T: Let's count them.

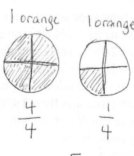

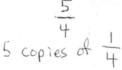

S: 1 fourth, 2 fourths, 3 fourths, (up to 8 fourths).

T: Are you sure our unit is still fourths? Talk with your partner.

S: No, it's in eighths because there are 8 pieces. → I disagree, because the unit is fourths in each orange. → Remember, each orange is a whole so the unit is fourths. 2 oranges aren't the whole!

T: I was so hungry I ate 1 whole orange and 1 piece of the second orange. Shade in the pieces I ate.

S: (Students shade.)

T: How many pieces did I eat?

S: 5 pieces.

T: And what's our unit?

S: Fourths.

T: So we can say that I ate 5 fourths of an orange for lunch. Let's count them.

S: 1 fourth, 2 fourths, 3 fourths, 4 fourths, 5 fourths.

T: On your personal board, work together to show 5 fourths as a number bond of unit fractions.

T: Compare the number of pieces I ate to 1 whole orange. What do you notice?

S: The number of pieces is bigger! → You ate more pieces than the whole.

T: Yes. If the number of parts is greater than the number of equal parts in the whole, then you know that the fraction describes more than 1 whole.

T: Can you make a number bond with 2 parts, one part showing the pieces that make up the whole and the other part showing the pieces that are more than the whole?

NOTES ON MULTIPLE MEANS OF ACTION AND EXPRESSION:

Turn-and-talk is an excellent way for ELLs to use English to discuss their math thinking. Let ELLs choose the language they wish to discuss their math reasoning, particularly if their English language fluency is limited.

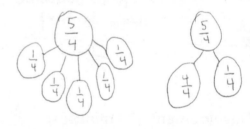

Demonstrate again using another concrete example. Follow by working with fraction strips. Fold fraction strips so that students have at least 2 strips representing halves, at least 2 strips representing each of the following fractions: thirds, fourths, sixths and eighths. Students can then build and identify fractions greater than 1 and less than 3 with the sets of fraction strips. Note that these fraction strips will be used again in Lesson 10. You may want to collect them or have students store them in a safe place.

NOTES ON MULTIPLE MEANS OF ENGAGEMENT:

For students below grade level, respectfully facilitate self-assessment of personal goals. Guide students to reflect upon questions such as, "Which fraction skills am I good at? What would I like to be better at? What is my plan to improve?" Celebrate improvement.

Lesson 9:   Build and write fractions greater than one whole using unit fractions.
Date: 11/19/13

5.B.49

Problem Set (10 minutes)

Students should do their personal best to complete the Problem Set within the allotted 10 minutes. For some classes, it may be appropriate to modify the assignment by specifying which problems they work on first. Some problems do not specify a method for solving. Students solve these problems using the RDW approach used for Application Problems.

Student Debrief (10 minutes)

Lesson Objective: Build and write fractions greater than one whole using unit fractions.

The Student Debrief is intended to invite reflection and active processing of the total lesson experience.

Invite students to review their solutions for the Problem Set. They should check work by comparing answers with a partner before going over answers as a class. Look for misconceptions or misunderstandings that can be addressed in the Debrief. Guide students in a conversation to debrief the Problem Set and process the lesson.

You may choose to use any combination of the questions below to lead the discussion.

- Problem 3 is likely to be challenging, and may result in confusion about whether the children ate $\frac{10}{8}$ or $\frac{10}{16}$. $\frac{10}{8}$ represents the amount of pans they ate, and $\frac{10}{16}$ represents the number of brownies they ate. The question asks for the number of pans. Have students share their work to spark a discussion that helps clarify this. The student work sample shows 2 different ways to write the answer.

- Although students have not been introduced to mixed fractions, it may be an intuitive way for them to answer the question. If so, you may have a natural opportunity to briefly examine and discuss the 2 'different' answers. Have students then return to clarify the lesson's objective. Have

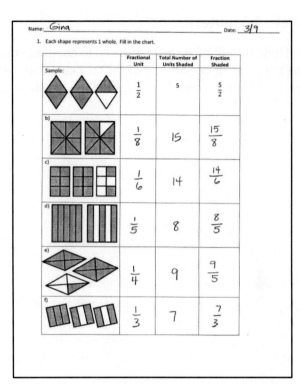

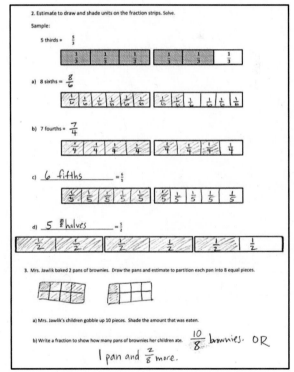

them discuss with a partner how to identify a fraction greater than one whole. If they are ready, advance to how they can identify a fraction greater than 2 wholes, etc.

| Lesson 9: | Build and write fractions greater than one whole using unit fractions. |
| Date: | 11/19/13 |

5.B.50

Exit Ticket (3 minutes)

After the Student Debrief, instruct students to complete the Exit Ticket. A review of their work will help you assess the students' understanding of the concepts that were presented in the lesson today and plan more effectively for future lessons. You may read the questions aloud to the students.

Lesson 9:   Build and write fractions greater than one whole using unit fractions.
Date: 11/19/13

5.B.51

A

Correct _____

Multiply.

1	8 x 1 =		23	9 x 8 =	
2	1 x 8 =		24	3 x 8 =	
3	8 x 2 =		25	8 x 8 =	
4	2 x 8 =		26	4 x 8 =	
5	8 x 3 =		27	7 x 8 =	
6	3 x 8 =		28	5 x 8 =	
7	8 x 4 =		29	6 x 8 =	
8	4 x 8 =		30	8 x 5 =	
9	8 x 5 =		31	8 x 10 =	
10	5 x 8 =		32	8 x 1 =	
11	8 x 6 =		33	8 x 6 =	
12	6 x 8 =		34	8 x 4 =	
13	8 x 7 =		35	8 x 9 =	
14	7 x 8 =		36	8 x 2 =	
15	8 x 8 =		37	8 x 7 =	
16	8 x 9 =		38	8 x 3 =	
17	9 x 8 =		39	8 x 8 =	
18	8 x 10 =		40	11 x 8 =	
19	10 x 8 =		41	8 x 11 =	
20	1 x 8 =		42	12 x 8 =	
21	10 x 8 =		43	8 x 12 =	
22	2 x 8 =		44	13 x 8 =	

B

Improvement _____   # Correct _____

Multiply.

1	1 x 8 =		23	10 x 8 =	
2	8 x 1 =		24	9 x 8 =	
3	2 x 8 =		25	4 x 8 =	
4	8 x 2 =		26	8 x 8 =	
5	3 x 8 =		27	8 x 3 =	
6	8 x 3 =		28	7 x 8 =	
7	4 x 8 =		29	6 x 8 =	
8	8 x 4 =		30	8 x 10 =	
9	5 x 8 =		31	8 x 5 =	
10	8 x 5 =		32	8 x 6 =	
11	6 x 8 =		33	8 x 1 =	
12	8 x 6 =		34	8 x 9 =	
13	7 x 8 =		35	8 x 4 =	
14	8 x 7 =		36	8 x 3 =	
15	8 x 8 =		37	8 x 2 =	
16	9 x 8 =		38	8 x 7 =	
17	8 x 9 =		39	8 x 8 =	
18	10 x 8 =		40	11 x 8 =	
19	8 x 10 =		41	8 x 11 =	
20	8 x 3 =		42	12 x 8 =	
21	1 x 8 =		43	8 x 12 =	
22	2 x 8 =		44	13 x 8 =	

Lesson 9:   Build and write fractions greater than one whole using unit fractions.
Date: 11/19/13

5.B.53

Name _____   Date _____

1. Each figure represents 1 whole. Fill in the chart.

	Unit Fraction	Total Number of Units Shaded	Fraction Shaded
a. Sample: 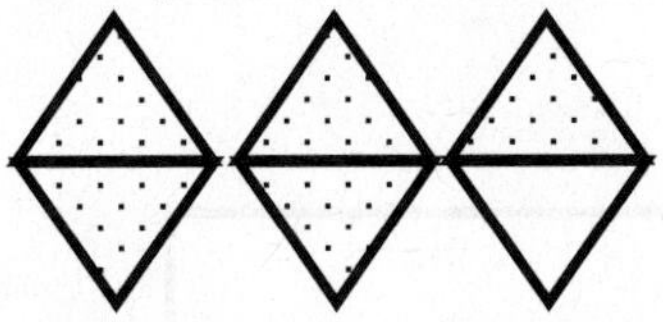	$\frac{1}{2}$	5	$\frac{5}{2}$
b. 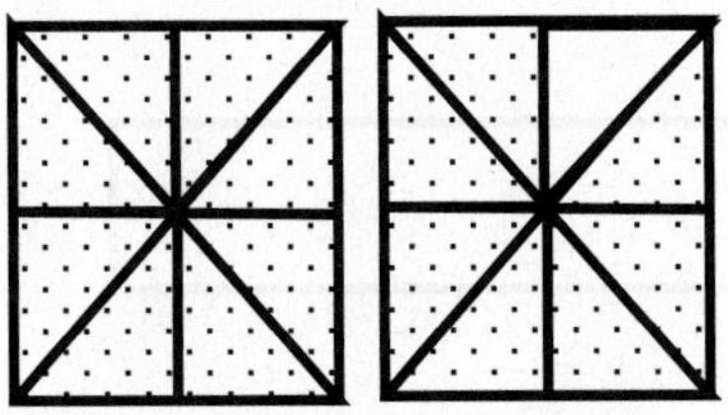			
c. 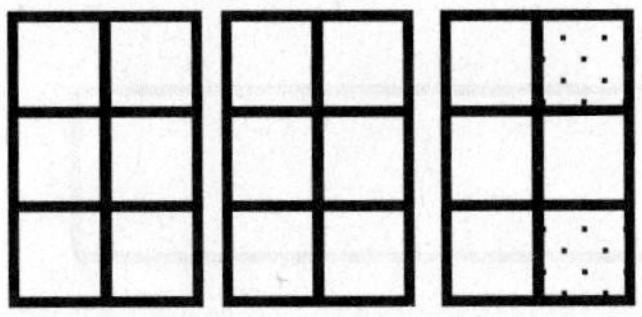			
d. 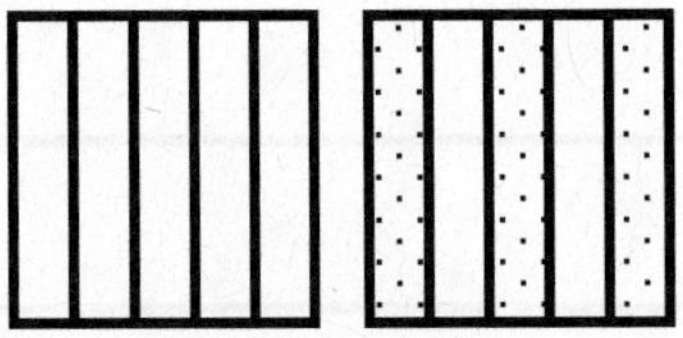			
e. 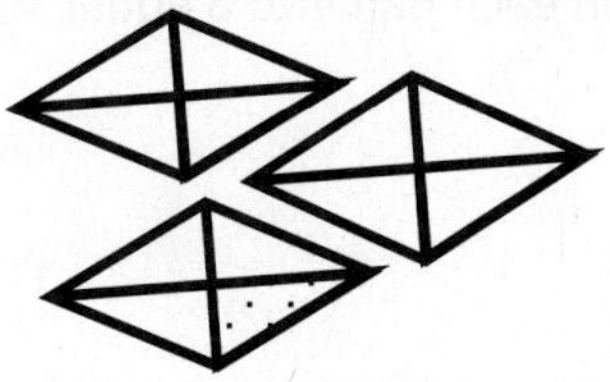			
f. 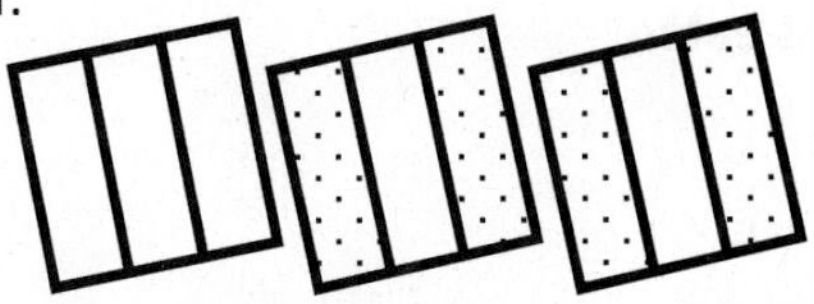			

COMMON CORE

Lesson 9:   Build and write fractions greater than one whole using unit fractions.
Date: 11/19/13

5.B.54

2. Estimate to draw and shade units on the fraction strips. Solve.

   Sample:

   5 thirds = $\dfrac{5}{3}$

   a. 8 sixths =

   b. 7 fourths =

   c. _____ = $\dfrac{6}{5}$

   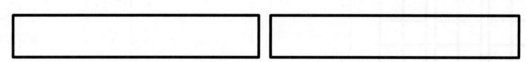

   d. _____ = $\dfrac{5}{2}$

3. Mrs. Jawlik baked 2 pans of brownies. Draw the pans and estimate to partition each pan into 8 equal pieces.

   a. Mrs. Jawlik's children gobble up 10 pieces. Shade the amount that was eaten.

   b. Write a fraction to show how many pans of brownies her children ate.

Name _____   Date _____

1. Each shape represents 1 whole. Fill in the chart.

	Fractional Unit	Total Number of Units Shaded	Fraction Shaded
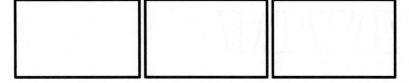			

2. Estimate to draw and shade units on the fraction strips. Solve.

a. 4 thirds =

b. _____ = $\frac{10}{4}$

COMMON CORE

Lesson 9:   Build and write fractions greater than one whole using unit fractions.
Date: 11/19/13

5.B.56

Name _____ Date _____

1. Each shape represents 1 whole. Fill in the chart.

	Fractional Unit	Total Number of Units Shaded	Fraction Shaded
a. Sample: 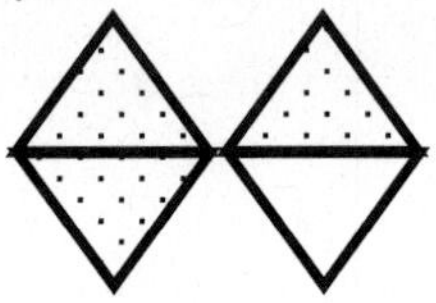	$\frac{1}{2}$	3	$\frac{3}{2}$
b. 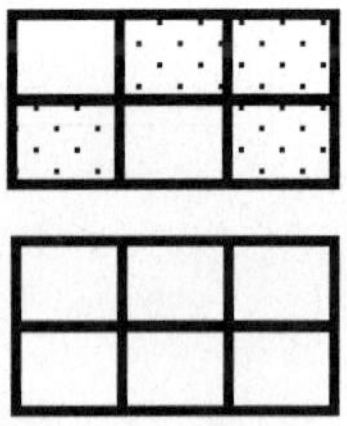			
c. 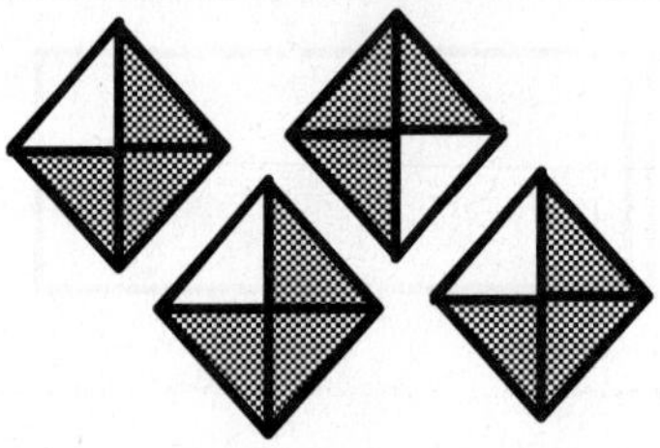			
d. 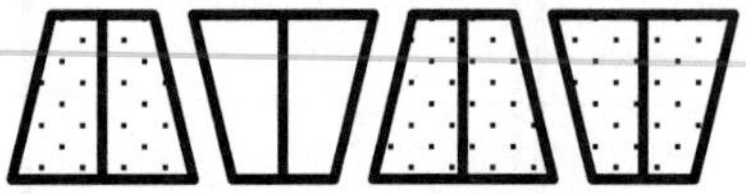			
e. 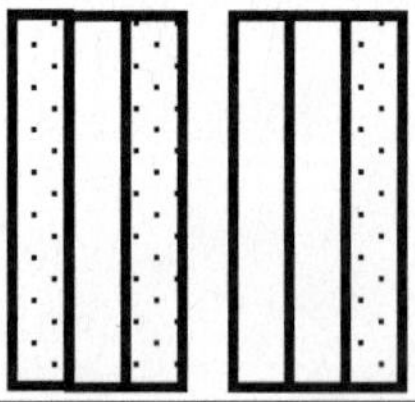			
f. 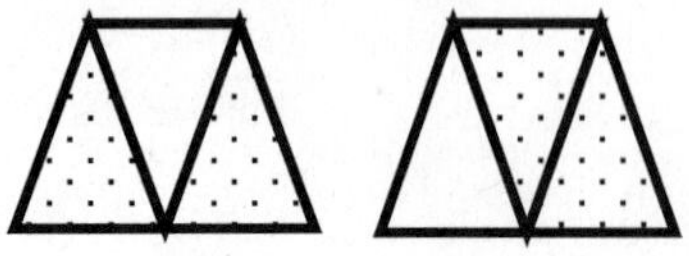			

Lesson 9: Build and write fractions greater than one whole using unit fractions.
Date: 11/19/13

5.B.57

2. Estimate to draw and shade units on the fraction strips. Solve.

Sample:

7 fourths = $\frac{7}{4}$

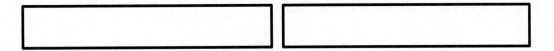

a. 5 thirds =

b. _____ = $\frac{9}{3}$

3. Reggie bought 2 candy bars. Draw the candy bars and estimate to partition each bar into 4 equal pieces.

a. Reggie ate 5 pieces. Shade the amount that was eaten.

b. Write a fraction to show how many pieces of the candy bar Reggie ate.

Topic C

Comparing Unit Fractions and Specifying the Whole

3.NF.3d, 3.NF.1, 3.NF.3a, 3.NF.3b, 3.NF.3c, 3.G.2

Focus Standard:	3.NF.3	Explain equivalence of fractions in special cases, and compare fractions by reasoning about their size.
		d. Compare two fractions with the same numerator or the same denominator by reasoning about their size. Recognize that comparisons are valid only when two fractions refer to the same whole. Record the results of comparisons with the symbols >, =, or <, and justify the conclusions, e.g., by using a visual fraction model.
Instructional Days:	4	
Coherence -Links from:	G2–M7	Recognizing Angles, Faces, and Vertices of Shapes, Fractions of Shapes
-Links to:	G4–M5	Order and Operations with Fractions

Students practiced identifying and labeling unit and non-unit fractions in Topic B. Now, in Topic C, they start out by comparing unit fractions. Using fraction strips, students recognize that when the same whole is folded into more equal parts, each part is smaller. Next, using real life examples and area models, students understand that when comparing fractions, the whole needs to be the same size. Next, students make corresponding wholes based on a given unit fraction using similar materials to those in Lesson 4's exploration: clay, yarn, two rectangles, and a square. They conduct a "museum walk" to study the wholes, identifying the unit fractions and observing part–whole relationships. Finally, students learn that redefining the whole can change the unit fraction that describes the shaded part.

A Teaching Sequence Towards Mastery of Comparing Unit Fractions and Specifying the Whole

Objective 1: Compare unit fractions by reasoning about their size using fraction strips.
(Lesson 10)

Objective 2: Compare unit fractions with different sized models representing the whole.
(Lesson 11)

Objective 3: Specify the corresponding whole when presented with one equal part.
(Lesson 12)

Objective 4: Identify a shaded fractional part in different ways depending on the designation of the whole.
(Lesson 13)

Lesson 10

Objective: Compare unit fractions by reasoning about their size using fraction strips.

Suggested Lesson Structure

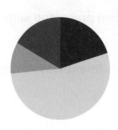

■ Fluency Practice   (12 minutes)
■ Application Problem   (6 minutes)
□ Concept Development   (32 minutes)
■ Student Debrief   (10 minutes)
   Total Time   **(60 minutes)**

Fluency Practice (12 minutes)

- Sprint: Divide by Eight **3.OA.4**   (9 minutes)
- Skip-Counting by Fourths on the Clock **3.G.2, 3.NF.1** (2 minutes)
- Greater or Less than 1 Whole **3.G.2, 3.NF.2**   (1 minute)

Sprint: Divide by Eight (9 minutes)

Materials: (S) Divide by Eight Sprint

Skip-Counting by Fourths on the Clock (2 minutes)

T: (Hold or project a clock.) Let's skip-count by fourths on the clock starting with 1.
S: 1, 1:15, 1:30, 1:45, 2, 2:15, 2:30, 2:45, 3.

Continue with possible sequences:

- 1, 1:15, half past 1, 1:45, 2, 2:15, half past 2, 2:45, 3.
- 1, quarter past 1, half past 1, quarter 'til 2, 2, quarter past 2, half past 2, quarter 'til 3, 3.

Greater or Less than 1 Whole (1 minute)

T: (Write $\frac{1}{2}$.) Greater or less than 1 whole?
S: Less!

Lesson 10:	Compare unit fractions by reasoning about their size using fraction strips.
Date:	11/19/13

5.C.3

Continue with possible sequence: $\frac{3}{2}, \frac{5}{4}, \frac{3}{4}, \frac{3}{7}, \frac{5}{3}, \frac{5}{2}$. It may be appropriate for some classes to draw responses on personal boards for extra support.

Application Problem (6 minutes)

Sarah makes soup. She divides each batch equally into thirds to give away. Each family that she makes soup for gets 1 third of a batch. Sarah needs to make enough soup for 5 families. How much soup does Sarah give away? Write your answer in terms of batches.

Bonus: What fraction will be left over for Sarah?

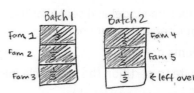

Concept Development (32 minutes)

Materials: (S) Folded fraction strips (halves, thirds, fourths, sixths, and eighths) from Lesson 9, personal white boards, 1 set of <, >, = cards per pair

MP.2

T: Take out the fraction strips you folded yesterday.

S: (Students take out strips folded into halves, thirds, fourths, sixths, and eighths.)

T: Look at the different units. Take a minute to arrange the strips in order from the largest to the smallest unit.

S: (Students place the fraction strips in order: halves, thirds, fourths, sixths and eighths.)

T: Turn and talk to your partner about what you notice.

S: Eighths are the smallest even though the number '8' is the biggest. → When the whole is folded into more units, then each unit is smaller. I only folded 1 time to get halves, and they're the biggest.

T: Look at 1 half and 1 third. Which unit is larger?

S: 1 half.

T: Explain to your partner how you know.

S: I can just see 1 half is bigger on the strip. → When you split it between 2 people, the pieces are bigger than if you split it between 3 people. → There are fewer pieces, so the pieces are bigger.

Continue with other examples using the fraction strips as necessary.

T: What happens when we aren't using fraction strips? What if we're talking about something round, like a pizza? Is 1 half still bigger than 1 third? Turn and talk to your partner about why or why not.

NOTES ON MUTLIPLE MEANS OF ENGAGEMENT:

Scaffold solving the application problem for students below grade level with step-by-step questioning. For example, ask, "How much soup does 1 family receive? (1 third of the batch of soup.) Two families? (2 thirds.) Three families? (3 thirds or 1 whole batch of soup.) Does Sarah have to make more than 1 batch? (Yes.) How much of the 2nd batch will she give? (2 thirds.) How much will remain?" (1 third.)

S: I'm not sure. → Sharing a pizza between 3 people is not as good as sharing it between 2 people. I think pieces that are halves are still bigger. → I agree because the number of parts doesn't change even if the shape of the whole changes.

T: Let's make a model and see what happens. Draw 5 circles that are the same size to represent pizzas on your personal white board.

S: (Students draw.)

T: Estimate to partition the first circle into halves. Label the unit fraction.

S: (Students draw and label.)

T: Estimate to partition the second circle into thirds. (Model if necessary.) Label the unit fraction.

S: (Students draw and label.)

T: What's happening to our pieces the more we cut?

S: They're getting smaller!

T: So is 1 third still smaller than 1 half?

S: Yes!

T: Partition your remaining circles into fourths, sixths, and eighths. Label each one.

S: (Students draw and label.)

T: Compare your drawings to your fraction strips. Do you notice the same pattern as with your fraction strips?

Continue with other real world examples if necessary.

T: Let's compare unit fractions. For each turn, you and your partner will both choose any 1 of your fraction strips. Choose now.

S: (Students each choose a strip to play.)

T: Now compare unit fractions by folding to show only the unit fraction and then placing the appropriate symbol card (<, >, or =) on the table between your strips.

S: (Students fold, compare and place symbol cards.)

T: (Hold symbol cards face down.) I will flip one of my symbol cards to see if the unit fraction that is 'greater than' or 'less than' wins this round. If I flip 'equals' it's a tie. (Flip a card.)

Continue at a rapid pace for a few rounds.

> **NOTES ON MULTIPLE MEANS OF ACTION AND EXPRESSION:**
>
> This partner activity benefits ELLs as it includes repeated use of math language in a reliable structure (e.g., "___ is greater than ___"). It also offers the ELL an opportunity to talk about the math with a peer, which may be more comfortable than speaking in front of the class or to the teacher.

Problem Set (10 minutes)

Students should do their personal best to complete the Problem Set within the allotted 10 minutes. For some classes, it may be appropriate to modify the assignment by specifying which problems they work on first. Some problems do not specify a method for solving. Students solve these problems using the RDW approach used for Application Problems.

Lesson 10:   Compare unit fractions by reasoning about their size using fraction strips.

Date: 11/19/13

5.C.5

Student Debrief (10 minutes)

Lesson Objective: Compare unit fractions by reasoning about their size using fraction strips.

The Student Debrief is intended to invite reflection and active processing of the total lesson experience.

Invite students to review their solutions for the Problem Set. They should check work by comparing answers with a partner before going over answers as a class. Look for misconceptions or misunderstandings that can be addressed in the Debrief. Guide students in a conversation to debrief the Problem Set and process the lesson.

You may choose to use any combination of the questions below to lead the discussion.

- How did Problem 3 help you answer Problem 5?
- How are Problems 3 and 5 the same and different?

The next lesson builds understanding that unit fractions can only be compared when they refer to the same whole. In this debrief you may want to lay the foundation for that work by drawing students' attention to the models they drew for questions 3 and 5. Discussion might include reasoning about why the models they drew facilitated comparison within each problem.

Exit Ticket (3 minutes)

After the Student Debrief, instruct students to complete the Exit Ticket. A review of their work will help you assess the students' understanding of the concepts that were presented in the lesson today and plan more effectively for future lessons. You may read the questions aloud to the students.

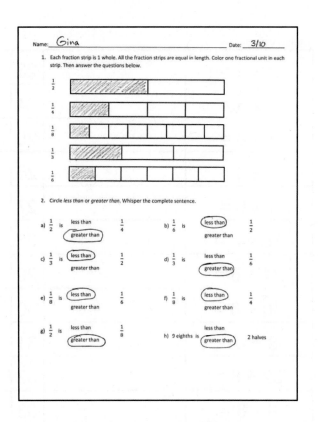

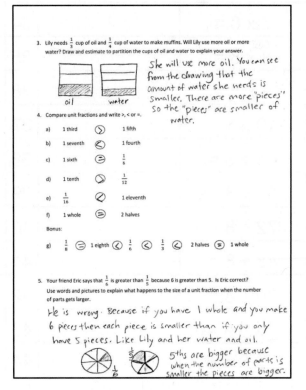

Lesson 10:   Compare unit fractions by reasoning about their size using fraction strips.
Date: 11/19/13

5.C.6

A

Multiply or divide.

Correct _____

1	$2 \times 8 =$		23	__ $\times 8 = 80$	
2	$3 \times 8 =$		24	__ $\times 8 = 16$	
3	$4 \times 8 =$		25	__ $\times 8 = 24$	
4	$5 \times 8 =$		26	$80 \div 8 =$	
5	$1 \times 8 =$		27	$40 \div 8 =$	
6	$16 \div 8 =$		28	$8 \div 8 =$	
7	$24 \div 8 =$		29	$16 \div 8 =$	
8	$40 \div 8 =$		30	$24 \div 8 =$	
9	$8 \div 8 =$		31	__ $\times 8 = 48$	
10	$32 \div 8 =$		32	__ $\times 8 = 56$	
11	$6 \times 8 =$		33	__ $\times 8 = 72$	
12	$7 \times 8 =$		34	__ $\times 8 = 64$	
13	$8 \times 8 =$		35	$56 \div 8 =$	
14	$9 \times 8 =$		36	$72 \div 8 =$	
15	$10 \times 8 =$		37	$48 \div 8 =$	
16	$64 \div 8 =$		38	$64 \div 8 =$	
17	$56 \div 8 =$		39	$11 \times 8 =$	
18	$72 \div 8 =$		40	$88 \div 8 =$	
19	$48 \div 8 =$		41	$12 \times 8 =$	
20	$80 \div 8 =$		42	$96 \div 8 =$	
21	__ $\times 8 = 40$		43	$14 \times 8 =$	
22	__ $\times 8 = 8$		44	$112 \div 8 =$	

Lesson 10:   Compare unit fractions by reasoning about their size using fraction
              strips.

Date: 11/19/13

5.C.7

B

Improvement _____   # Correct _____

Multiply or divide.

1	1 x 8 =		23	__ x 8 = 16	
2	2 x 8 =		24	__ x 8 = 80	
3	3 x 8 =		25	__ x 8 = 24	
4	4 x 8 =		26	16 ÷ 8 =	
5	5 x 8 =		27	8 ÷ 8 =	
6	24 ÷ 8 =		28	80 ÷ 8 =	
7	16 ÷ 8 =		29	40 ÷ 8 =	
8	32 ÷ 8 =		30	24 ÷ 8 =	
9	8 ÷ 8 =		31	__ x 8 = 24	
10	40 ÷ 8 =		32	__ x 8 = 32	
11	10 x 8 =		33	__ x 8 = 72	
12	6 x 8 =		34	__ x 8 = 56	
13	7 x 8 =		35	64 ÷ 8 =	
14	8 x 8 =		36	72 ÷ 8 =	
15	9 x 8 =		37	48 ÷ 8 =	
16	56 ÷ 8 =		38	56 ÷ 8 =	
17	48 ÷ 8 =		39	11 x 8 =	
18	64 ÷ 8 =		40	88 ÷ 8 =	
19	80 ÷ 8 =		41	12 x 8 =	
20	72 ÷ 8 =		42	96 ÷ 8 =	
21	__ x 8 = 8		43	13 x 8 =	
22	__ x 8 = 40		44	104 ÷ 8 =	

Lesson 10:   Compare unit fractions by reasoning about their size using fraction strips.

Date: 11/19/13

5.C.8

Name _____   Date _____

1. Each fraction strip is 1 whole. All the fraction strips are equal in length. Color one fractional unit in each strip. Then answer the questions below.

$\frac{1}{2}$

$\frac{1}{4}$

$\frac{1}{8}$

$\frac{1}{3}$

$\frac{1}{6}$

2. Circle *less than* or *greater than*. Whisper the complete sentence.

a. $\frac{1}{2}$ is   less than $\frac{1}{4}$ b. $\frac{1}{6}$ is   less than $\frac{1}{2}$
                    greater than   greater than

c. $\frac{1}{3}$ is   less than $\frac{1}{2}$ d. $\frac{1}{3}$ is   less than $\frac{1}{6}$
                    greater than   greater than

e. $\frac{1}{8}$ is   less than $\frac{1}{6}$ f. $\frac{1}{8}$ is   less than $\frac{1}{4}$
                    greater than   greater than

g. $\frac{1}{2}$ is   less than $\frac{1}{8}$ h. 9 eighths is   less than   2 halves
                    greater than   greater than

Lesson 10:   Compare unit fractions by reasoning about their size using fraction strips.
Date: 11/19/13

3. Lily needs $\frac{1}{3}$ cup of oil and $\frac{1}{4}$ cup of water to make muffins. Will Lily use more oil or more water? Draw and estimate to partition the cups of oil and water to explain your answer.

4. Compare unit fractions and write >, <, or =.

   a. 1 third $\bigcirc$ 1 fifth

   b. 1 seventh $\bigcirc$ 1 fourth

   c. 1 sixth $\bigcirc$ $\frac{1}{6}$

   d. 1 tenth $\bigcirc$ $\frac{1}{12}$

   e. $\frac{1}{16}$ $\bigcirc$ 1 eleventh

   f. 1 whole $\bigcirc$ 2 halves

   Bonus:

   g. $\frac{1}{8}$ $\bigcirc$ 1 eighth $\bigcirc$ $\frac{1}{6}$ $\bigcirc$ $\frac{1}{3}$ $\bigcirc$ 2 halves $\bigcirc$ 1 whole

5. Your friend Eric says that $\frac{1}{6}$ is greater than $\frac{1}{5}$ because 6 is greater than 5. Is Eric correct? Use words and pictures to explain what happens to the size of a unit fraction when the number of parts gets larger.

Name _____   Date _____

1. Each fraction strip is 1 whole. All the fraction strips are equal in length. Color one fractional unit in each strip. Then, circle the largest fraction and draw a star to the right of the smallest fraction.

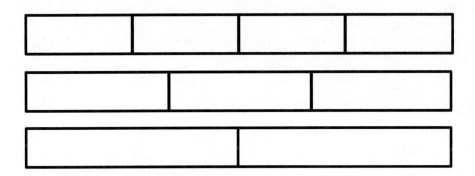

2. Compare unit fractions and write >, <, or =.

   a.   1 eighth   ◯   1 tenth

   b.   1 whole   ◯   5 fifths

   c. $\dfrac{1}{7}$ ◯ $\dfrac{1}{6}$

COMMON CORE | **Lesson 10:**   Compare unit fractions by reasoning about their size using fraction strips.

Date: 11/19/13

5.C.11

Name _____   Date _____

1. Each fraction strip is 1 whole. All the fraction strips are equal in length. Color one fractional unit in each strip. Then answer the questions below.

$\frac{1}{2}$

$\frac{1}{3}$

$\frac{1}{5}$

$\frac{1}{4}$

$\frac{1}{9}$

2. Circle *less than* or *greater than*. Whisper the complete sentence.

a. $\frac{1}{2}$ is   less than / greater than $\frac{1}{3}$

b. $\frac{1}{9}$ is   less than / greater than $\frac{1}{2}$

c. $\frac{1}{4}$ is   less than / greater than $\frac{1}{2}$

d. $\frac{1}{4}$ is   less than / greater than $\frac{1}{9}$

e. $\frac{1}{5}$ is   less than / greater than $\frac{1}{3}$

f. $\frac{1}{5}$ is   less than / greater than $\frac{1}{4}$

g. $\frac{1}{2}$ is   less than / greater than $\frac{1}{5}$

h. 6 fifths is   less than / greater than   3 thirds

Lesson 10: Compare unit fractions by reasoning about their size using fraction strips.
Date: 11/19/13

5.C.12

3. After his football game, Malik drinks $\frac{1}{2}$ liter of water and $\frac{1}{3}$ liter of juice. Did Malik drink more water or juice? Draw and estimate to partition. Explain your answer.

4. Compare unit fractions and write >, <, or =.

    a. 1 fourth $\bigcirc$ 1 eighth

    b. 1 seventh $\bigcirc$ 1 fifth

    c. 1 eighth $\bigcirc$ $\frac{1}{8}$

    d. 1 twelfth $\bigcirc$ $\frac{1}{10}$

    e. $\frac{1}{15}$ $\bigcirc$ 1 thirteenth

    f. 3 thirds $\bigcirc$ 1 whole

5. Write a word problem using comparing fractions for your friends to solve. Be sure to show the solution so that your friends can check their work.

COMMON CORE

Lesson 10: Compare unit fractions by reasoning about their size using fraction strips.

Date: 11/19/13

5.C.1

Lesson 11

Objective: Compare unit fractions with different sized models representing the whole.

Suggested Lesson Structure

■ Fluency Practice   (8 minutes)
■ Application Problem   (6 minutes)
■ Concept Development   (32 minutes)
■ Student Debrief   (14 minutes)
  Total Time   **(60 minutes)**

Fluency Practice (8 minutes)

- Skip-Count by Fourths on the Clock **3.G.2, 3.NF.1**   (3 minutes)
- Greater or Less Than 1 Whole **3.G.2, 3.NF.2b**   (2 minutes)
- Write Fractions Greater Than 1 Whole **3.NF.2b**   (3 minutes)

Skip-Count by Fourths on the Clock (3 minutes)

Materials: (T) Clock

> T: (Hold or project a clock.) Let's skip-count by fourths on the clock starting with 5.
>
> S: 5, 5:15, 5:30, 5:45, 6, 6:15, 6:30, 6:45, 7.

Continue with possible sequences:

- 5, 5:15, half past 5, 5:45, 6, 6:15, half past 6, 6:45, 7.
- 5, quarter past 5, half past 5, quarter 'til 6, 6, quarter past 6, half past 6, quarter 'til 7, 7.

Greater or Less Than 1 Whole (2 minutes)

> T: (Write $\frac{1}{2}$.) Greater or less than 1 whole?
>
> S: Less!

**NOTES ON
MULTIPLE MEANS OF
ACTION AND
EXPRESSION:**

"Skip-Count by Fourths on the Clock" is a valuable opportunity for ELLs to practice everyday math language (time on the clock) within the comforts of the choral response.

Scaffold this quick oral fluency activity with hand clocks. As students move the minute hand to reflect the count, they are tangibly partitioning fourths of the clock (the whole).

Continue with possible sequence: $\frac{1}{2}, \frac{3}{2}, \frac{1}{3}, \frac{2}{3}, \frac{4}{3}, \frac{5}{3}, \frac{3}{4}, \frac{5}{4}, \frac{11}{10}, \frac{9}{10}, \frac{11}{8}, \frac{5}{8}, \frac{11}{6}, \frac{5}{6}, \frac{11}{12}, \frac{13}{12}$.

It may be appropriate for some classes to draw responses on personal white boards for extra support.

Lesson 11:	Compare unit fractions with different sized models representing the whole.	
Date:	11/19/13	5.C.14

Write Fractions Greater Than 1 Whole (3 minutes)

Materials: (S) Personal white boards

 T: How many halves are in 1 whole?

 S: 2 halves.

 T: What's one more half than 2 halves?

 S: 3 halves.

 T: Write it as a fraction on your personal white board.

 S: (Write $\frac{3}{2}$.)

Continue with possible sequence: $\frac{1}{3}$, $\frac{1}{4}$, $\frac{1}{5}$, $\frac{1}{10}$, $\frac{1}{6}$, $\frac{1}{8}$.

As students build confidence, omit the first 2 questions in the vignette.

Application Problem (6 minutes)

Rachel, Silvia, and Lola each received the same homework assignment but they only completed part of it. Rachel completed $\frac{1}{6}$ of hers, Silvia completed $\frac{1}{2}$ of hers, and Lola completed $\frac{1}{4}$ of hers. Write the amount of homework each girl completed from least to greatest. Draw a picture to prove your answer.

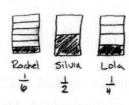

Rachel completed the least, Lola was next, and Silvia did the most out of the girls.

Concept Development (32 minutes)

Materials: (T) Two different sized clear plastic cups, food coloring, water (S) Personal white boards

 T: (Write 1 is the same as 1.) Show thumbs up if you agree, thumbs down if you disagree.

 S: (Most students show thumbs up.)

 T: 1 liter of soda and 1 can of soda. (Draw pictures or show objects.) Is 1 still the same as 1? Turn and talk to your partner.

MP.6 S: Yes, they're still the same amount. → No, a liter and a can are different. → How *many* stays the same, but a liter is bigger than a can so how *much* in each is different.

 T: How *many* and how *much* are important to our question. In this case, *what* each thing is changes it too. A liter is bigger so it has more soda than a can.

 T: How does this change your thinking about "1 is the same as 1?" Tell your partner.

 S: If the thing is bigger, then it has more. → Even though the number of things is the same, *what* it is might change how *much* of it there is. → If *what* it is and how *much* it is are different, then 1 and 1 aren't exactly the same.

Lesson 11:   Compare unit fractions with different sized models representing the whole.

Date: 11/19/13

5.C.15

T: As you compare 1 and 1, I hear you say that the size of the whole and how much is in it matters.

T: The same is true when comparing fractions.

T: For breakfast this morning, my brother and I each had a glass of juice. (Present different sized glasses partitioned into halves and fourths.)

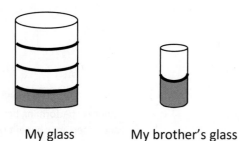

My glass   My brother's glass

T: What fraction of my glass has juice?

S: 1 fourth.

T: What fraction of my brother's glass has juice?

S: 1 half.

T: When the wholes are the same, 1 half is greater than 1 fourth. Does this picture prove that? Discuss it with your partner.

S: 1 half is always bigger than 1 fourth. → It looks like you might have drunk more, but the wholes aren't the same. → The glasses are different sizes like the can and the liter. We can't really compare.

T: I'm hearing you say that we have to consider the size of the whole when we compare fractions.

You may choose to further illustrate the point by pouring each glass of juice into containers that are the same size. It may be helpful to purposefully select your containers so that 1 fourth of the large glass is the larger quantity.

To transition into the pictorial work with wholes that are the same, demonstrate with another concrete example. This time use rectangular shaped 'wholes' that are different in size like those shown below.

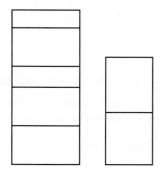

T: Let's see how comparison changes when our wholes are the same. Draw two rectangles that are the same size on your board. Partition them both into thirds.

S: (Draw and partition rectangles.)

Lesson 11: Compare unit fractions with different sized models representing the whole.
Date: 11/19/13

5.C.16

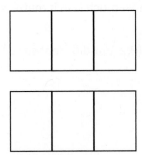

T: Now partition the first rectangle into sixths.

S: (Partition the first rectangle from thirds to sixths.)

T: Shade the unit fraction in each rectangle. Label your models and use the words 'greater than' or 'less than' to compare.

S: (Draw models.)

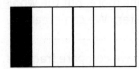

is less than

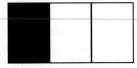

$\frac{1}{6}$ is less than $\frac{1}{3}$.

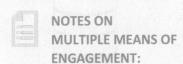

NOTES ON MULTIPLE MEANS OF ENGAGEMENT:

Students performing below grade level and others may benefit from having prepared Problem Sets that have pre-drawn wholes of the same shape and size to ease the task for those who may struggle.

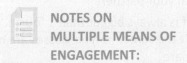

NOTES ON MULTIPLE MEANS OF ENGAGEMENT:

The open-ended nature of this activity helps meet students above grade level where they are. Encourage their creative solutions and maintain high expectations for precision and reasoning.

T: Does this picture prove that 1 sixth is less than 1 third? Why or why not? Discuss with your partner.

S: Yes, because the shapes are the same size. → One is just cut into more pieces than the other. → We know the pieces are smaller if there are more of them, as long as the whole is the same.

Demonstrate with more examples if necessary, perhaps rotating one of the shapes so that it appears different but does not change in size.

Lesson 11:   Compare unit fractions with different sized models representing the whole.

Date: 11/19/13

5.C.17

Problem Set (10 minutes)

Students should do their personal best to complete the Problem Set within the allotted 10 minutes. For some classes, it may be appropriate to modify the assignment by specifying which problems they work on first. Some problems do not specify a method for solving. Students solve these problems using the RDW approach used for Application Problems.

Student Debrief (14 minutes)

Lesson Objective: Compare unit fractions with different sized models representing the whole.

The Student Debrief is intended to invite reflection and active processing of the total lesson experience.

Invite students to review their solutions for the Problem Set. They should check work by comparing answers with a partner before going over answers as a class. Look for misconceptions or misunderstandings that can be addressed in the Debrief. Guide students in a conversation to debrief the Problem Set and process the lesson.

You may choose to use any combination of the questions below to lead the discussion.

- Problem Set Problem 10 presents wholes that are clearly different sizes, and also different shapes. Students may already have questioned this as they moved through the Problem Set. If so, you may want to credit the student(s) who asked and pose the question to the rest of the class for discussion. Know that the question of shape need not be answered today since it will be specifically addressed in Lesson 20. Allowing the class to grapple with the question now may provide useful information that guides your delivery of Lesson 20.

- Guide a conversation through which students understand that to compare wholes numerically, they must be the same size. You may want to close by having students redraw the diagrams in Problem 9 so that Elizabeth is correct, and in Problem 10 so that Manny is correct.

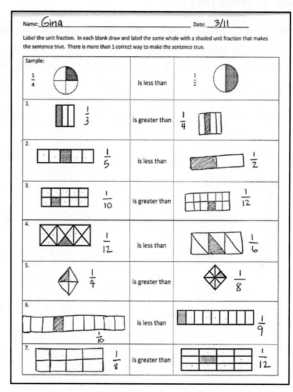

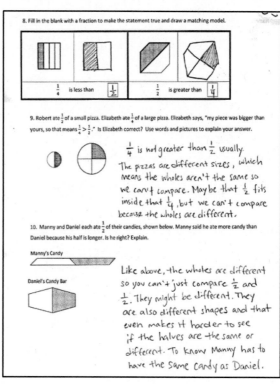

Lesson 11:   Compare unit fractions with different sized models representing the whole.

Date: 11/19/13

5.C.18

Exit Ticket (3 minutes)

After the Student Debrief, instruct students to complete the Exit Ticket. A review of their work will help you assess the students' understanding of the concepts that were presented in the lesson today and plan more effectively for future lessons. You may read the questions aloud to the students.

Lesson 11:	Compare unit fractions with different sized models representing the whole.
Date:	11/19/13

5.C.19

Name _____ Date _____

Label the unit fraction. In each blank, draw and label the same whole with a shaded unit fraction that makes the sentence true. There is more than 1 correct way to make the sentence true.

Sample: $\dfrac{1}{4}$	is less than	$\dfrac{1}{2}$
1.	is greater than	
2.	is less than	
3.	is greater than	
4.	is less than	

5.	is greater than	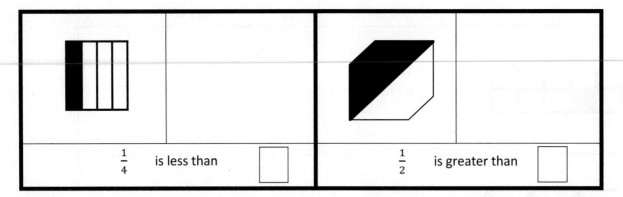
6.	is less than	
7.	is greater than	

8. Fill in the blank with a fraction to make the statement true and draw a matching model.

$\frac{1}{4}$	is less than	$\frac{1}{2}$	is greater than

COMMON CORE

Lesson 11: Compare unit fractions with different sized models representing the whole.

Date: 11/19/13

5.C.21

9. Robert ate $\frac{1}{2}$ of a small pizza. Elizabeth ate $\frac{1}{4}$ of a large pizza. Elizabeth says, "My piece was bigger than yours, so that means $\frac{1}{4} > \frac{1}{2}$." Is Elizabeth correct? Use words and pictures to explain your answer.

10. Manny and Daniel each ate $\frac{1}{2}$ of their candies, shown below. Manny said he ate more candy than Daniel because his half is longer. Is he right? Explain.

Manny's Candy

Daniel's Candy Bar
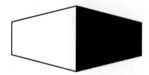

COMMON CORE

Lesson 11: Compare unit fractions with different sized models representing the whole.
Date: 11/19/13

5.C.22

Name _____   Date _____

1. Fill in the blank with a fraction to make the statement true and draw a matching model.

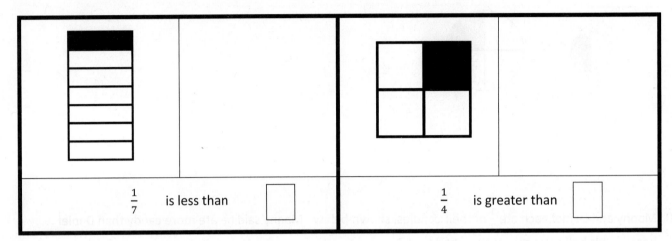

2. Tatiana ate $\frac{1}{2}$ of a small carrot. Louis ate $\frac{1}{4}$ of a large carrot. Who ate more carrot? Use words and pictures to explain your answer.

COMMON CORE   **Lesson 11:**   Compare unit fractions with different sized models representing the whole.

Date: 11/19/13

5.C.23

Name _____ Date _____

Label the unit fraction. In each blank draw and label the same whole with a shaded unit fraction that makes the sentence true. There is more than 1 correct way to make the sentence true.

Sample: $\frac{1}{3}$	is less than	$\frac{1}{2}$
1.	is greater than	
2.	is less than	
3.	is greater than	
4.	is less than	

5.	is greater than	
6.	is less than	
7.	is greater than	

8. Fill in the blank with a fraction to make the statement true and draw a matching model.

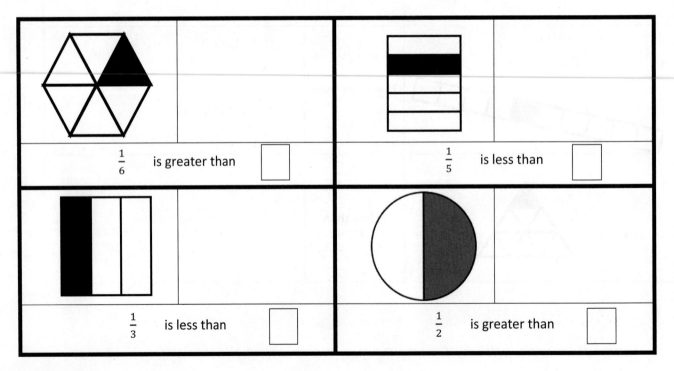

COMMON CORE   Lesson 11:   Compare unit fractions with different sized models representing the whole.

Date: 11/19/13   5.C.2

© 2013 Common Core, Inc. All rights reserved. **commoncore.org**

9. Debbie ate $\frac{1}{8}$ of a large brownie. Julian ate $\frac{1}{2}$ of a small brownie. Julian says, "I ate more brownies than you because $\frac{1}{2} > \frac{1}{8}$."

     a. Use pictures and words to explain Julian's mistake.

     b. How could you change the problem so that Julian is correct? Use pictures and words to explain.

COMMON CORE | **Lesson 11:**   Compare unit fractions with different sized models representing the whole.
Date: 11/19/13

5.C.26

Lesson 12

Objective: Specify the corresponding whole when presented with one equal part.

Suggested Lesson Structure

■ Fluency Practice	(12 minutes)
■ Application Problem	(8 minutes)
■ Concept Development	(32 minutes)
■ Student Debrief	(8 minutes)
Total Time	**(60 minutes)**

Fluency Practice (12 minutes)

- Sprint: Multiply by 9 **3.OA.4** (6 minutes)
- Unit and Non-Unit Fractions of 1 Whole **3.G.2, 3.NF.2** (3 minutes)
- More Units Than 1 Whole **3.NF.2b** (3 minutes)

Sprint: Multiply by 9 (6 minutes)

Materials: (S) Sprint: Multiply by 9

Unit and Non-Unit Fractions of 1 Whole (3 minutes)

Materials: (S) Personal white boards

T: (Draw a shape partitioned in halves with 1 half shaded.) Write the fraction that is shaded.
S: (Write $\frac{1}{2}$.)
T: Write the fraction that is not shaded.
S: (Write $\frac{1}{2}$.)
T: Write the number bond.
S: (Draw number bond showing that 1 half and 1 half equals 2 halves.)

Continue with a possible sequence that includes the following shaded or non-shaded parts:

$\frac{2}{3}$ and $\frac{1}{3}$, $\frac{4}{5}$ and $\frac{1}{5}$, $\frac{9}{10}$ and $\frac{1}{10}$, $\frac{7}{8}$ and $\frac{1}{8}$.

Lesson 12:	Specify the corresponding whole when presented with one equal part.	5.C.27
Date:	11/19/13	

More Units Than 1 Whole (3 minutes)

Materials: (S) Personal white boards (optional)

T: What's 1 more fifth than 1 whole?
S: 6 fifths.
T: 2 fifths more than 1 whole?
S: 7 fifths.

Continue for possible sequence: 4 fifths, 3 fifths, one tenth, 7 tenths, 1 third, 2 thirds, 1 eighth, 5 eighths, 1 sixth, 5 sixths.

It may be appropriate for some classes to draw responses on personal boards for extra support.

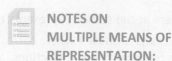

NOTES ON MULTIPLE MEANS OF REPRESENTATION:

Support students below grade level as they participate in "More Units Than 1 Whole" with pictorial models—teacher drawn or student drawn (on personal white boards).

Or you may begin with halves, thirds, and fourths, gradually progressing to tenths.

Application Problem (8 minutes)

Jennifer hid half her birthday money in the top drawer of her dresser. The other half she put in her jewelry box. If she hid $8 in her top drawer, how much money did she get for her birthday?

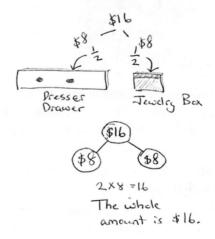

Concept Development (32 minutes)

Materials: (S) Use similar materials to those used in Lesson 4 (at least 75 copies of each), 10 centimeter length of yarn, 4 inch x 1 inch rectangular piece of yellow construction paper, 3 inch x 1 inch brown paper, 1 inch x 1 inch orange square

Exploration: Designate the following stations for three students per station (more than three not suggested).

    Station A: 1 half and 1 fourth
    Station B: 1 half and 1 third
    Station C: 1 third and 1 fourth
    Station D: 1 third and 1 sixth
    Station E: 1 fourth and 1 sixth
    Station F: 1 fourth and 1 eighth
    Station G: 1 fifth and 1 tenth
    Station H: 1 fifth and 1 sixth

NOTES ON MULTIPLE MEANS OF ENGAGEMENT:

Organize students below grade level at the stations with the easier fractional units and students above grade level stations with the most challenging fractional units.

The students are to represent 1 whole using the materials at their station.

Lesson 12:   Specify the corresponding whole when presented with one equal part.
Date: 11/19/13

5.C.28

Note:

- Each item at the station represents the indicated unit fractions.

- Students are to show 1 whole corresponding to the given unit fraction. Each station includes 2 objects representing unit fractions, and therefore 2 different whole amounts.

- The entire quantity of each item must be used as the fraction indicated. For example, if showing 1 third with the orange square, the whole must use 3 thirds or 3 of the orange squares.

T: (Hold up the same size ball of clay, 200 g, from Lesson 4.) This piece of clay represents 1 third. What does 1 whole look like? Discuss with your partner.

S: (Discuss.)

T: (After discussion, model the whole as 3 equal lumps of clay (600 g).)

T: (Hold up a 12 inch by 1 inch yellow strip.) This strip represents 1 fourth. What does 1 whole look like?

S: (Discuss.)

T: (After discussion, model the whole using 4 equal strips laid end to end: 48 inches.)

T: (Show a 12oz cup of water.) This cup represents 1 fifth. What does the whole look like? What if it represents 1 fourth? (Measure the 2 quantities into 2 separate containers.)

Give the students five minutes to create their display. Next, conduct a "museum walk" where they tour the work of the other stations. As they tour, students should identify the fractions and think about the relationships they are seeing. Use the following points to guide student thinking.

- Identify the unit fraction.

- Think about how the whole amount relates to your own and to other whole amounts.

- At 1 station, think about how the 2 whole amounts relate to each other.

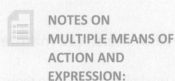

NOTES ON MULTIPLE MEANS OF ACTION AND EXPRESSION:

The museum walk is a rich opportunity for students to practice language. Pair students and give them sentence frames or prompts to use at each station to help them discuss what they see with their partner.

NOTES ON MULTIPLE MEANS OF REPRESENTATION:

Give ELLs a little more time to respond as they formulate their math thinking into English language. Offer a choice of responding in writing or in their first language.

Lesson 12: Specify the corresponding whole when presented with one equal part.
Date: 11/19/13

5.C.2

- Compare the yarn to the yellow strip.
- Compare the yellow strip to the brown paper.

Problem Set (10 minutes)

Students should do their personal best to complete the Problem Set within the allotted 10 minutes. For some classes, it may be appropriate to modify the assignment by specifying which problems they work on first. Some problems do not specify a method for solving. Students solve these problems using the RDW approach used for Application Problems.

Student Debrief (8 minutes)

Lesson Objective: Specify the corresponding whole when presenting with one equal part**.**

The Student Debrief is intended to invite reflection and active processing of the total lesson experience.

Invite students to review their solutions for the Problem Set. They should check work by comparing answers with a partner before going over answers as a class. Look for misconceptions or misunderstandings that can be addressed in the Debrief. Guide students in a conversation to debrief the Problem Set and process the lesson.

You may choose to use any combination of the questions below to lead the discussion.

- What were the different wholes we saw at each station that were the same?
- What different unit fractions did you see as you went from station to station?
- What did you notice about different unit fractions at the stations?
- Which unit fractions had the most equal parts?
- Which unit fractions had the least equal parts?
- What surprised you about the different representations of thirds, or any other fraction?
- How does the water compare to the clay? The clay to the yarn?

MP.2

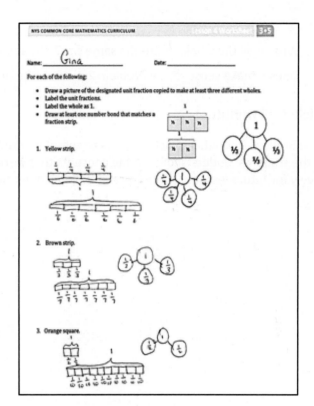

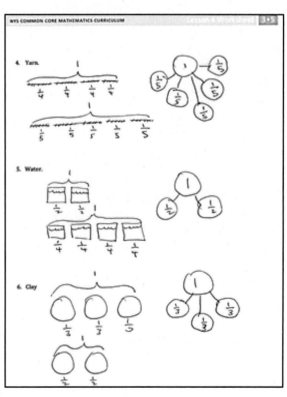

Lesson 12:　　Specify the corresponding whole when presented with one equal part.
Date:　　　11/19/13

5.C.30

MP.2
- What if all the wholes were the same size? What would happen to the equal parts?\
- Does it make sense to use Problem 2 picture (the brown strip) to compare $\frac{1}{3}$ and $\frac{1}{7}$? Why not?

Exit Ticket (3 minutes)

After the Student Debrief, instruct students to complete the Exit Ticket. A review of their work will help you assess the students' understanding of the concepts that were presented in the lesson today and plan more effectively for future lessons. You may read the questions aloud to the students.

Lesson 12:	Specify the corresponding whole when presented with one equal part.
Date:	11/19/13

5.C.3

A

Correct _____

Multiply.

1	9 x 1 =		23	9 x 9 =	
2	1 x 9 =		24	3 x 9 =	
3	9 x 2 =		25	8 x 9 =	
4	2 x 9 =		26	4 x 9 =	
5	9 x 3 =		27	7 x 9 =	
6	3 x 9 =		28	5 x 9 =	
7	9 x 4 =		29	6 x 9 =	
8	4 x 9 =		30	9 x 5 =	
9	9 x 5 =		31	9 x 10 =	
10	5 x 9 =		32	9 x 1 =	
11	9 x 6 =		33	9 x 6 =	
12	6 x 9 =		34	9 x 4 =	
13	9 x 7 =		35	9 x 9 =	
14	7 x 9 =		36	9 x 2 =	
15	9 x 8 =		37	9 x 7 =	
16	8 x 9 =		38	9 x 3 =	
17	9 x 9 =		39	9 x 8 =	
18	9 x 10 =		40	11 x 9 =	
19	10 x 9 =		41	9 x 11 =	
20	1 x 9 =		42	12 x 9 =	
21	10 x 9 =		43	9 x 12 =	
22	2 x 9 =		44	13 x 9 =	

Lesson 12:   Specify the corresponding whole when presented with one equal part.
Date: 11/19/13

5.C.32

B

Multiply.

Improvement _____   # Correct _____

1	1 x 9 =		23	10 x 9 =	
2	9 x 1 =		24	9 x 9 =	
3	2 x 9 =		25	4 x 9 =	
4	9 x 2 =		26	8 x 9 =	
5	3 x 9 =		27	3 x 9 =	
6	9 x 3 =		28	7 x 9 =	
7	4 x 9 =		29	6 x 9 =	
8	9 x 4 =		30	9 x 10 =	
9	5 x 9 =		31	9 x 5 =	
10	9 x 5 =		32	9 x 6 =	
11	6 x 9 =		33	9 x 1 =	
12	9 x 6 =		34	9 x 9 =	
13	7 x 9 =		35	9 x 4 =	
14	9 x 7 =		36	9 x 3 =	
15	8 x 9 =		37	9 x 2 =	
16	9 x 8 =		38	9 x 7 =	
17	9 x 9 =		39	9 x 8 =	
18	10 x 9 =		40	11 x 9 =	
19	9 x 10 =		41	9 x 11 =	
20	9 x 3 =		42	12 x 9 =	
21	1 x 9 =		43	9 x 12 =	
22	2 x 9 =		44	13 x 9 =	

Lesson 12:   Specify the corresponding whole when presented with one equal part.
Date: 11/19/13

5.C.3

Name _____ Date _____

For each of the following:

- Draw a picture of the designated unit fraction copied to make at least two different wholes.
- Label the unit fractions.
- Label the whole as 1.
- Draw at least one number bond that matches a drawing.

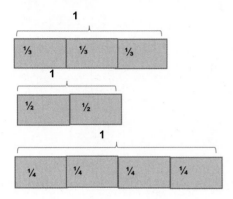

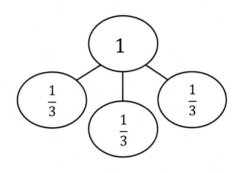

1. Yellow strip

2. Brown strip

| Lesson 12: | Specify the corresponding whole when presented with one equal part. |
| Date: | 11/19/13 |

5.C.34

3. Orange square

4. Yarn

5. Water

6. Clay

 Lesson 12:   Specify the corresponding whole when presented with one equal part.
Date: 11/19/13

5.C.3

Name _____   Date _____

Each shape represents the unit fraction. Draw a possible picture representing 1 whole.

1. $\dfrac{1}{7}$ 2. $\dfrac{1}{9}$

3. Aileen and Jack used the same triangle representing the unit fraction $\frac{1}{4}$ to create 1 whole. Who did it correctly? Explain.

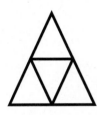

Aileen's
drawing

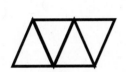

Jack's
drawing

Name _____ Date _____

Each shape represents the given unit fraction. Estimate to draw the whole.

1. $\frac{1}{2}$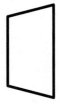

2. $\frac{1}{6}$

3. 1 third

4. 1 fourth

Each shape represents the given unit fraction. Estimate to draw the corresponding whole, label the unit fractions, then write a number bond that matches the drawing. The first one is done for you.

5. $\frac{1}{3}$

    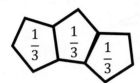   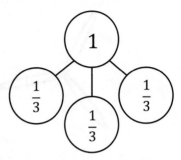

6. $\frac{1}{2}$

7. $\frac{1}{5}$

8. $\frac{1}{7}$

COMMON CORE   **Lesson 12:**   Specify the corresponding whole when presented with one equal part.
Date: 11/19/13   5.C.38

9. Evan and Yong used this shape , representing the unit fraction $\frac{1}{3}$, to draw 1 whole. Shania thinks both of them did it correctly. Do you agree with her? Explain.

COMMON CORE | **Lesson 12:**   Specify the corresponding whole when presented with one equal part.
                    | **Date:**   11/19/13

5.C.3

Lesson 13

Objective: Identify a shaded fractional part in different ways depending on the designation of the whole.

Suggested Lesson Structure

■ Fluency Practice   (11 minutes)
■ Application Problem   (5 minutes)
■ Concept Development   (33 minutes)
■ Student Debrief   (11 minutes)

   Total Time   **(60 minutes)**

Fluency Practice (11 minutes)

- Skip-Count by Fourths on the Clock **3.G.2, 3.NF.1**   (2 minutes)
- Unit Fraction Counting **3.NF.1**   (3 minutes)
- Division **3.OA.2**   (3 minutes)
- Draw a Unit Whole **3.NF.3c**   (3 minutes)

Skip-Count by Fourths on the Clock (2 minutes)

Materials: (T) Clock

   T: (Hold or project a clock.) Let's skip-count by fourths on the clock starting with 1.
   S: 1, quarter past 1, half past 1, quarter 'til 2, 2, quarter past 2, half past 2, quarter 'til 3, 3.
   T: Stop. From 3:00, skip-count by fourths backwards.
   S: 3, quarter 'til 3, half past 2, quarter past 2, 2, quarter 'til 2, half past 1, quarter past 1, 1.

Unit Fraction Counting (3 minutes)

   T: (Draw a number line.) Count by halves to 2 halves, then back to zero.
   S: 1 half, 2 halves, 1 half, 0.
   T: This time count by halves to 2 halves.
   S: 1 half, 2 halves.
   T: Good. Count backwards by halves starting with one whole.
   S: 1 whole, 1 half, 0.

Lesson 13:	Identify a shaded fractional part in different ways depending on the designation of the whole.	5.C.40
Date:	11/19/13	

Continue, possibly with thirds, fourths, and eighths.

Division (3 minutes)

T: (Write 4 ÷ 2 =_____.) Say the number sentence and the answer.

S: 4 divided by 2 equals 2.

Continue with possible sequence: 6 ÷ 2, 6 ÷ 3, 8 ÷ 2, 8 ÷ 4, 10 ÷ 2, 10 ÷ 5, 12 ÷ 2, 12 ÷ 6, 12 ÷ 4, 12 ÷ 3.

Draw a Unit Whole (3 minutes)

Materials: (S) Personal white boards

T: Draw 1 unit on your personal board.

S: (Students draw 1 unit.)

T: Label the unit $\frac{1}{3}$. Now draw the whole that corresponds to your unit of $\frac{1}{3}$.

Continue with possible sequence: $\frac{1}{5}$, $\frac{1}{6}$, $\frac{1}{4}$, and $\frac{1}{2}$.

Application Problem (5 minutes)

Davis wants to make a picture using 9 square tiles. What fraction of the picture does 1 tile represent? Draw 3 different ways Davis could make his picture.

I block represents $\frac{1}{9}$ of the tower.

Concept Development (33 minutes)

Materials: (S) 1 index card per student or partners, black markers, fraction strips, personal white boards

T: Fold your index card to make 4 equal units. Shade and label the first unit. Each part is equal to what fraction of the whole?

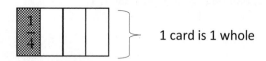

1 card is 1 whole

S: 1 fourth.

T: What is the whole?

S: The index card.

T: Take a black marker and trace the outside of your card to show what is the whole.

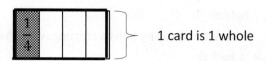

1 card is 1 whole

T: Flip your index card over so you cannot see the fraction you wrote. The new whole is half of the card. Outline it with marker. Use your pencil to shade the same amount of space you shaded on the other side. Talk with your partner about how to label the shaded amount on this side of the card.

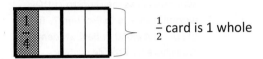 $\frac{1}{2}$ card is 1 whole

NOTES ON
MULTIPLE MEANS OF
ENGAGEMENT:

Instead of discussing with a partner "What you should label?", have above grade level students answer an open-ended question that requires higher-level thinking. For example, ask, "What number patterns (or relationships) do you notice?"

S: The shaded part is $\frac{1}{2}$ because the new whole is different. I see the whole. The shaded part is just half of that.

T: Changing the whole changed the unit fraction that we use to describe the shaded part. What was 1 fourth of the whole card is 1 half of the new, smaller whole.

Display the following figure, and give students a fraction strip of the same length.

T: This time the whole is the entire rectangle. Trace the outline of your fraction strip and then shade to draw the model on your board.

S: (Draw the model.)

T: Tell your partner how you can figure out what fraction is shaded.

S: I can estimate and draw lines to partition the rectangle. → I can fold my fraction strip to figure out the unit fraction. → Either way 2 thirds are shaded.

T: Now use your fraction strip to measure, partition and label.

| $\frac{1}{3}$ | $\frac{1}{3}$ | $\frac{1}{3}$ |

T: (Show the figure below and have students draw it on boards using fraction strips for accuracy.) If both of the outlined rectangles represent 1 whole, then what fraction is shaded? Discuss with your partner.

S: I can fold my fraction strip to measure the parts. → I can estimate to draw lines inside the small rectangles and partition each into 3 equal pieces. → Then 1 whole rectangle and 1 third are shaded, or $\frac{4}{3}$.

| Lesson 13: | Identify a shaded fractional part in different ways depending on the designation of the whole. |
| Date: | 11/19/13 |

5.C.42

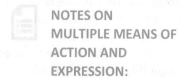

T: Talk with your partner about why it's important to know the whole.

Display the following picture.

MP.3

 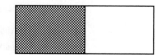

T: Kyle's mom brought his class cake for his birthday. When she picked up the 2 cake pans at the end of the day, she said, "Wow, your friends ate $\frac{3}{4}$ of the cake." Kyle said, "No mom, we ate $\frac{6}{4}$ cakes." Who is right? Talk about it with your partner. Use your personal boards to help prove your answer.

Problem Set (10 minutes)

Students should do their personal best to complete the Problem Set within the allotted 10 minutes. For some classes, it may be appropriate to modify the assignment by specifying which problems they work on first. Some problems do not specify a method for solving. Students solve these problems using the RDW approach used for Application Problems.

Distribute the Problem Set. Students work independently until there are 11 minutes remaining in the lesson.

Student Debrief (11 minutes)

Lesson Objective: Identify a shaded fractional part in different ways depending on the designation of the whole.

The Student Debrief is intended to invite reflection and active processing of the total lesson experience.

Invite students to review their solutions for the Problem Set. They should check work by comparing answers with a partner before going over answers as a class. Look for misconceptions or misunderstandings that can be addressed in the Debrief. Guide students in a conversation to debrief the Problem Set and process the lesson.

NOTES ON MULTIPLE MEANS OF ACTION AND EXPRESSION:

Support ELLs as they construct their written response to Problem 7. Read the prompt aloud or have students read chorally. Provide sentence starters and a word bank.

Sentence starters may include:

- "I agree with….because…"
- "I think ____ is right because…."

Possible words for the word bank may include:

specify   shaded   rectangle
whole   fourths   halves

NOTES ON MULTIPLE MEANS OF ENGAGEMENT:

Model a few examples of the Problem Set activities to support students working below grade level. Make sure they can specify the whole. Ask, "Trace the whole with your finger."

To aid partitioning in Part B, cover all but the shaded part.

For Problem 6, have students organize the data with a chart or table to facilitate comparisons, if needed.

COMMON CORE

Lesson 13: Identify a shaded fractional part in different ways depending on the designation of the whole.
Date: 11/19/13

5.C.43

You may choose to use any combination of the questions below to lead the discussion.

- In Problems A–D, box the rope that represents the whole and circle the rope that represents the part.
- Compare Problems E and F to illustrate the part-whole relationship.
- Compare Rope C in Problems A and D.
- Compare Rope B in Problems A and B.

Exit Ticket (3 minutes)

After the Student Debrief, instruct students to complete the Exit Ticket. A review of their work will help you assess the students' understanding of the concepts that were presented in the lesson today and plan more effectively for future lessons. You may read the questions aloud to the students.

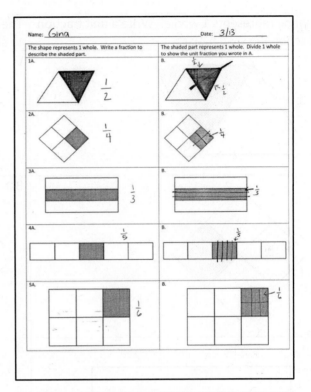

Lesson 13:	Identify a shaded fractional part in different ways depending on the designation of the whole.
Date:	11/19/13

Name _____   Date _____

The shape represents 1 whole. Write a unit fraction to describe the shaded part.	The shaded part represents 1 whole. Divide 1 whole to show the same unit fraction you wrote in A.
1A. 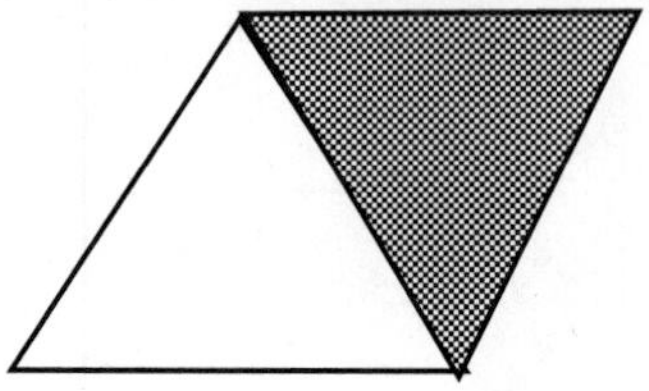	B. 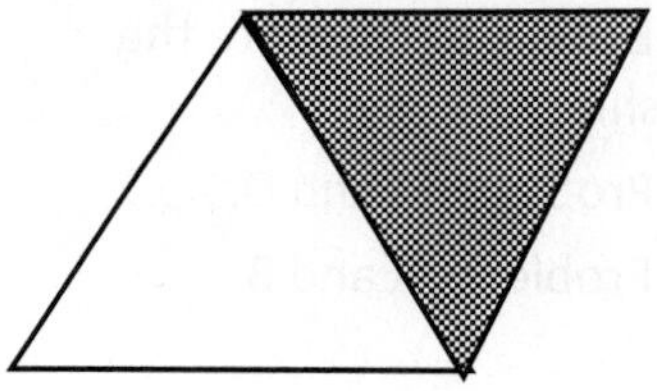
2A. 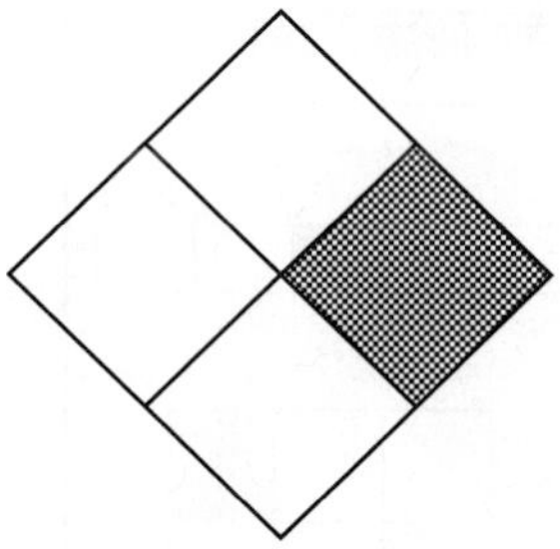	B. 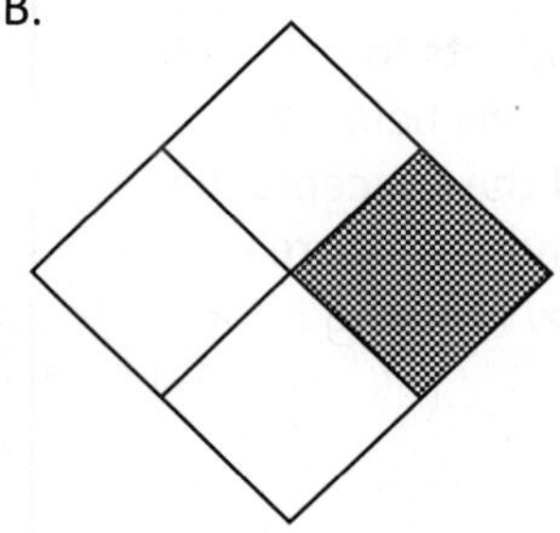
3A. 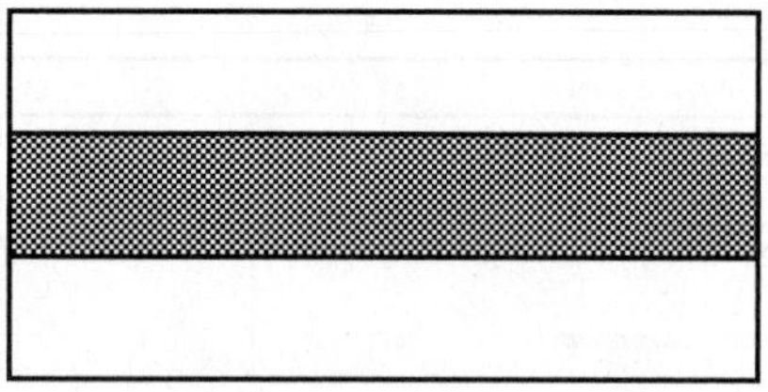	B. 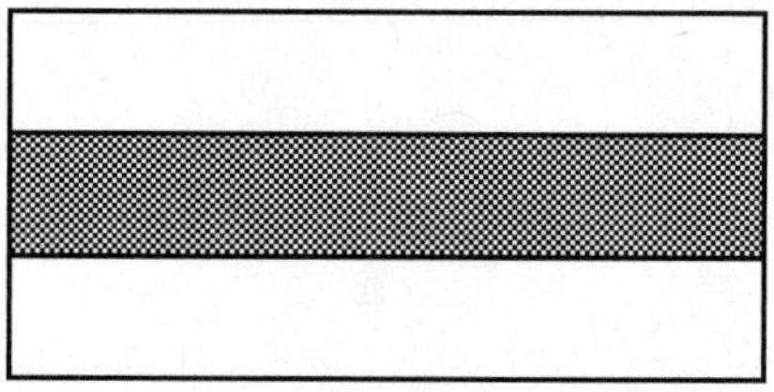
4A. 	B. 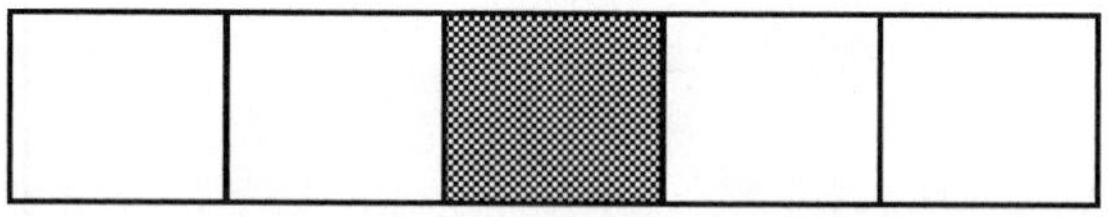
5A. 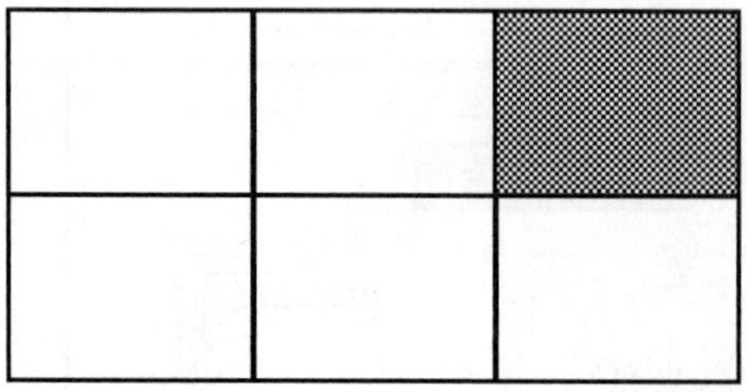	B. 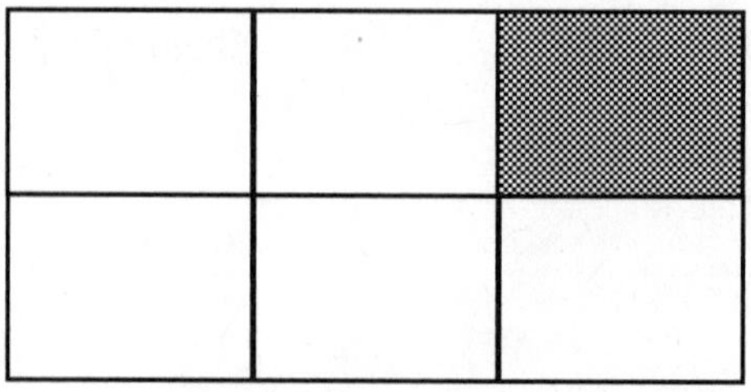

COMMON CORE

Lesson 13:   Identify a shaded fractional part in different ways depending on the designation of the whole.

Date: 11/19/13

5.C.4

6. Use the diagram below to complete the following statements.

Rope A

Rope B

Rope C

a. Rope _____ is $\frac{1}{2}$ the length of Rope B.   b. Rope _____ is $\frac{1}{2}$ the length of Rope A.

c. Rope B is $\frac{1}{2}$ the length of Rope _____.   d. Rope C is $\frac{1}{4}$ the length of Rope _____.

e. If Rope B measures 1m long, then Rope A is _____ m long and Rope C is _____ m long.

f. If Rope A measures 1m long, Rope B is _____ m long and Rope C is _____ m long.

7. Ms. Fan drew the figure below on the board. She asked the class to name the shaded fraction. Charlie answered $\frac{3}{4}$. Janice answered $\frac{3}{2}$. Jenna thinks they're both right. With whom do you agree? Explain your thinking.

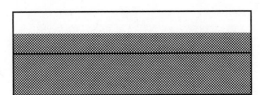

Lesson 13: Identify a shaded fractional part in different ways depending on the designation of the whole.

Date: 11/19/13

5.C.46

Name _____   Date _____

Ms. Silverstein asked the class to draw a model showing $\frac{2}{3}$ shaded. Karol and Deb drew the models below.
Which is correct? Explain how you know.

Karol's   Deb's

Name _____   Date _____

The shape represents 1 whole. Write a fraction to describe the shaded part.	The shaded part represents 1 whole. Divide 1 whole to show the same unit fraction you wrote in A.
1A. 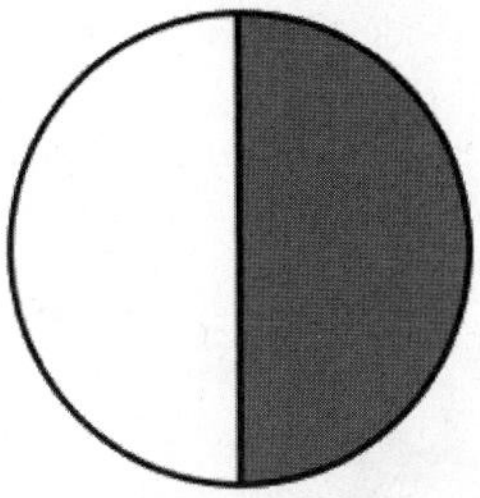	B. 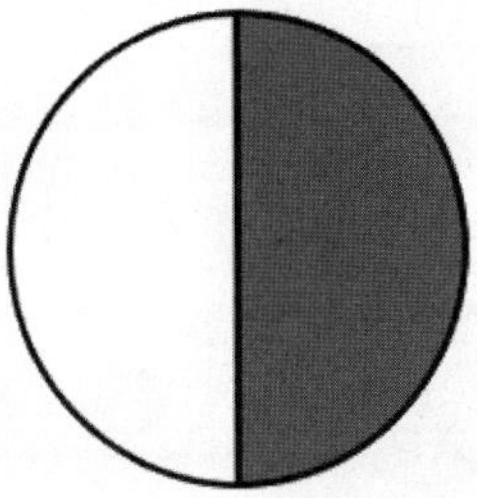
2A. 	B. 
3A. 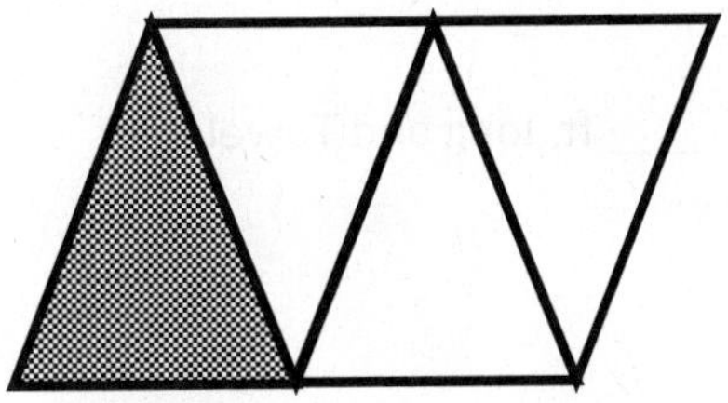	B. 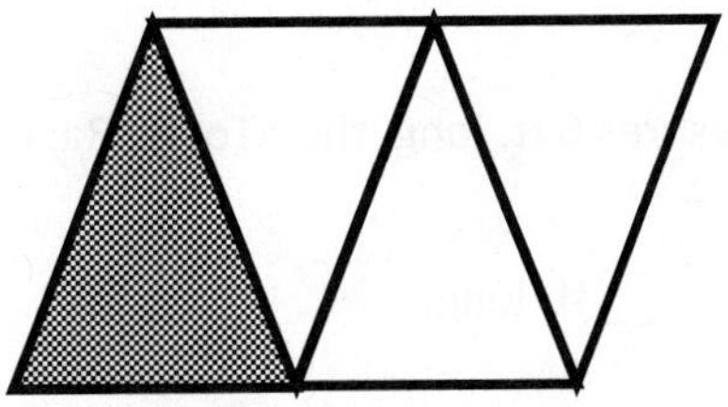
4A. 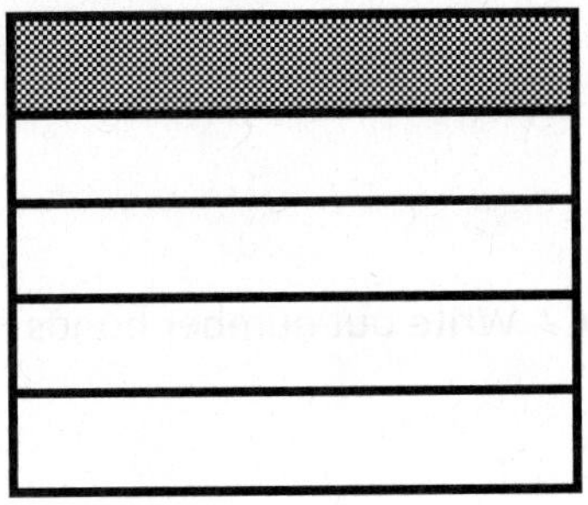	B. 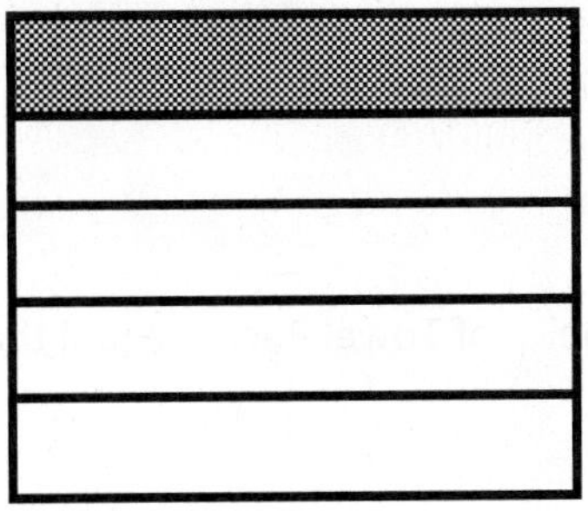

COMMON CORE

Lesson 13:   Identify a shaded fractional part in different ways depending on the designation of the whole.

Date: 11/19/13

5.C.48

5.   Use the pictures below to complete the following statements.

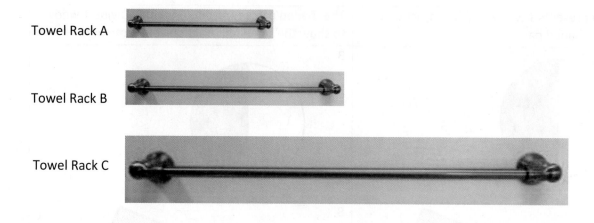

Towel Rack A

Towel Rack B

Towel Rack C

a.   _____ is about $\frac{1}{2}$ the length of Towel Rack C.

b.   _____ is about $\frac{1}{3}$ the length of Towel Rack C.

c.   If Towel Rack C measures 6 ft. long, then Towel Rack B is about _____ ft. long and Towel Rack

A is about _____ ft. long.

d.   About how many copies of Towel Rack A equal the length of Towel Rack C? Write number bonds to
help you.

e.   About how many copies of Towel Rack B equal the length of Towel Rack C? Write out number bonds
to help you.

6. Draw 4 strings, A, B, C, and D by following the directions below. String A is already done for you.

- String B is $\frac{1}{3}$ of String A.
- String C is $\frac{1}{2}$ of String B.
- String D is $\frac{1}{3}$ of String C.

BONUS: String E is 5 times the length of String D.

String A

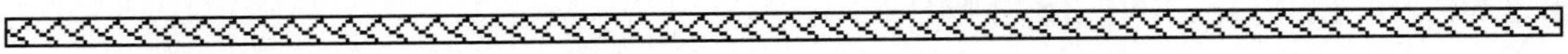

Lesson 13: Identify a shaded fractional part in different ways depending on the designation of the whole.
Date: 11/19/13

5.C.50

Topic D
Fractions on the Number Line

3.NF.2a, 3.NF.2b, 3.NF.3c, 3.NF.3d, 3.MD.4

Focus Standard:	3.NF.2	Understand a fraction as a number on the number line; represent fractions on a number line diagram.
		a. Represent a fraction 1/*b* on a number line diagram by defining the interval from 0 to 1 as the whole and partitioning it into *b* equal parts. Recognize that each part has size 1/*b* and that the endpoint of the part based at 0 locates the number 1/*b* on the number line.
		b. Represent a fraction *a*/*b* on a number line diagram by marking off *a* lengths 1/*b* from 0. Recognize that the resulting interval has size *a*/*b* and that its endpoint locates the number *a*/*b* on the number line.
	3.NF.3	Explain equivalence of fractions in special cases, and compare fractions by reasoning about their size.
		c. Express whole numbers as fractions, and recognize factions that are equivalent to whole numbers. *Examples: Express 3 in the form 3 = 3/1; recognize that 6/1 = 6; locate 4/4 and 1 at the same point of a number line diagram.*
		d. Compare two fractions with the same numerator or the same denominator by reasoning about their size. Recognize that comparisons are valid only when the two fractions refer to the same whole. Record the results of comparisons with the symbols >, =, <, and justify the conclusions, e.g., by using a visual fraction model.
Instructional Days:	6	
Coherence -Links from:	G2–M7	Time, Shapes, and Fractions as Equal Parts of Shapes
-Links to:	G4–M5	Fraction Equivalence, Ordering, and Operations

In Topic C, students compared unit fractions and explored the importance of specifying the whole when doing so. In Topic D, they apply their learning to the number line. Number bonds and fraction strips serve as bridges into this work. Students see intervals on the number line as wholes. They initially measure equal lengths between 0 and 1 with their fraction strips. They then work with number lines that have endpoints other than 0 and 1, or that include multiple whole number intervals. This naturally leads into comparing fractions with the same denominator, and fractions and whole numbers on the number line. As they compare, students reason about the size of fractions and contextualize their learning within real world applications.

A Teaching Sequence Towards Mastery of Fractions on the Number Line

Objective 1: Place unit fractions on a number line with endpoints 0 and 1.
(Lesson 14)

Objective 2: Place any fraction on a number line with endpoints 0 and 1.
(Lesson 15)

Objective 3: Place whole number fractions and unit fractions between whole numbers on the number line.
(Lesson 16)

Objective 4: Practice placing various fractions on the number line.
(Lesson 17)

Objective 5: Compare fractions and whole numbers on the number line by reasoning about their distance from 0.
(Lesson 18)

Objective 6: Understand distance and position on the number line as strategies for comparing fractions.
(Optional.)
(Lesson 19)

Lesson 14

Objective: Place unit fractions on a number line with endpoints 0 and 1.

Suggested Lesson Structure

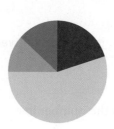

■ Fluency Practice	(12 minutes)
■ Application Problem	(7 minutes)
■ Concept Development	(33 minutes)
■ Student Debrief	(8 minutes)
Total Time	**(60 minutes)**

Fluency Practice (12 minutes)

- Division **3.OA.2**   (8 minutes)
- Unit Fraction Counting **3.NF.1, 3.NF.3**   (3 minutes)
- Unit Fractions in 1 Whole **3.NF.1**   (1 minute)

Division (8 minutes)

T: Write as many different division facts as you can in the next 2 minutes. Take your mark, get set, go.

S: (Students work independently.)

T: (At three minutes.) Share your work with your partner. Check to see if their problems are correct.

T: Try again for three minutes. Take your mark, get set, go.

T: Check your work with your partner. Tell them what division facts are easy for you.

T: Who improved? How did you improve? What helped you do more problems correctly?

Unit Fraction Counting (3 minutes)

T: (Project a number line.) Count by 1 eighth to 8 eighths.

S: $\frac{1}{8}, \frac{2}{8}, \frac{3}{8}, \frac{4}{8}, \frac{5}{8}, \frac{6}{8}, \frac{7}{8}, \frac{8}{8}, \frac{7}{8}, \frac{6}{8}, \frac{5}{8}, \frac{4}{8}, \frac{3}{8}, \frac{2}{8}, \frac{1}{8}$

Continue with possible sequence: fifths, thirds, and fourths.

> **NOTES ON**
> **MULTIPLE MEANS**
> **FOR ENGAGEMENT:**
>
> - Change directions so that the sequence stays unpredictable.
> - React to misunderstandings by repeating transitions until mastery.
> - Support by recording on a number line as students count.
> - Extend by having students say "1" or "1 whole" instead of a fraction. (E.g., "...6 eighths, 7 eighths, 1, 7 eighths, 6 eighths...")

Unit Fractions in 1 Whole (1 minute)

T: I'll say a unit. You say how many there are in 1 whole. 1 fifth.

S: 5 fifths are in 1 whole.

Continue with possible sequence: 1 tenth, 1 fourth, 1 third, 1 eighth, 1 half.

Application Problem (7 minutes)

Mr. Ray is knitting a scarf. He says that he has completed 1 fifth of the total length of the scarf.

Draw a picture of the final scarf. Label what he has finished and what he still has to make. Draw a number bond with 2 parts to show the fraction he has made and the fraction he has not made.

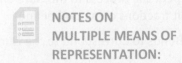

> **NOTES ON MULTIPLE MEANS OF REPRESENTATION:**
>
> Empower ELLs to solve word problems by activating prior knowledge. Guide students to make personal connections. Discuss their own experiences with knitting and scarves.

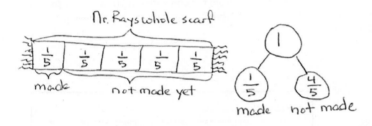

Concept Development (33 minutes)

Materials: (T) Board space, yard stick, large fraction strip for modeling (S) Fraction kit, blank paper, rulers, pencils

Measure a Line of Length 1 Whole:

1. Draw a horizontal line with your ruler that is a bit longer than 1 of your fraction strips.
2. Place a whole fraction strip just above the line you drew.
3. Make a small mark on the left end of your strip.
4. Label that mark 0 above the line. This is where we start measuring the length of the strip.
5. Make a small mark on the right end of your strip.
6. Label that mark 1 above the line. If we start at 0, the 1 tells us when we've travelled 1 whole length of the strip.

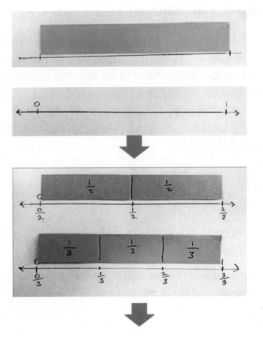

Measure the Unit Fractions:

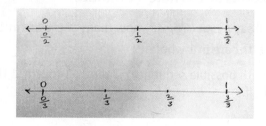

MP.7

1. Place your fraction strip with halves above the line.

2. Make a mark on the number line at the right end of 1 half. This is the length of 1 half of the fraction strip.

3. Label that mark $\frac{1}{2}$. Label 0 halves and 2 halves.

4. Repeat the process to measure and make other unit fractions on a number line.

Draw Number Bonds to Correspond to the Number Lines:

Once students have gotten good at making and labeling fraction number lines using strips to measure, have them draw number bonds to correspond. Use questioning as you circulate to help them see similarities and differences between the bonds, the fraction strips, and the fractions on the number line. You may want to use the following suggestions:

- What do both the number bond and number line show?

- Which model shows you how big the unit fraction is in relation to the whole? Explain how.

- How do your number lines help you to make number bonds?

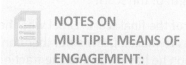

NOTES ON
MULTIPLE MEANS OF
ENGAGEMENT:

This lesson gradually leads the student from the concrete level (fraction strips) to the pictorial level (number lines).

Problem Set (10 minutes)

Students should do their personal best to complete the Problem Set within the allotted 10 minutes. For some classes, it may be appropriate to modify the assignment by specifying which problems they work on first. Some problems do not specify a method for solving. Students solve these problems using the RDW approach used for Application Problems.

Student Debrief (8 minutes)

Lesson Objective: Place unit fractions on a number line with endpoints 0 and 1.

The Student Debrief is intended to invite reflection and active processing of the total lesson experience.

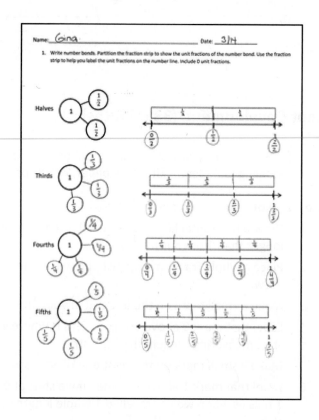

Invite students to review their solutions for the Problem Set. They should check work by comparing answers with a partner before going over answers as a class. Look for misconceptions or misunderstandings that can be addressed in the Debrief. Guide students in a conversation to debrief the Problem Set and process the lesson.

You may choose to use any combination of the questions below to lead the discussion.

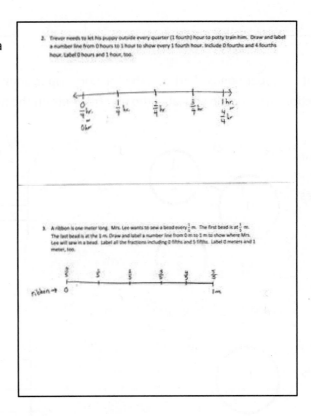

- Describe the process for labeling unit fractions on the number line.

- Why is the fraction strip an important tool to use when labeling unit fractions?

- What does the fraction strip help you measure?

- Look at the number line you made for Problem 3 on the Problem Set. What does each point on the number line mean? (Possible response: "$\frac{1}{5}$ marks the distance from 0 – the end of the ribbon – to where Mrs. Lee sews on the first bead.")

- In the puppy-walking problem, the point is a point in time, not the whole length. In the ribbon problem, the point describes the length of the ribbon. Let them have fun with the difference between these two problems.
  The puppy is in one location, like the mark on the line. The ribbon is the entire length. You may want to use the following suggestions to guide the discussion:

  - Think about the units of measure in Problem Set Problems 2 and 3. How are they the same? How are they different?

  - How does the unit of measure change what's happening in the problem? How does that change what the number line shows?

  - How does what each number line shows stay the same?

Exit Ticket (3 minutes)

After the Student Debrief, instruct students to complete the Exit Ticket. A review of their work will help you assess the students' understanding of the concepts that were presented in the lesson today and plan more effectively for future lessons. You may read the questions aloud to the students.

Lesson 14:   Place unit fractions on a number line with endpoints 0 and 1.
Date: 11/19/13

5.D.6

Name _____   Date _____

1. Write number bonds. Partition the fraction strip to show the unit fractions of the number bond. Use the fraction strip to help you label the unit fractions on the number line. Include 0 unit fractions.

Halves

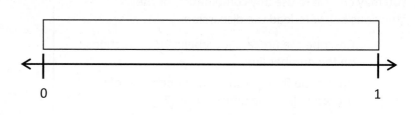

Thirds

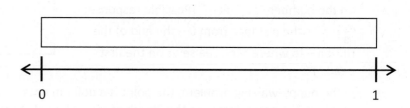

Fourths

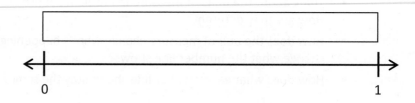

Fifths

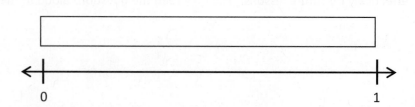

2. Trevor needs to let his puppy outside every quarter (1 fourth) hour to potty train him. Draw and label a number line from 0 hours to 1 hour to show every 1 fourth hour. Include 0 fourths and 4 fourths hour. Label 0 hours and 1 hour, too.

3. A ribbon is one meter long. Mrs. Lee wants to sew a bead every $\frac{1}{5}$ m. The first bead is at $\frac{1}{5}$ m. The last bead is at the 1 m. Draw and label a number line from 0 m to 1 m to show where Mrs. Lee will sew in a bead. Label all the fractions including 0 fifths and 5 fifths. Label 0 meters and 1 meter, too.

Name _____   Date _____

1. Write a number bond. Partition the fraction strip and draw and label the fractional units on the number line. Be sure to label 0 unit fractions.

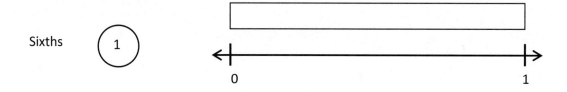

Write number bonds and draw a number line to help explain Problem 2.

2. Ms. Metcalf wants to share $1 equally between 5 students.

    a. What fraction of a dollar will each student get?

    b. How much money will each student get?

Name _____   Date _____

1. Write number bonds. Partition the fraction strip to show the unit fractions of the number bond. Use the fraction strip to help you label the unit fractions on the number line. Include 0 unit fractions.

Sample:

a. Halves

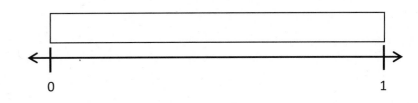

b. Eighths

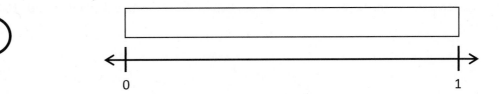

c. Fifths

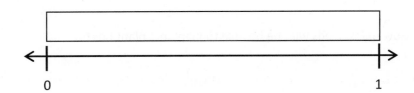

2. Carter needs to wrap 6 presents. He lays the ribbon out flat and says, "If I make 6 equally spaced cuts, I'll have just enough pieces. I can use 1 piece for each package, and I won't have any pieces left over." Does he have enough pieces to wrap all the presents?

3. Mrs. Rivera is planting flowers in her 1 meter long rectangular plant box. She divides the plant box into sections $\frac{1}{9}$ m in length, and plants 1 seed in each section. Draw and label a fraction strip representing the plant box from 0m to 1m. Represent each section where Mrs. Rivera will plant a seed. Label all the fractions.

a. How many seeds will she be able to plant in 1 plant box?

b. How many seeds will she be able to plant in 4 plant boxes?

c. Draw a number line below your fraction strip and mark all the fractions.

Lesson 15

Objective: Place any fraction on a number line with endpoints 0 and 1.

Suggested Lesson Structure

- ■ Fluency Practice   (9 minutes)
- ■ Application Problem   (7 minutes)
- ■ Concept Development   (35 minutes)
- ■ Student Debrief   (9 minutes)
-    **Total Time**   **(60 minutes)**

Fluency Practice (9 minutes)

- Unit Fraction Counting **3.NF.1, 3.NF.3c**   (3 minutes)
- Division **3.OA.2**   (3 minutes)
- Place Unit Fractions on a Number Line Between 0 and 1 **3.NF.2a**   (3 minutes)

Unit Fraction Counting (3 minutes)

T: (Draw a number line.) Count by fourths from 1 fourth to 8 fourths and back to 0.

S: $\frac{1}{4}, \frac{2}{4}, \frac{3}{4}, \frac{4}{4}, \frac{5}{4}, \frac{6}{4}, \frac{7}{4}, \frac{8}{4}, \frac{7}{4}, \frac{6}{4}, \frac{5}{4}, \frac{4}{4}, \frac{3}{4}, \frac{2}{4}, \frac{1}{4},$ 0.

Continue with possible sequence: thirds, halves, and fifths.

Division (3 minutes)

T: (Write $\frac{4}{4} = $ _____.) Say the number sentence and answer.

S: 4 divided by 4 equals 1.

Continue with possible sequence: 4 ÷ 2, 4 ÷ 1, 10 ÷ 10, 10 ÷ 5, 10 ÷ 2, 10 ÷ 1, 6 ÷ 6, 6 ÷ 3, 6 ÷ 1, 8 ÷ 8, 8 ÷ 4, 8 ÷ 2, 8 ÷ 1, 15 ÷ 15, 15 ÷ 5, 15 ÷ 3, 15 ÷ 1, 12 ÷ 12, 12 ÷ 6, 12 ÷ 4, 12 ÷ 3, 12 ÷ 2, 12 ÷ 1, 16 ÷ 16, 16 ÷ 8, 16 ÷ 4, 16 ÷ 2, 16 ÷ 1.

Lesson 15:   Place any fraction on a number line with endpoints 0 and 1.

Date: 11/19/13   5.D.12

Place Unit Fractions on a Number Line
Between 0 and 1 (3 minutes)

Materials: (S) Personal white boards

> T: (Draw a number line with endpoints 0 and 1.) Draw my
>   number line on your board.
> S: (Draw.)
> T: Estimate to show and label 1 half.
> S: (Estimate the halfway point between 0 and 1 and write
> $\frac{1}{2}$.)

Continue with possible sequence: $\frac{1}{2}$, $\frac{1}{10}$, $\frac{1}{2}$, $\frac{1}{4}$, $\frac{1}{8}$, $\frac{1}{3}$, $\frac{1}{5}$, $\frac{1}{6}$.

**NOTES ON
MULTIPLE MEANS OF
REPRESENTATION:**

As students estimate to equally
partition fractional units on the
number line, guide them to begin by
finding the midpoint, first drawing 2
equal parts and then continuing
"halving" until the desired unit fraction
is created.

Application Problem (7 minutes)

In baseball, it is about 30 yards from home plate to first base. The
batter got tagged out about half way to first base. About how
many yards from home plate was he when he got tagged out?
Draw a number line to show the point where he was when tagged
out.

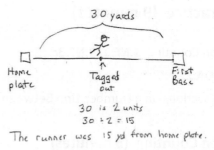

Concept Development (35 minutes)

Materials: (S) Personal white boards

Problem 1: Locate the point 2 thirds.

> T: 2 thirds. How many equal parts in the whole?
> S: Three.
> T: How many of those equal parts have been counted?
> S: Two.
> T: Count up to 2 thirds by unit fractions.
> S: 1 third, 2 thirds.
> T: Show me a 2-part number bond of 1 whole with one
>   part as 2 thirds.
> S: (Students show.)
> T: What is the missing part?
> S: 1 third.
> T: Show me a number line with end points of 0 and 1, and with 0 thirds and 3 thirds, to match your
>   number line.

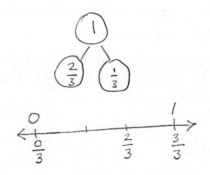

T: Mark off your thirds without labeling the unit fractions.

T: Slide your finger along the length of the first part of your number bond. Speak the fraction as you do.

S: 2 thirds (Sliding up to the point 2 thirds.).

T: Label that point as 2 thirds.

T: Put your finger back on 2 thirds. Slide and speak the next part.

S: 1 third.

T: At what point are you now?

S: 3 thirds or 1 whole.

T: Our number bond is complete.

Problem 2: Locate the point 3 fifths.

T: 3 fifths. How many equal parts in the whole?

S: Five.

T: How many of those equal parts have been counted?

S: Three.

T: Count up to 3 fifths by unit fractions.

S: 1 fifth, 2 fifths, 3 fifths.

T: Show me a 2-part number bond of 1 whole with one part as 3 fifths.

S: (Students show.)

T: What is the missing part?

S: 2 fifths.

T: Show me a number line with end points of 0 and 1, and with 0 fifths and 5 fifths, to match your number bond.

T: Mark off your fifths without labeling the unit fractions.

T: Slide your finger along the length of the first part of your number. Speak the fraction as you do.

S: 3 fifths (Sliding up to the point 3 fifths.).

T: Label that point as 3 fifths.

T: Put your finger back on 3 fifths. Slide and speak the next part.

S: 2 fifths.

T: At what point are you now?

S: 5 fifths or 1 whole.

T: Our number bond is complete.

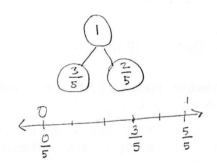

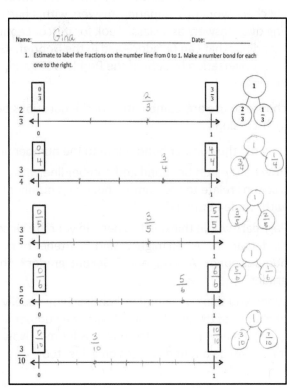

Repeat the process with other fractions such as 3 fourths, 6 eighths, 2 sixths, and 1 seventh. Release the students to work independently as they demonstrate the skill and understanding.

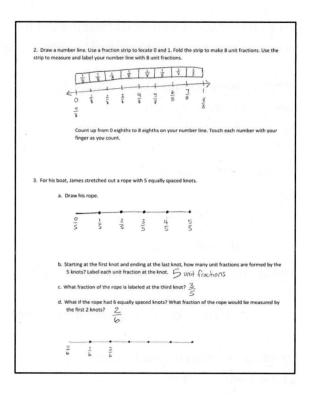

Problem Set (10 minutes)

Students should do their personal best to complete the Problem Set within the allotted 10 minutes. For some classes, it may be appropriate to modify the assignment by specifying which problems they work on first. Some problems do not specify a method for solving. Students solve these problems using the RDW approach used for Application Problems.

Student Debrief (9 minutes)

Lesson Objective: Place any fraction on a number line with endpoints 0 and 1.

The Student Debrief is intended to invite reflection and active processing of the total lesson experience.

Invite students to review their solutions for the Problem Set. They should check work by comparing answers with a partner before going over answers as a class. Look for misconceptions or misunderstandings that can be addressed in the Debrief. Guide students in a conversation to debrief the Problem Set and process the lesson.

You may choose to use any combination of the questions below to lead the discussion.

- How did the number bond relate to the number line?
- How do the number bond and number line with fractions relate to the number bond and number line with whole numbers?
- Part-part-whole thinking has been in your life since Kindergarten. When might a kindergartener draw a number bond? A first grader? Second grader? Third grader?
- When you think of a number bond, do you usually think of chunks of things? Is using it with the number line giving it a new meaning to you? It is for me. Now I see it also can be about distances on a line, too.

NOTES ON MULTIPLE MEANS OF ENGAGEMENT:

The Problem set offers practice of increasing difficulty. Expect and coach students above grade level to complete the entire Problem Set with excellence.

NOTES ON MULTIPLE MEANS OF ACTION AND EXPRESSION:

Facilitate math meaning-making for ELLs through discussion. The daily debriefs and frequent turn-and-talks in each lesson benefit the ELLs' understanding of math concepts and language. Build confidence and comfort, and communicate high expectations for the ELLs' participation.

Exit Ticket (3 minutes)

After the Student Debrief, instruct students to complete the Exit Ticket. A review of their work will help you assess the students' understanding of the concepts that were presented in the lesson today and plan more effectively for future lessons. You may read the questions aloud to the students.

Name _____   Date _____

1. Estimate to label the fractions on the number line from 0 to 1. Make a number bond for each one to the right. This time, the fractions are written above the number line.

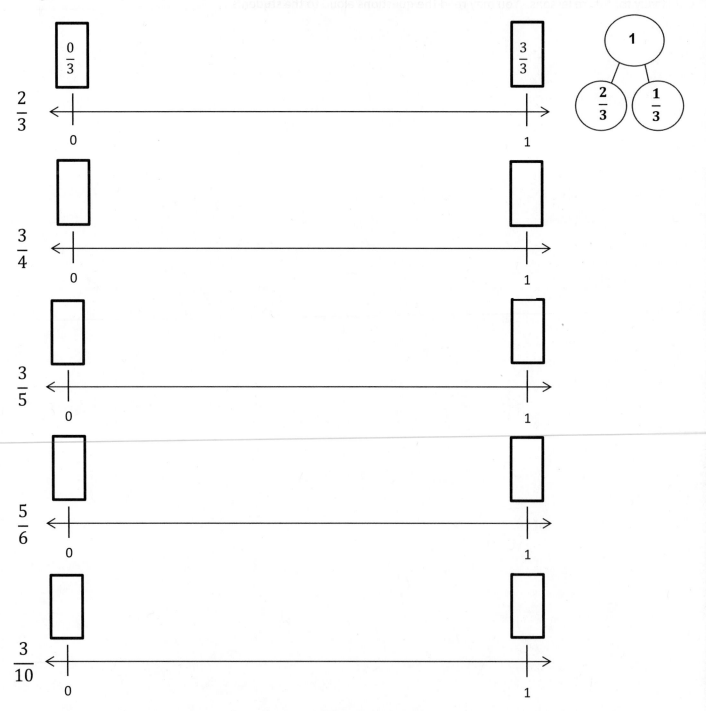

2. Draw a number line. Use a fraction strip to locate 0 and 1. Fold the strip to make 8 equal parts. Use the strip to measure and label your number line with 8 unit fractions.

Count up from 0 eighths to 8 eighths on your number line. Touch each number with your finger as you count.

3. For his boat, James stretched out a rope with 5 equally spaced knots as shown.

a. Starting at the first knot and ending at the last knot, how many equal parts are formed by the 5 knots? Label each unit fraction at the knot.

b. What fraction of the rope is labeled at the third knot?

c. What if the rope had 6 equally spaced knots along the same length? What fraction of the rope would be measured by the first 2 knots?

Lesson 15:   Place any fraction on a number line with endpoints 0 and 1.
Date: 11/19/13

5.D.18

Name _____   Date _____

1. Estimate to label the fraction on the number line from 0 to 1. Draw a number bond to match your number line.

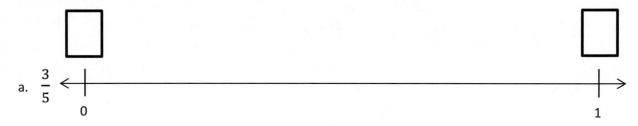

a. $\dfrac{3}{5}$

2. Partition the number line. Then place each fraction on the number line: $\dfrac{3}{6}, \dfrac{1}{6}, \dfrac{5}{6}$.

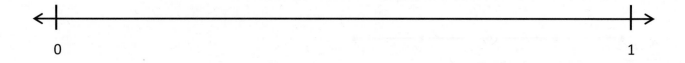

Name _____   Date _____

1. Estimate to label the fractions on the number line from 0 to 1. The first one is done for you. Draw a number bond to match.

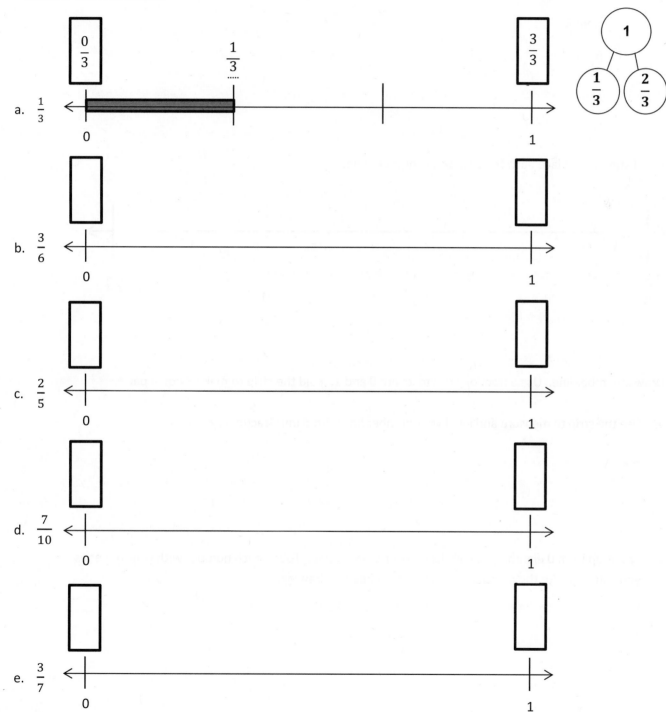

a. $\frac{1}{3}$

b. $\frac{3}{6}$

c. $\frac{2}{5}$

d. $\frac{7}{10}$

e. $\frac{3}{7}$

2. Henry has 5 dimes. Ben has 9 dimes. Tina has 2 dimes.

   a. Write the value of each person's money as a fraction of a dollar:

      Henry:

      Ben:

      Tina:

   b. Estimate to place each fraction on the number line.

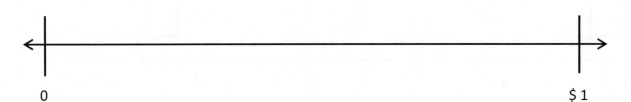

   0 $ 1

3. Draw a number line. Use a fraction strip to locate 0 and 1. Fold the strip to make 8 equal parts.

   a. Use the strip to measure and label your number line with 8 unit fractions.

   b. Count up from 0 eighths to 8 eighths on your number line. Touch each number with your finger as you count. Write the number bonds that matches the drawing.

Lesson 16

Objective: Place whole number fractions and unit fractions between whole numbers on the number Line.

Suggested Lesson Structure

■ Fluency Practice   (12 minutes)
■ Application Problem   (7 minutes)
■ Concept Development   (31 minutes)
■ Student Debrief   (10 minutes)

   Total Time   **(60 minutes)**

Fluency Practice (12 minutes)

▪ Dividing by 9 Sprint **3.OA.4**   (7 minutes)
▪ Counting by Unit Fractions **3.NF.1, 3.NF.3c**   (2 minutes)
▪ Place Fractions on a Number Line Between 0 and 1 **3.NF.2a**   (3 minutes)

Dividing by 9 Sprint (7 minutes)

Materials: (S) Dividing by 9 Sprint

Counting by Unit Fractions (2 minutes)

T: (Project a number line.) Count by halves from 1 half to 6 halves and back to 0.

S: $\frac{1}{2}$, $\frac{2}{2}$, $\frac{3}{2}$, $\frac{4}{2}$, $\frac{5}{2}$, $\frac{6}{2}$, $\frac{5}{2}$, $\frac{4}{2}$, $\frac{3}{2}$, $\frac{2}{2}$, $\frac{1}{2}$, 0.

Continue with possible sequence for: thirds, fifths, and fourths.

Place Fractions on a Number Line Between 0 and 1 (3 minutes)

Materials: (S) Personal white boards

T: (Project a number line with endpoints 0 and 1.) Draw my number line on your board.

S: (Draw.)

T: Estimate to show and label 1 fifth.

NOTES ON MULTIPLE MEANS OF REPRESENTATION:

Check ELL students' listening comprehension of math language as during the fluency activity, Place Fractions on a Number Line Between 0 and 1. Celebrate improvement! "You heard 1 fifth and showed 1 fifth. Great job!"

Lesson 16:	Place whole number fractions and unit fractions between whole numbers on the number line.	**5.D.22**
Date:	11/19/13	

S: (Estimate 1 fifth of the distance between 0 and 1 and write $\frac{1}{5}$.)

T: Estimate to show and label 4 fifths.

S: (Estimate 4 fifths of the distance between 0 and 1 and write $\frac{4}{5}$.)

Continue with the following possible sequence: $\frac{1}{8}$, $\frac{7}{8}$, $\frac{3}{8}$, $\frac{5}{8}$, $\frac{3}{4}$, $\frac{1}{4}$.

Application Problem (7 minutes)

Hannah bought 1 yard of ribbon to wrap 4 small presents. She wants to cut the ribbon into equal parts. Draw and label a number line from 0 yd. to 1 yd. to show where Hannah will cut the ribbon. Label all the fractions including 0 fourths and 4 fourths. Label 0 yd. and 1 yd., also.

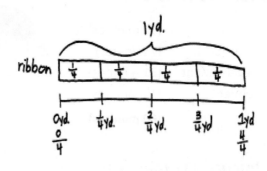

Concept Development (31 minutes)

Materials: (S) Personal white boards

T: Let's draw a number line on our personal boards with the endpoints 1 and 2. The last few days our left endpoint was 0. Where has 0 gone? Tell your partner.

S: It didn't disappear; it is to the left of the 1. → The arrow on the number line tells us that there are more numbers, but we just didn't show them.

T: It's as if we took a picture of a piece of the number line but those missing numbers still exist.

T: We are going to partition this whole into 4 equal lengths.

T: Go ahead and partition your whole into 4 equal lengths.

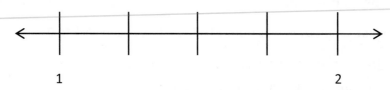

1   2

MP.7

T: Our number line doesn't start at 0 so we can't start at 0 fourths. How many fourths are in 1 whole?

S: 4 fourths.

T: So we will label 4 fourths at whole number 1. Label the rest of the fractions up to 2. Check with your partner to see if you have the same number line. What are the whole number fractions, the fractions equal to 1 and 2?

S: 4 fourths and 8 fourths.

NOTES ON MULTIPLE MEANS OF ENGAGEMENT:

If you gauge that students below grade level need it, build understanding with pictures or concrete materials. Extend the number line back to 0. Have students shade in fourths as they count. Use fraction strips as in Lesson 14, if needed.

Lesson 16:   Place whole number fractions and unit fractions between whole numbers on the number line.

Date: 11/19/13

5.D.2

P.7

T: Let's draw a box around those fractions.

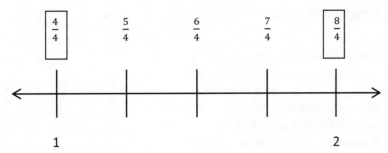

T: 4 fourths is the same point on the number line as 1. We call that equivalence. How many fourths would be equivalent to, or at the same point as 2?

S: 8 fourths.

T: Discuss what fraction is equivalent to – at the same point as – 3 with your partner.

S: (After discussion.) 12 fourths.

T: Draw a number line with the end points 2 and 4. What whole number is missing from this number line?

S: The number 3.

T: Let's place the number 3. It should be equally spaced between 2 and 4. Let's draw that in. (Model.)

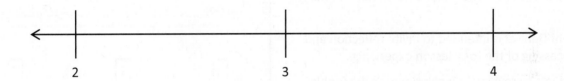

T: We will partition this line into 3 equal lengths. Tell your partner what your number line will look like.

T: To label the number line that starts at 2, we have to know how many thirds are equivalent to 2 wholes. Discuss with your partner how to find the number of thirds in 2 wholes.

S: 3 thirds made 1 whole. So, 6 units of thirds makes 2 wholes. → 6 thirds are equivalent to 2 wholes.

T: Fill in the rest of your number line.

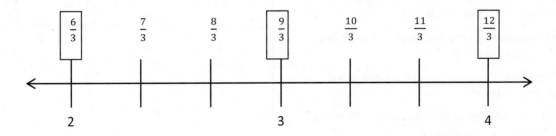

COMMON CORE

| **Lesson 16:** | Place whole number fractions and unit fractions between whole numbers on the number line. |
| **Date:** | 11/19/13 |

5.D.24

Follow with an example using endpoints 3 and 6 so students place 2 whole numbers on the number line, and then partition into halves.

Close the guided practice by having students work in pairs. Partner A names a number line with endpoints between 0 and 5, and a unit fraction. Partners begin with halves and thirds. When they have demonstrated to you that they have done 2 number lines correctly, they may try fourths and fifths, etc. Partner B draws and Partner A assesses. Then partners switch roles.

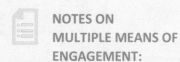

NOTES ON MULTIPLE MEANS OF ENGAGEMENT:

Students above grade level may quickly solve with mental math. Push students to notice and articulate patterns and relationships. As they work in pairs to partition number lines, have students make and analyze their predictions.

Problem Set (10 minutes)

Students should do their personal best to complete the Problem Set within the allotted 10 minutes. For some classes, it may be appropriate to modify the assignment by specifying which problems they work on first. Some problems do not specify a method for solving. Students solve these problems using the RDW approach used for Application Problems.

Student Debrief (10 minutes)

Lesson Objective: Place whole number fractions and unit fractions between whole numbers on the number line.

The Student Debrief is intended to invite reflection and active processing of the total lesson experience.

Invite students to review their solutions for the Problem Set. They should check work by comparing answers with a partner before going over answers as a class. Look for misconceptions or misunderstandings that can be addressed in the Debrief. Guide students in a conversation to debrief the Problem Set and process the lesson.

You may choose to use any combination of the questions below to lead the discussion.

- What number shares the exact same point as 3 on the number line?
- What number shares the exact same point with 12 fourths?"
- Point out Problem 3, which counts 3 thirds, 6 thirds, 9 thirds, 12 thirds:
  - Look at the fractions you boxed in problem 3. What pattern do you notice?

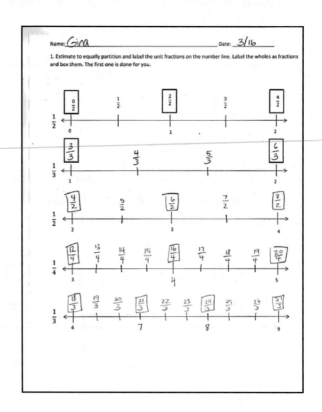

Lesson 16:   Place whole number fractions and unit fractions between whole numbers on the number line.

Date: 11/19/13

5.D.2

- What is the connection between multiplication and fractions equal to whole numbers?
- How do you think that strategy might help you to find other whole number fractions?

Exit Ticket (3 minutes)

After the Student Debrief, instruct students to complete the Exit Ticket. A review of their work will help you assess the students' understanding of the concepts that were presented in the lesson today and plan more effectively for future lessons. You may read the questions aloud to the students.

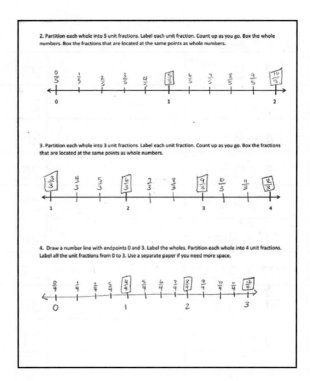

Lesson 16:

Place whole number fractions and unit fractions between whole numbers on the number line.

Date: 11/19/13

5.D.26

A

Correct _____

Multiply or divide.

1	2 x 9 =		23	__ x 9 = 90	
2	3 x 9 =		24	__ x 9 = 18	
3	4 x 9 =		25	__ x 9 = 27	
4	5 x 9 =		26	90 ÷ 9 =	
5	1 x 9 =		27	45 ÷ 9 =	
6	18 ÷ 9 =		28	9 ÷ 9 =	
7	27 ÷ 9 =		29	18 ÷ 9 =	
8	45 ÷ 9 =		30	27 ÷ 9 =	
9	9 ÷ 9 =		31	__ x 9 = 54	
10	36 ÷ 9 =		32	__ x 9 = 63	
11	6 x 9 =		33	__ x 9 = 81	
12	7 x 9 =		34	__ x 9 = 72	
13	8 x 9 =		35	63 ÷ 9 =	
14	9 x 9 =		36	81 ÷ 9 =	
15	10 x 9 =		37	54 ÷ 9 =	
16	72 ÷ 9 =		38	72 ÷ 9 =	
17	63 ÷ 9 =		39	11 x 9 =	
18	81 ÷ 9 =		40	99 ÷ 9 =	
19	54 ÷ 9 =		41	12 x 9 =	
20	90 ÷ 9 =		42	108 ÷ 9 =	
21	__ x 9 = 45		43	14 x 9 =	
22	__ x 9 = 9		44	126 ÷ 9 =	

Lesson 16: Place whole number fractions and unit fractions between whole numbers on the number line.

Date: 11/19/13

5.D.2

B

Improvement _____   # Correct _____

Multiply or divide.

1	1 x 9 =		23	__ x 9 = 18	
2	2 x 9 =		24	__ x 9 = 90	
3	3 x 9 =		25	__ x 9 = 27	
4	4 x 9 =		26	18 ÷ 9 =	
5	5 x 9 =		27	9 ÷ 9 =	
6	27 ÷ 9 =		28	90 ÷ 9 =	
7	18 ÷ 9 =		29	45 ÷ 9 =	
8	36 ÷ 9 =		30	27 ÷ 9 =	
9	9 ÷ 9 =		31	__ x 9 = 27	
10	45 ÷ 9 =		32	__ x 9 = 36	
11	10 x 9 =		33	__ x 9 = 81	
12	6 x 9 =		34	__ x 9 = 63	
13	7 x 9 =		35	72 ÷ 9 =	
14	8 x 9 =		36	81 ÷ 9 =	
15	9 x 9 =		37	54 ÷ 9 =	
16	63 ÷ 9 =		38	63 ÷ 9 =	
17	54 ÷ 9 =		39	11 x 9 =	
18	72 ÷ 9 =		40	99 ÷ 9 =	
19	90 ÷ 9 =		41	12 x 9 =	
20	81 ÷ 9 =		42	108 ÷ 9 =	
21	__ x 9 = 9		43	13 x 9 =	
22	__ x 9 = 45		44	117 ÷ 9 =	

Name _____ Date _____

1. Estimate to equally partition and label the unit fractions on the number line. Label the wholes as fractions and box them. The first one is done for you.

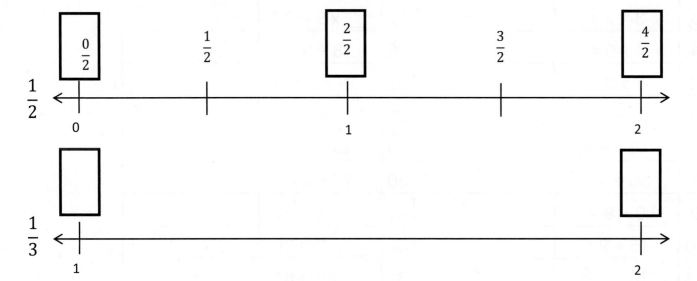

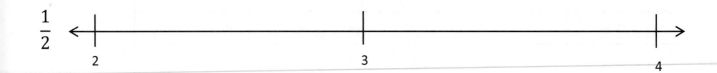

2. Partition each whole into 5 unit fractions. Label each fraction. Count up as you go. Box the whole numbers. Box the fractions that are located at the same points as whole numbers.

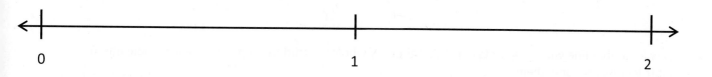

3. Partition each whole into 3 unit fractions. Label each fraction. Count up as you go. Box the fractions that are located at the same points as whole numbers.

4. Draw a number line with endpoints 0 and 3. Label the wholes. Partition each whole into 4 unit fractions. Label all the fractions from 0 to 3. Use a separate paper if you need more space.

Lesson 16:   Place whole number fractions and unit fractions between whole
              numbers on the number line.
Date: 11/19/13

5.D.30

Name _____   Date _____

1. Estimate to equally partition and label the unit fractions on the number line. Label the wholes as fractions and box them.

2. Draw a number line with endpoints 0 and 2. Label the wholes. Estimate to partition each whole into 6 unit fractions and label them.

COMMON CORE

Lesson 16: Place whole number fractions and unit fractions between whole numbers on the number line.

Date: 11/19/13

5.D.3

Name _____   Date _____

1. Estimate to equally partition and label the fractional units on the number line. Label the wholes as fractions and box them. The first one is done for you.

a. $\frac{1}{3}$

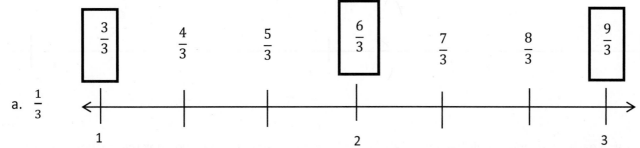

b. $\frac{1}{8}$

c. $\frac{1}{4}$

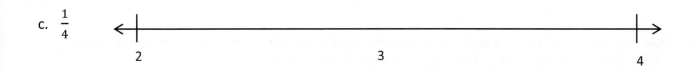

d. $\frac{1}{2}$

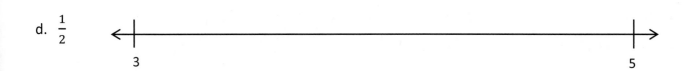

e. $\frac{1}{5}$

COMMON CORE   Lesson 16:   Place whole number fractions and unit fractions between whole numbers on the number line.   **5.D.32**

Date: 11/19/13

2. Partition each whole into 6 unit fractions. Label each fraction. Count up as you go. Box the whole numbers. Box the fractions that are located at the same points as whole numbers.

3. Partition each whole into 2 unit fractions. Label each fraction. Count up as you go. Box the fractions that are located at the same points as whole numbers.

4. Draw a number line with endpoints 0 and 3. Label the wholes. Partition each whole into 5 unit fractions. Label all the fractions from 0 to 3. Use a separate paper if you need more space.

COMMON CORE | **Lesson 16:** Place whole number fractions and unit fractions between whole numbers on the number line.

Date: 11/19/13

5.D.3

Lesson 17

Objective: Practice placing various fractions on the number line.

Suggested Lesson Structure

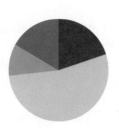

■ Fluency Practice   (12 minutes)
■ Application Problem   (6 minutes)
■ Concept Development   (32 minutes)
■ Student Debrief   (10 minutes)

Total Time   **(60 minutes)**

Fluency Practice (12 minutes)

- Division Sprint **3.OA.2**   (8 minutes)
- Place Whole Number and Unit Fractions on a Number Line **3.NF.2b**   (3 minutes)
- Compare Unit Fractions **3.NF.3d**   (1 minutes)

Division Sprint (8 minutes)

Materials: (S) Division Sprint

Place Whole Number and Unit Fractions on a Number Line (3 minutes)

Materials: (S) Personal white boards

T: (Draw a number line marked at 0, 1, 2, and 3.) Draw my number line on your board.
S: (Draw.)
T: Estimate to show and label 1 half within the interval 0 to 1.
S: (Estimate the halfway point between 0 and 1 and write $\frac{1}{2}$.)
T: Estimate to show 2 halves. Label 2 halves as a fraction.
S: (Write $\frac{2}{2}$ above the 1 on the number line.)

Continue with possible sequence: $\frac{4}{2}$, $\frac{6}{2}$, $\frac{1}{5}$, $\frac{5}{5}$, $\frac{10}{5}$, $\frac{15}{5}$, $\frac{1}{3}$, $\frac{3}{3}$, $\frac{9}{3}$, $\frac{6}{3}$, $\frac{1}{4}$, $\frac{8}{4}$, $\frac{12}{4}$, $\frac{4}{4}$.

Compare Unit Fractions (1 minute)

T: (Write: $\frac{1}{2}$ $\frac{1}{10}$.) Say the largest fraction.

Lesson 17:   Practice placing various fractions on the number line.
Date: 11/19/13

5.D.34

S: 1 half.

Continue with possible sequence: $\frac{1}{2}$ $\frac{1}{3}$, $\frac{1}{3}$ $\frac{1}{4}$, $\frac{1}{4}$ $\frac{1}{6}$, $\frac{1}{4}$ $\frac{1}{2}$, $\frac{1}{6}$ $\frac{1}{8}$, $\frac{1}{6}$ $\frac{1}{5}$, $\frac{1}{5}$ $\frac{1}{10}$.

Application Problem (6 minutes)

Sammy goes to the pool. She sees a black line at the bottom stretching from one end of the pool to the other. She wonders how long it is. The black line is the same length as 9 concrete slabs that make the sidewalk at the edge of the pool. One concrete slab is 5 meters long. What is the length of the black line at the bottom of the pool?

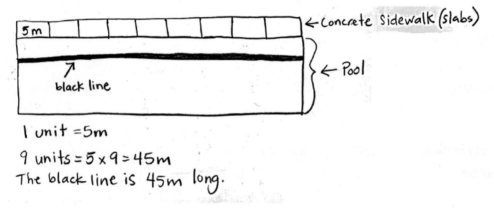

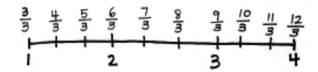

Concept Development (32 minutes)

Materials: (S) Personal white boards

T: Draw a number line with endpoints 1 and 4. Label the wholes. Partition each whole into 3 unit fractions. Label all the fractions from 1 to 4.

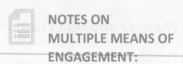

NOTES ON MULTIPLE MEANS OF ENGAGEMENT:

To help students below grade level locate and label fractions on the number line, elicit answers that specify the whole and the unit fraction. Ask, "Point to and count the unit intervals (with me). How many wholes (unit intervals)? What unit (fraction) are we partitioning the whole into? Label as we count the unit fraction."

T: After you labeled your whole numbers, what did you think about to place your fractions?

S: Evenly spacing the marks between whole numbers to make 3 unit fractions. → Writing the numbers in order: 3 thirds, 4 thirds, 5 thirds, etc. → Starting with 3 thirds because the endpoint was 1.

T: What do the fractions have in common? What do you notice?

Lesson 17:   Practice placing various fractions on the number line.
Date: 11/19/13

5.D.3

S: All the fractions have a 3 on the bottom. → All are equal to or greater than 1 whole. → The number of thirds that name whole numbers count by threes: 1 = 3 thirds, 2 = 6 thirds, 3 = 9 thirds. → $\frac{3}{3}$, $\frac{6}{3}$, $\frac{9}{3}$ and $\frac{12}{3}$ are at the same point on the number line as 1, 2, 3 and 4. Those fractions are equivalent to whole numbers.

T: Draw a number line on your board with endpoints 1 and 4.

T: (Write $\frac{2}{2}$, $\frac{5}{2}$, $\frac{7}{2}$, $\frac{8}{2}$.) Look at these fractions. What do you notice?

S: They are all halves. → They are all equal to or greater than 1. → They are in order but some are missing.

T: Place these fractions on your number line.

T: Compare with your partner. Check that your number lines are the same.

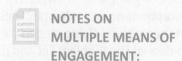

NOTES ON MULTIPLE MEANS OF ENGAGEMENT:

Ask students above grade level the more open-ended question: "How many unit fractions will we place on the number line?"

Follow a similar sequence with the following:

- Number line with endpoints 1 and 4, marking fractions in thirds
- Number line with endpoints 2 and 5, marking fractions in fifths
- Number line with endpoints 4 and 6, marking fractions in thirds (if necessary)

Close the lesson by having pairs of students generate collections of fractions to place on number lines with specified endpoints. Students might then exchange problems, challenging each other to place fractions on the number line. Students should reason aloud about how the partitioned unit fraction is chosen for each number line.

Problem Set (10 minutes)

Students should do their personal best to complete the Problem Set within the allotted 10 minutes. For some classes, it may be appropriate to modify the assignment by specifying which problems they work on first. Some problems do not specify a method for solving. Students solve these problems using the RDW approach used for Application Problems.

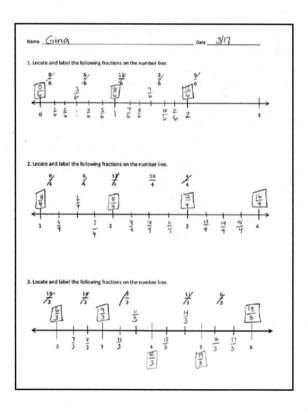

Lesson 17:   Practice placing various fractions on the number line.
Date: 11/19/13

5.D.36

Student Debrief (10 minutes)

Lesson Objective: Practice placing various fractions on the number line.

The Student Debrief is intended to invite reflection and active processing of the total lesson experience.

Invite students to review their solutions for the Problem Set. They should check work by comparing answers with a partner before going over answers as a class. Look for misconceptions or misunderstandings that can be addressed in the Debrief. Guide students in a conversation to debrief the Problem Set and process the lesson.

You may choose to use any combination of the questions below to lead the discussion.

- What did you think about first to help you place the fractions?
- Did you label all the marks on your number line or just the fractions on the list? Why?
- What was the first fraction that you placed on your number line? Why did you start with that one?
- What advice would you give an absent classmate about completing this activity sheet? What is the most important thing to remember when placing fractions on the number line?

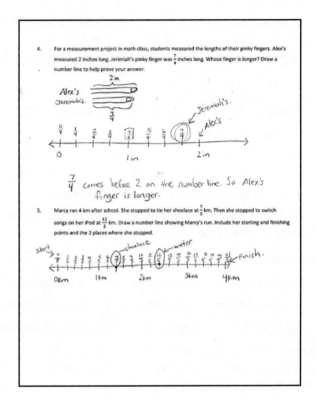

Exit Ticket (3 minutes)

After the Student Debrief, instruct students to complete the Exit Ticket. A review of their work will help you assess the students' understanding of the concepts that were presented in the lesson today and plan more effectively for future lessons. You may read the questions aloud to the students.

 NOTES ON MULTIPLE MEANS OF ACTION AND EXPRESSION:

Support ELLs as they construct written responses. Read the prompt aloud or have students read chorally. Provide sentence starters and a word bank.

Sentence starters may include:

- "I think _____ has a longer pinky finger than _____ because...."

Possible words for the word bank may include:

less than   eighths   closer to

greater than   zero

Lesson 17: Practice placing various fractions on the number line.
Date: 11/19/13

5.D.3

A

Divide.

Correct _____

1	3 ÷ 3 =		23	24 ÷ 3 =	
2	4 ÷ 4 =		24	16 ÷ 2 =	
3	5 ÷ 5 =		25	30 ÷ 10 =	
4	19 ÷ 19 =		26	30 ÷ 3 =	
5	0 ÷ 1 =		27	27 ÷ 3 =	
6	0 ÷ 2 =		28	18 ÷ 2 =	
7	0 ÷ 3 =		29	40 ÷ 10 =	
8	0 ÷ 19 =		30	40 ÷ 4 =	
9	6 ÷ 3 =		31	20 ÷ 4 =	
10	9 ÷ 3 =		32	20 ÷ 5 =	
11	12 ÷ 3 =		33	24 ÷ 4 =	
12	15 ÷ 3 =		34	30 ÷ 5 =	
13	4 ÷ 2 =		35	28 ÷ 4 =	
14	6 ÷ 2 =		36	40 ÷ 5 =	
15	8 ÷ 2 =		37	32 ÷ 4 =	
16	10 ÷ 2 =		38	45 ÷ 5 =	
17	18 ÷ 3 =		39	44 ÷ 4 =	
18	12 ÷ 2 =		40	36 ÷ 4 =	
19	21 ÷ 3 =		41	48 ÷ 6 =	
20	14 ÷ 2 =		42	63 ÷ 7 =	
21	20 ÷ 10 =		43	64 ÷ 8 =	
22	20 ÷ 2 =		44	72 ÷ 9 =	

Lesson 17:   Practice placing various fractions on the number line.
Date: 11/19/13

5.D.38

B

Improvement _____   # Correct _____

Divide.

1	2 ÷ 2 =		23	16 ÷ 2 =	
2	3 ÷ 3 =		24	24 ÷ 3 =	
3	4 ÷ 4 =		25	30 ÷ 3 =	
4	17 ÷ 17 =		26	30 ÷ 10 =	
5	0 ÷ 2 =		27	18 ÷ 2 =	
6	0 ÷ 3 =		28	27 ÷ 3 =	
7	0 ÷ 4 =		29	40 ÷ 4 =	
8	0 ÷ 17 =		30	40 ÷ 10 =	
9	4 ÷ 2 =		31	20 ÷ 5 =	
10	6 ÷ 2 =		32	20 ÷ 4 =	
11	8 ÷ 2 =		33	30 ÷ 5 =	
12	10 ÷ 2 =		34	24 ÷ 4 =	
13	6 ÷ 3 =		35	40 ÷ 5 =	
14	9 ÷ 3 =		36	28 ÷ 4 =	
15	12 ÷ 3 =		37	45 ÷ 5 =	
16	15 ÷ 3 =		38	32 ÷ 4 =	
17	12 ÷ 2 =		39	55 ÷ 5 =	
18	18 ÷ 3 =		40	36 ÷ 4 =	
19	14 ÷ 2 =		41	54 ÷ 6 =	
20	21 ÷ 3 =		42	56 ÷ 7 =	
21	20 ÷ 2 =		43	72 ÷ 8 =	
22	20 ÷ 10 =		44	63 ÷ 9 =	

COMMON CORE

Lesson 17: Practice placing various fractions on the number line.
Date: 11/19/13

5.D.3

Name _____   Date _____

1. Locate and label the following fractions on the number line.

$$\frac{0}{6} \qquad \frac{6}{6} \qquad \frac{12}{6} \qquad \frac{3}{6} \qquad \frac{9}{6}$$

2. Locate and label the following fractions on the number line.

$$\frac{8}{4} \qquad \frac{6}{4} \qquad \frac{12}{4} \qquad \frac{16}{4} \qquad \frac{4}{4}$$

3. Locate and label the following fractions on the number line.

$$\frac{18}{3} \qquad \frac{14}{3} \qquad \frac{9}{3} \qquad \frac{11}{3} \qquad \frac{6}{3}$$

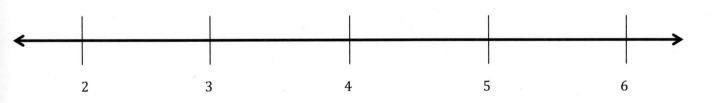

COMMON CORE   **Lesson 17:**   Practice placing various fractions on the number line.

             Date: 11/19/13   **5.D.40**

4. For a measurement project in math class, students measured the lengths of their pinky fingers. Alex's measured 2 inches long. Jerimiah's pinky finger was $\frac{7}{4}$ inches long. Whose finger is longer? Draw a number line to help prove your answer.

5. Marcy ran 4 km after school. She stopped to tie her shoelace at $\frac{7}{5}$ km. Then she stopped to switch songs on her iPod at $\frac{12}{5}$ km. Draw a number line showing Marcy's run. Include her starting and finishing points and the 2 places where she stopped.

Lesson 17: Practice placing various fractions on the number line.
Date: 11/19/13

5.D.4

Name _____   Date _____

1. Locate and label the following fractions on the number lines.

$$\frac{7}{3} \qquad\qquad\qquad \frac{2}{3} \qquad\qquad\qquad \frac{4}{3}$$

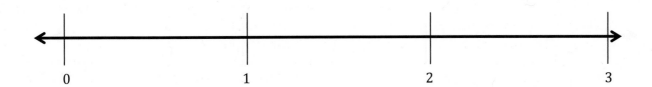

        0   1   2   3

2. Katie bought 2 one-gallon bottles of juice for a party. Her guests drank $\frac{8}{4}$ gallons of juice. What fraction of juice didn't they drink? Draw a number line to show and explain your answer.

COMMON CORE   Lesson 17:   Practice placing various fractions on the number line.
Date: 11/19/13

5.D.42

Name _____   Date _____

Locate and label the following fractions on the number lines.

1. $\dfrac{1}{2}$ $\dfrac{4}{2}$ $\dfrac{5}{2}$

2. $\dfrac{11}{3}$ $\dfrac{6}{3}$ $\dfrac{8}{3}$

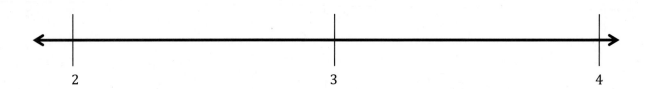

3. $\dfrac{20}{4}$ $\dfrac{13}{4}$ $\dfrac{23}{4}$

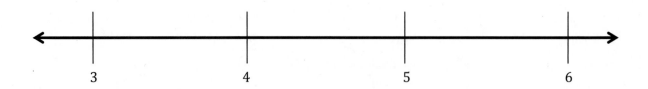

4. Wayne went on a 4 km hike. He took a break at $\frac{4}{3}$ km. He took a drink of water at $\frac{10}{3}$ km. Show Wayne's hike on the number line. Include his starting and finishing place, and the 2 points where he stopped.

5. Ali wants to buy a piano. The piano measures $\frac{19}{4}$ ft. long. She has a space 5 ft. long for the piano in her house. Does she have enough room? Draw a number line to show and explain your answer.

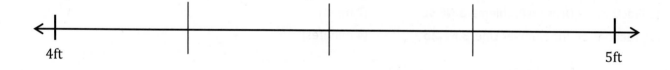

4ft   5ft

Lesson 18

Objective: Compare fractions and whole numbers on the number line by reasoning about their distance from 0.

Suggested Lesson Structure

■ Fluency Practice	(10 minutes)
■ Application Problem	(8 minutes)
■ Concept Development	(32 minutes)
■ Student Debrief	(10 minutes)
Total Time	**(60 minutes)**

Fluency Practice (10 minutes)

- Draw Number Bonds of 1 Whole **3.NF.1**   (4 minutes)
- State Fractions as Division Problems **3.NF.3c**   (2 minutes)
- Place Fractions on the Number Line **3.NF.2b**   (4 minutes)

Draw Number Bonds of 1 Whole (4 minutes)

Materials: (S) Personal white boards

    T: Draw a number bond to partition 1 whole into halves.

    S: (Students write.)

NOTES ON
MULTIPLE MEANS OF
REPRESENTATION:

Students who have not mastered fraction comparisons at an abstract level may benefit from a pictorial reference tool, such as a chart of unit fraction models.

    T: How many copies of 1 half did you draw to make 1 whole?

    S: 2 copies.

Continue with possible sequence: thirds, fourths, fifths, sixths, sevenths, and eighths. Have students draw the models side by side and compare to notice patterns at the end.

COMMON CORE	**Lesson 18:** Compare fractions and whole numbers on the number line by reasoning about their distance from 0.
	Date: 11/19/13

5.D.45

State Fractions as Division Problems (2 minutes)

T: 5 fifths.

S: $5 \div 5 = 1$.

T: 10 fifths.

S: $10 \div 5 = 2$.

T: 25 fifths.

S: $25 \div 5 = 5$.

Continue with possible sequence: 2 halves, 4 halves, 10 halves, 14 halves, 3 thirds, 6 thirds, 9 thirds, 21 thirds, 15 thirds, 4 fourths, 8 fourths, 12 fourths, 36 fourths, and 28 fourths.

Place Fractions on the Number Line (4 minutes)

Materials: (S) Personal white boards

T: (Project a number line marked at 0, 1, 2, and 3.) Draw my number line on your board.

S: (Students draw the projected number line.)

T: Estimate to show and label 1 half in the interval 0 to 1.

S: (Students estimate the point between 0 and 1 and write $\frac{1}{3}$.)

T: Write 3 thirds on your number line. Label the point as a fraction.

S: (Students write $\frac{3}{3}$ above the 1 on the number line.)

Continue with possible sequence: $\frac{6}{3}, \frac{9}{3}, \frac{4}{3}, \frac{7}{3}, \frac{2}{3}, \frac{8}{3}$.

Application Problem (8 minutes)

Third grade students are growing peppers for their Earth Day gardening project. The student with the longest pepper wins the "Green Thumb" award. Jackson's pepper measured 3 inches long. Drew's measured $\frac{10}{4}$ inches long. Who won the award? Draw a number line to help prove your answer.

Jackson won the award since 3 in. is greater than 10/4 in.

Concept Development (32 minutes)

Materials: (T) Large-scale number line partitioned into thirds (description to the right), 4 containers, 4 beanbags (or balled up pieces of paper), sticky notes (S) Work from Application Problem

NOTES ON
MATERIALS:

Before the lesson use painter's tape to make a large-scale number line from 0 to 1 on the floor or in the hallway. Partition the interval evenly into thirds. Try and make the 0 and 1 far apart.

COMMON CORE

Lesson 18:   Compare fractions and whole numbers on the number line by reasoning about their distance from 0.

Date: 11/19/13

5.D.46

T: Look at the number line I've created on the floor. Let's use it to measure and compare.

T: This number line shows the interval from 0 to 1 (Place sticky notes with '0' and '1' written on them in the appropriate places.). What unit does the number line show?

S: Thirds.

T: Let's place containers on $\frac{1}{3}$ and $\frac{2}{3}$. (Select volunteers to place containers.)

S: (Student places containers.)

T: How can we use our thirds to help us place $\frac{1}{6}$ on this number line?

S: $\frac{1}{6}$ is right in the middle of the first third. (Student places a container.)

T: Looking at the number line, where can we place our last container so that it is the greatest distance from 0?

NOTES ON MULTIPLE MEANS OF REPRESENTATION:

S: On 1! → On this number line it has to be 1 because the interval is from 0 to 1. → 1 is the furthest point from 0 on this number line. (Student places a container on 1.)

You may want to pre-teach the vocabulary by adding it to a math word wall before the lesson starts. Helping students connect terms like 'more than,' 'fewer,' and 'the same' to familiar symbols or often used words (greater than, less than, equal to) will make the language more accessible during the lesson.

T: Suppose we invite 4 volunteers to come up. Each volunteer takes a turn to stand at 0 and toss a beanbag into one of the containers. Which container will be the hardest and which will be the easiest to toss the beanbag into? Why?

S: The container at 1 will be the hardest because it's the furthest away from 0. → The container at $\frac{1}{6}$ will be easy. It's close to 0.

T: Let's have volunteers toss. (Each different volunteer tosses a beanbag into a given container. They toss in order: $\frac{1}{6}, \frac{1}{3}, \frac{2}{3}, 1$ whole.)

S: (Volunteers toss, others observe.)

Guide students to discuss how each toss shows the different distances from 0 that each beanbag travelled. Emphasize the distance from 0 as an important feature of the comparison.

T: Why is a fraction's distance from 0 important for comparison?

T: How would the comparison change if each volunteer stood at a different place on the number line?

S: It would be hard to compare because distances would be different. → The distance the beanbag flew wouldn't tell you how big the fraction is. → It's like measuring. When you use a ruler, you start at 0 to measure. Then you can compare the measurements. → The number line is like a giant ruler.

T: Suppose we tossed bean bags to containers at the same points from 0 to 1 on a different number line, but the distance from 0 to 1 was different. How would the comparison of the fractions change if the distance from 0 to 1 was shorter? Longer?

S: If the whole changes, the distance between fractions also changes → So, if it was shorter, then tossing the bean bags to each distance would be shorter. → The same for if it was longer. → True, but the position of each fraction within the number lines stays the same.

Lesson 18:   Compare fractions and whole numbers on the number line by reasoning about their distance from 0.

Date: 11/19/13

5.D.47

Students return to their seats.

T: Think back to our application problem. What in the application problem relates to the length of the toss?

S: How big they are. → The length of the peppers.

T: Talk to your partner. How did we use the distance from 0 to show the length of the peppers?

S: We saw 3 is bigger than $\frac{10}{4}$. → We used the number line sort of like a ruler. We put the measurements on it. Then we saw which one was furthest from the 0. → On the number line you can see the length from 0 to 3 is longer than the length from 0 to $\frac{10}{4}$.

T: Let's do the same thing we did with our big number line on the floor, pretending we measured *giant* peppers with yards instead of inches. 1 pepper measured 3 yards long and the other measured $\frac{10}{4}$ yards. How would the comparison of the fractions change using yards rather than inches?

S: Yards are much bigger than inches. → But even though the lengths changed, $\frac{10}{4}$ yards is still less than 3 yards just like $\frac{10}{4}$ inches is less than 3 inches.

NOTES ON MULTIPLE MEANS OF ENGAGEMENT:

As students compare the giant peppers, you may want to give students a third pepper to include in the comparison. You might make the length of the pepper equal to $\frac{12}{4}$.

Problem Set (10 minutes)

Students should do their personal best to complete the Problem Set within the allotted 10 minutes. For some classes, it may be appropriate to modify the assignment by specifying which problems they work on first. Some problems do not specify a method for solving. Students solve these problems using the RDW approach used for Application Problems.

Student Debrief (10 minutes)

Lesson Objective: Compare fractions and whole numbers on the number line by reasoning about their distance from 0.

The Student Debrief is intended to invite reflection and active processing of the total lesson experience.

Invite students to review their solutions for the Problem Set. They should check work by comparing answers with a partner before going over answers as a class. Look for misconceptions or misunderstandings that can be

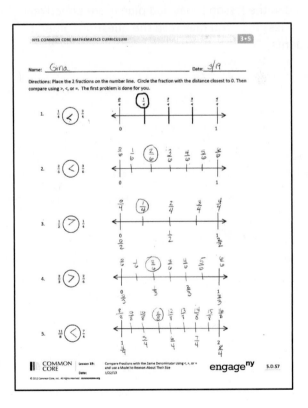

Lesson 18: Compare fractions and whole numbers on the number line by reasoning about their distance from 0.

Date: 11/19/13

5.D.48

addressed in the Debrief. Guide students in a conversation to debrief the Problem Set and process the lesson.

You may choose to use any combination of the questions below to lead the discussion.

- If necessary, review the "toss" portion of the lesson by having students draw each toss on a separate number line, and then place the fractions on the same number line to compare.

- Invite students to share their work on Problems 6, 7 and 8. Make sure that each student can articulate how the distance from 0 helped them to figure out which fraction was greater or less.

- Extend the lesson by having students work through the same comparison given at the end of the Concept Development, this time altering the measurements to centimeters and inches.

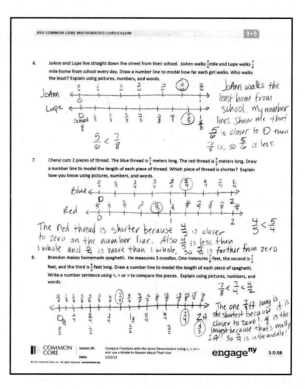

Exit Ticket (3 minutes)

After the Student Debrief, instruct students to complete the Exit Ticket. A review of their work will help you assess the students' understanding of the concepts that were presented in the lesson today and plan more effectively for future lessons. You may read the questions aloud to the students.

Lesson 18:   Compare fractions and whole numbers on the number line by reasoning about their distance from 0.

Date: 11/19/13

5.D.49

Name _____ Date _____

Directions: Place the 2 fractions on the number line. Circle the fraction with the distance closest to 0. Then compare using >, <, or =. The first problem is done for you.

1.

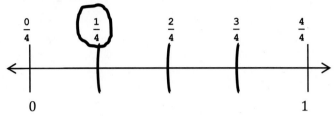

2.

3.

4.

5.

COMMON CORE

Lesson 18: Compare fractions and whole numbers on the number line by reasoning about their distance from 0.

Date: 11/19/13

5.D.50

6. JoAnn and Lupe live straight down the street from their school. JoAnn walks $\frac{5}{6}$ mile and Lupe walks $\frac{7}{8}$ mile home from school every day. Draw a number line to model how far each girl walks. Who walks the least? Explain using pictures, numbers, and words.

7. Cheryl cuts 2 pieces of thread. The blue thread is $\frac{5}{4}$ meters long. The red thread is $\frac{4}{5}$ meters long. Draw a number line to model the length of each piece of thread. Which piece of thread is shorter? Explain how you know using pictures, numbers, and words.

8. Brandon makes homemade spaghetti. He measures 3 noodles. One measures $\frac{7}{8}$ feet, the second is $\frac{7}{4}$ feet, and the third is $\frac{4}{2}$ feet long. Draw a number line to model the length of each piece of spaghetti. Write a number sentence using <, >, or = to compare the pieces. Explain using pictures, numbers, and words.

COMMON CORE | Lesson 18: Compare fractions and whole numbers on the number line by reasoning about their distance from 0.

Date: 11/19/13

5.D.51

Name _____   Date _____

Directions: Place the two fractions on the number line. Circle the fraction with the distance closest to 0.
Then compare using >, <, or =.

1. $\frac{3}{5}$ $\bigcirc$ $\frac{1}{5}$

2. $\frac{1}{2}$ $\bigcirc$ $\frac{3}{4}$

3. Mr. Brady draws a fraction on the board. Ken said it's $\frac{2}{3}$, and Dan said it's $\frac{3}{2}$. Do both of these fractions mean the same thing? If not, which fraction is larger? Draw a number line to model $\frac{2}{3}$ and $\frac{3}{2}$. Use words, pictures, and numbers to explain your comparison.

COMMON CORE   Lesson 18:   Compare fractions and whole numbers on the number line by   5.D.52
                                  reasoning about their distance from 0.
                   Date: 11/19/13

Name _____   Date _____

Directions: Place the two fractions on the number line. Circle the fraction with the distance closest to 0.
Then compare using >, <, or =.

1. $\frac{1}{3}$ ◯ $\frac{2}{3}$

2. $\frac{4}{6}$ ◯ $\frac{1}{6}$

3. $\frac{1}{4}$ ◯ $\frac{1}{8}$

4. $\frac{4}{5}$ ◯ $\frac{4}{10}$

5. $\frac{8}{6}$ ◯ $\frac{5}{3}$

COMMON CORE | Lesson 18:   Compare fractions and whole numbers on the number line by
                    reasoning about their distance from 0.
              | Date: 11/19/13

© 2013 Common Core, Inc. All rights reserved. **commoncore.org**

5.D.53

6. Liz and Jay each have a piece of string. Liz's string is $\frac{4}{6}$ yard long, and Jay's string is $\frac{5}{7}$ yard long. Whose string is longer? Draw a number line to model the length of both strings. Explain the comparison using pictures, numbers, and words.

7. In a long jump competition, Wendy jumped $\frac{9}{10}$ meter and Judy jumped $\frac{10}{9}$ meters. Draw a number line to model the distance of each girl's long jump. Who jumped the shorter distance? Explain how you know using pictures, numbers, and words.

8. Nikki has 3 pieces of yarn. The first piece is $\frac{5}{6}$ feet long, the second piece is $\frac{5}{3}$ feet long, and the third piece is $\frac{3}{2}$ feet long. She wants to arrange them from the shortest to the longest. Draw a number line to model the length of each piece of yarn. Write a number sentence using <, >, or = to compare the pieces. Explain using pictures, numbers, and words.

COMMON CORE

Lesson 18:   Compare fractions and whole numbers on the number line by reasoning about their distance from 0.
Date: 11/19/13

5.D.54

Lesson 19

Objective: Understand distance and position on the number line as strategies for comparing fractions. (Optional)

Suggested Lesson Structure

- ■ Fluency Practice   (12 minutes)
- ■ Application Problem   (10 minutes)
- ■ Concept Development   (28 minutes)
- ■ Student Debrief   (10 minutes)
-   **Total Time**   **(60 minutes)**

Fluency Practice (12 minutes)

- Express Fractions as Whole Numbers Sprint **3.NF.3c**   (9 minutes)
- Place Fractions on the Number Line **3.NF.2b**   (3 minutes)

Express Fractions as Whole Numbers Sprint (9 minutes)

Materials: (S) Express Fractions as Whole Numbers Sprint

Place Fractions on the Number Line (3 minutes)

Materials: (S) Personal white boards

    T: (Draw a number line marked at 0, 1, 2, and 3.) Draw my number line on your board.
    S: (Draw.)
    T: Estimate to show and label 1 third on the interval 0 to 1.
    S: Students estimate the point between 0 and 1 and write $\frac{1}{3}$.
    T: Estimate to show 3 thirds.
    S: (Write $\frac{3}{3}$ above the 1 on the number line.)

Continue with possible sequence: $\frac{6}{3}, \frac{9}{3}, \frac{4}{3}, \frac{7}{3}, \frac{2}{3}, \frac{8}{3}, \frac{1}{2}, \frac{2}{2}, \frac{4}{2}, \frac{3}{2}, \frac{5}{2}, \frac{6}{2}.$

Lesson 19:	Understand distance and position on the number line as strategies for comparing fractions. (Optional.)	5.D.55
Date:	11/19/13	

Application Problem (10 minutes)

Thomas has 2 sheets of paper. He wants to punch 4 equally spaced holes along the edge of each sheet.

Draw Thomas' 2 sheets of paper next to each other so the ends meet. Label a number line from 0 at the start of his first paper to 2 at the end of his second paper. Show Thomas where to hole-punch his papers and label the unit fractions. What unit fraction is labeled on the eighth hole?

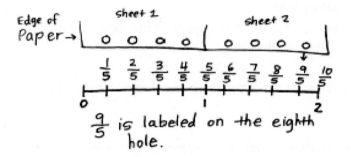

NOTES ON MULTIPLE MEANS OF ACTION AND EXPRESSION:

Students below grade level may benefit from acting out the Application Problem, lining up 2 sheets of paper to make a concrete example.

Note that this problem is different from the problem with the rope in Lesson 16 and the nails in Lesson 17. The first hole is not marking zero. Zero is the edge of the paper. Students below grade level may not pick up on this. For all students, it is important when measuring to be clear about the location of zero.

Concept Development (28 minutes)

Materials: (S) Personal white boards

T: Draw 2 same-sized rectangles on your board and partition both into 4 equal parts. Shade your top rectangle to show 1 fourth and shade the bottom to show 3 copies of 1 fourth.

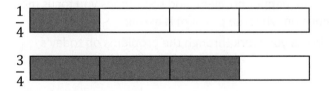

T: Compare the models. Which shaded fraction is larger? Tell your partner how you know.

S: I know 3 fourths is larger because 3 parts is greater than just 1 part of the same size.

T: Use your rectangles to measure and draw a number line from 0 to 1. Partition it into 4 equal size segments. Label all parts of your number line.

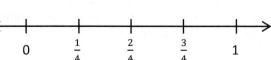

NOTES ON MULTIPLE MEANS OF ACTION AND EXPRESSION:

For ELLs, model the directions or use gestures to clarify English language. E.g., extend your arms to demonstrate "long."

Give ELLs a little more time to discuss with a partner their math thinking in English.

T: Talk with your partner to compare 1 fourth to 3 fourths using the number line. How do you know which is the larger fraction?

S: 1 fourth is less distance from 0, so it is the smaller fraction. 3 fourths is a greater distance away from 0, so it is the larger fraction.

T: Many of you are comparing the fractions by seeing their distance from 0. You're right, 1 unit is a smaller distance from 0 than 3 units. If we know where 0 is on the number line, how can it help us to find the smaller or larger fraction?

S: The smaller fraction will always be to the left of the larger fraction.

T: How do you know?

S: Because the further you go to the right on the number line, the further the distance from 0. → That means the fraction to the left is always smaller. It's closer to 0.

T: Think back to our application problem. What were we trying to find? The length of the page from the edge to each hole? Or were we simply finding the location of each hole?

S: The location of each hole.

T: Remember the pepper problem from yesterday? What were we comparing? The length of the peppers or the location of the peppers?

S: We were looking for the length of each pepper.

T: Talk with your partner. What is the same and what is different about the way we solved these problems?

S: In both we placed fractions on the number line. → To do that we actually had to find the distance of each from 0, too. → Yes, but in Thomas' we were more worried about the position of each fraction so he'd put the holes in the right places. → And in the pepper problem the distance from 0 to the fraction told us the length of each pepper, and then we compared that.

T: How do distance and position relate to each other when we compare fractions on the number line?

S: You use the distance from 0 to find the fraction's placement. → Or you use the placement to find the distance. → So they're both part of comparing. The part you focus on just depends on what you're trying to find out.

T: Relate that to your work on the pepper and hole-punch problems.

S: Sometimes you focus more on the distance like in the pepper problem, and sometimes you focus more on the position like in Thomas' problem. It depends on what the problem is asking.

T: Try and use both ways of thinking about comparing as you work through the problems on today's Problem Set.

Problem Set (10 minutes)

Students should do their personal best to complete the Problem Set within the allotted 10 minutes. For some classes, it may be appropriate to modify the assignment by specifying which problems they work on first. Some problems do not specify a method for solving. Students solve these problems using the RDW approach used for Application Problems.

Lesson 19:   Understand distance and position on the number line as strategies for
comparing fractions. (Optional.)

Date: 11/19/13

Student Debrief (10 minutes)

Lesson Objective: Understand distance and position the number line as strategies for comparing fractions.

The Student Debrief is intended to invite reflection and active processing of the total lesson experience.

Invite students to review their solutions for the Problem Set. They should check work by comparing answers with a partner before going over answers as a class. Look for misconceptions or misunderstandings that can be addressed in the Debrief. Guide students in a conversation to debrief the Problem Set and process the lesson.

You may choose to use any combination of the questions below to lead the discussion.

- Invite students to share their work on the final 3 problems. Students should have slightly different explanations for Problems 4 and 5. Invite a variety of responses so that both explanations are heard.
- Extend the lesson by having students work together (or guide them) to create word problems with real world contexts that emphasize different types of comparisons:
- Create word problems with a context that emphasizes placement of the fraction on a number line (like the hole-punch problem).
- Create word problems with a context that emphasizes the distance of the fraction from 0 (like the pepper problem).
- Have students solve the problems together and discuss how the context of the problem affects the way in which the solution is delivered.

Exit Ticket (3 minutes)

After the Student Debrief, instruct students to complete the Exit Ticket. A review of their work will help you assess the students' understanding of the concepts that were presented in the lesson today and plan more effectively for future lessons. You may read the questions aloud to the students.

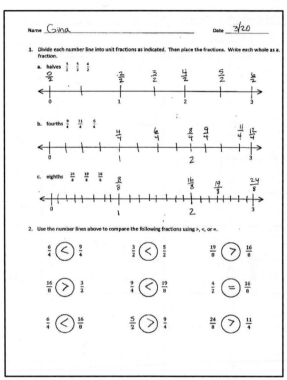

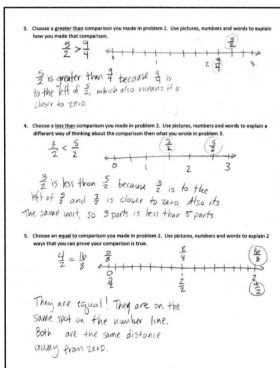

Lesson 19:   Understand distance and position on the number line as strategies for comparing fractions. (Optional.)

Date: 11/19/13

5.D.58

A

Correct _____

Write each fraction as a whole number.

1	$\frac{2}{1} =$		23	$\frac{6}{3} =$	
2	$\frac{2}{2} =$		24	$\frac{3}{3} =$	
3	$\frac{4}{2} =$		25	$\frac{3}{1} =$	
4	$\frac{6}{2} =$		26	$\frac{9}{3} =$	
5	$\frac{10}{2} =$		27	$\frac{16}{4} =$	
6	$\frac{8}{2} =$		28	$\frac{20}{4} =$	
7	$\frac{5}{1} =$		29	$\frac{12}{3} =$	
8	$\frac{5}{5} =$		30	$\frac{15}{3} =$	
9	$\frac{10}{5} =$		31	$\frac{70}{10} =$	
10	$\frac{15}{5} =$		32	$\frac{12}{2} =$	
11	$\frac{25}{5} =$		33	$\frac{14}{2} =$	
12	$\frac{20}{5} =$		34	$\frac{90}{10} =$	
13	$\frac{10}{10} =$		35	$\frac{30}{5} =$	
14	$\frac{50}{10} =$		36	$\frac{35}{5} =$	
15	$\frac{30}{10} =$		37	$\frac{60}{10} =$	
16	$\frac{10}{1} =$		38	$\frac{18}{2} =$	
17	$\frac{20}{10} =$		39	$\frac{40}{5} =$	
18	$\frac{40}{10} =$		40	$\frac{80}{10} =$	
19	$\frac{8}{4} =$		41	$\frac{16}{2} =$	
20	$\frac{4}{4} =$		42	$\frac{45}{5} =$	
21	$\frac{4}{1} =$		43	$\frac{27}{3} =$	
22	$\frac{12}{4} =$		44	$\frac{32}{4} =$	

Lesson 19: Understand distance and position on the number line as strategies for
comparing fractions. (Optional.)

Date: 11/19/13

5.D.5

B

Improvement _____   # Correct _____

Write each fraction as a whole number.

1	$\frac{5}{1} =$		23	$\frac{8}{4} =$	
2	$\frac{5}{5} =$		24	$\frac{4}{4} =$	
3	$\frac{10}{5} =$		25	$\frac{4}{1} =$	
4	$\frac{15}{5} =$		26	$\frac{12}{4} =$	
5	$\frac{25}{5} =$		27	$\frac{12}{3} =$	
6	$\frac{20}{5} =$		28	$\frac{15}{3} =$	
7	$\frac{2}{1} =$		29	$\frac{16}{4} =$	
8	$\frac{2}{2} =$		30	$\frac{20}{4} =$	
9	$\frac{4}{2} =$		31	$\frac{90}{10} =$	
10	$\frac{6}{2} =$		32	$\frac{30}{5} =$	
11	$\frac{10}{2} =$		33	$\frac{35}{5} =$	
12	$\frac{8}{2} =$		34	$\frac{70}{10} =$	
13	$\frac{10}{1} =$		35	$\frac{12}{2} =$	
14	$\frac{10}{10} =$		36	$\frac{14}{2} =$	
15	$\frac{50}{10} =$		37	$\frac{80}{10} =$	
16	$\frac{30}{10} =$		38	$\frac{45}{5} =$	
17	$\frac{20}{10} =$		39	$\frac{16}{2} =$	
18	$\frac{40}{10} =$		40	$\frac{60}{10} =$	
19	$\frac{6}{3} =$		41	$\frac{18}{2} =$	
20	$\frac{3}{3} =$		42	$\frac{40}{5} =$	
21	$\frac{3}{1} =$		43	$\frac{36}{4} =$	
22	$\frac{9}{3} =$		44	$\frac{24}{3} =$	

Lesson 19:   Understand distance and position on the number line as strategies for
comparing fractions. (Optional.)
Date: 11/19/13

5.D.60

Name _____ Date _____

1. Divide each number line into unit fractions as indicated. Then place the fractions. Write each whole as a fraction.

   a. halves $\frac{3}{2}$ $\frac{5}{2}$ $\frac{4}{2}$

   b. fourths $\frac{9}{4}$ $\frac{11}{4}$ $\frac{6}{4}$

   c. eighths $\frac{24}{8}$ $\frac{19}{8}$ $\frac{16}{8}$

2. Use the number lines above to compare the following fractions using >, <, or =.

$\frac{6}{4}$ ◯ $\frac{9}{4}$	$\frac{3}{2}$ ◯ $\frac{5}{2}$	$\frac{19}{8}$ ◯ $\frac{16}{8}$
$\frac{16}{8}$ ◯ $\frac{3}{2}$	$\frac{9}{4}$ ◯ $\frac{19}{8}$	$\frac{4}{2}$ ◯ $\frac{16}{8}$
$\frac{6}{4}$ ◯ $\frac{16}{8}$	$\frac{5}{2}$ ◯ $\frac{9}{4}$	$\frac{24}{8}$ ◯ $\frac{11}{4}$

COMMON CORE | Lesson 19: | Understand distance and position on the number line as strategies for comparing fractions. (Optional.)

Date: 11/19/13

5.D.6

3. Choose a <u>greater than</u> comparison you made in Problem 2. Use pictures, numbers, and words to explain how you made that comparison.

4. Choose a <u>less than</u> comparison you made in Problem 2. Use pictures, numbers, and words to explain a different way of thinking about the comparison than what you wrote in Problem 3.

5. Choose an <u>equal to</u> comparison you made in Problem 2. Use pictures, numbers, and words to explain two ways that you can prove your comparison is true.

COMMON CORE

Lesson 19:   Understand distance and position on the number line as strategies for comparing fractions. (Optional.)

Date: 11/19/13

5.D.62

Name _____   Date _____

1. Divide each number line into unit fractions as indicated. Then place the fractions. Write each whole as a fraction.

    a.   fourths $\frac{2}{4}$ $\frac{10}{4}$ $\frac{7}{4}$

2. Use the number line above to compare the following fractions using >, <, or =.

    $\frac{3}{4}$ ◯ $\frac{5}{4}$ $\frac{7}{4}$ ◯ $\frac{4}{4}$ 3 ◯ $\frac{6}{4}$

3. Use the number line from Problem 1. Which is larger, 2 wholes or $\frac{9}{4}$? Use words, pictures, and numbers to explain your answer.

COMMON CORE   **Lesson 19:**   Understand distance and position on the number line as strategies for
                                  comparing fractions. (Optional.)   5.D.6
                Date: 11/19/13

Name _____   Date _____

1. Divide each number line into the given unit fractions. Then place the fractions. Write each whole as a fraction.

   a. thirds $\frac{6}{3}$ $\frac{5}{3}$ $\frac{8}{3}$

   b. sixths $\frac{10}{6}$ $\frac{18}{6}$ $\frac{15}{6}$

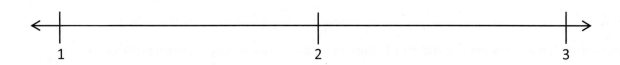

   c. fifths $\frac{14}{5}$ $\frac{7}{5}$ $\frac{11}{5}$

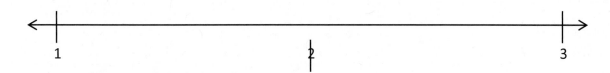

2. Use the number lines above to compare the following fractions using >, <, or =.

   $\frac{17}{6}$ ◯ $\frac{15}{6}$ $\frac{7}{3}$ ◯ $\frac{9}{3}$ $\frac{11}{5}$ ◯ $\frac{8}{5}$

   $\frac{4}{3}$ ◯ $\frac{8}{6}$ $\frac{13}{6}$ ◯ $\frac{8}{3}$ $\frac{11}{6}$ ◯ $\frac{5}{3}$

   $\frac{10}{6}$ ◯ $\frac{3}{3}$ $\frac{6}{3}$ ◯ $\frac{12}{6}$ $\frac{15}{5}$ ◯ $\frac{5}{3}$

COMMON CORE

Lesson 19:   Understand distance and position on the number line as strategies for comparing fractions. (Optional.)

Date: 11/19/13

5.D.64

3. Use fractions from the number lines in Problem 1. Complete the sentence. Use a words, pictures, or numbers to explain how you made that comparison.

_____ is greater than _____.

4. Use fractions from the number lines in Problem 1. Complete the sentence. Use a words, pictures, or numbers to explain how you made that comparison.

_____ is less than _____.

5. Use fractions from the number lines in Problem 1. Complete the sentence. Use a words, pictures, or numbers to explain how you made that comparison.

_____ is equal to _____.

Topic E

Equivalent Fractions

3.NF.3a, 3.NF.3b, 3.NF.3c

Focus Standards:	3.NF.3	Explain equivalence of fractions in special cases, and compare fractions by reasoning about their size.
		a. Understand two fractions as equivalent (equal) if they are the same size, or the same point on a number line.
		b. Recognize and generate simple equivalent fractions, e.g., 1/2 = 2/4, 4/6 = 2/3). Explain why the fractions are equivalent, e.g., by using a visual fraction model.
		c. Express whole numbers as fractions, and recognize factions that are equivalent to whole numbers. *Examples: Express 3 in the form 3 = 3/1; recognize that 6/1 = 6; locate 4/4 and 1 at the same point of a number line diagram.*
Instructional Days:	8	
Coherence -Links from:	G2–M7	Recognizing Angles, Faces, and Vertices of Shapes, Fractions of Shapes
-Links to:	G4–M5	Time, Shapes, and Fractions as Equal Parts of Shapes

In Topic D, students practiced placing and comparing fractions on a number line. In Topic E, they identify equivalent fractions using fraction strips, number bonds, and the number line as models. Students compare fractions on the number line to recognize that equivalent fractions refer to the same whole and to the same point on the line. Initially, students find equivalence in fractions less than 1 whole, e.g., 1 half = 2 fourths. They then express whole numbers as fractions using number bonds and number lines to show how many copies of a unit are needed to make the whole, e.g., 4 copies of 1 fourth equals 1 whole. They reason about why whole numbers can be written as fractions with a denominator of 1. Finally, students explain equivalence through manipulating units.

A Teaching Sequence Towards Mastery of Equivalent Fractions

Objective 1: Recognize and show that equivalent fractions have the same size, though not necessarily the same shape.
(Lesson 20)

Objective 2: Recognize and show that equivalent fractions refer to the same point on the number line.
(Lesson 21)

Objective 3: Generate simple equivalent fractions by using visual fraction models and the number line.
(Lesson 22–23)

Objective 4: Express whole numbers as fractions and recognize equivalence with different units.
(Lesson 24)

Objective 5: Express whole number fractions on the number line when the unit interval is 1.
(Lesson 25)

Objective 6: Decompose whole number fractions greater than 1 using whole number equivalence with various models.
(Lesson 26)

Objective 7: Explain equivalence by manipulating units and reasoning about their size.
(Lesson 27)

Lesson 20

Objective: Recognize and show that equivalent fractions have the same size, though not necessarily the same shape.

Suggested Lesson Structure

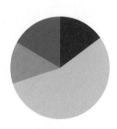

■ Fluency Practice   (9 minutes)
■ Application Problem   (8 minutes)
■ Concept Development   (33 minutes)
■ Student Debrief   (10 minutes)

   Total Time   **(60 minutes)**

Fluency Practice (9 minutes)

▪ Multiply by 7 Sprint **3.OA.4**   (9 minutes)

Multiply by 7 Sprint (9 minutes)

Materials: (S) Multiply by 7 Sprint

   T: Skip-count by sevens. (Write multiples horizontally as students count.)
   S: 7, 14, 21, 28, 35, 42, 49, 56, 63, 70.
   T: (Write 7 x 5 = _____.) Let's skip-count by sevens to find the answer. (Count with fingers to 5 as students count.)
   S: 7, 14, 21, 28, 35.
   T: (Circle 35 and write 7 x 5 = 35 above it. Write 7 x 3 = _____.) Let's skip-count up by sevens again. (As students count show your fingers to count with them.)
   S: 7, 14, 21.
   T: Let's see how we can skip-count down to find the answer too. Start at 35. (Count down with your fingers as students say numbers.)
   S: 35, 28, 21.
   T: (Write 7 x 9 = _____.) Let's skip-count up by sevens. (Count with fingers to 9 as students count.)
   S: 7, 14, 21, 28, 35, 42, 49, 56, 63.
   T: Let's see how we can skip-count down to find the answer too. Start at 70. (Count down with your fingers as student say numbers.)
   S: 70, 63.
   T: Let's get some practice multiplying by 7. Be sure to work left to right across the page. (Distribute Multiply by 7 Sprint.)

 **COMMON CORE**

Lesson 20:   Recognize and show that equivalent fractions have the same size, though not necessarily the same shape.
Date: 11/19/13

5.E.3

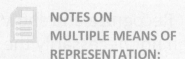

Application Problem (8 minutes)

Max ate $\frac{2}{3}$ of his pizza for lunch. He wanted to eat a small snack in the afternoon, so he cut the leftover pizza in half and ate 1 slice. How much of the pizza was left? Draw a picture to help you think about the pizza.

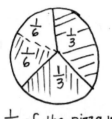

$\frac{1}{6}$ of the pizza was left.

NOTES ON
MULTIPLE MEANS OF
REPRESENTATION:

Empower ELLs to solve the Application Problem by connecting its context to their prior knowledge. Discuss their experiences at lunch, eating pizza, having leftovers, and eating a snack.

Concept Development (33 minutes)

Materials: (S) Personal white boards, linking cubes, coins, rods

Show Model 1:

NOTES ON
MULTIPLE MEANS OF
REPRESENTATION:

Students who have not mastered fraction comparisons at an abstract level may benefit from a pictorial reference tool, such as a chart of unit fraction models for the sprint.

T: The whole is all the blocks. Whisper the fraction of cubes that are blue to your partner.

S: (Whisper $\frac{1}{4}$.)

Show Model 2:

T: Again, the whole is all the blocks. Whisper the fraction of cubes that are blue to your partner.

S: (Whisper $\frac{1}{4}$.)

 Lesson 20:   Recognize and show that equivalent fractions have the same size, though not necessarily the same shape.
Date: 11/19/13

5.E.4

T: Discuss with your partner whether or not the fraction of cubes that are blue is equal, even though the models are not the same shape.

S: They don't look the same, so they are different. → I disagree. They are equal because they are both $\frac{1}{4}$ blue. → They are equal because the units are still the same size, and the wholes have the same number of units. They are just in a different shape.

T: I hear you noticing that the units make a different shape in the second model. It's square rather than rectangular. Good observation. Take another minute to notice what is similar about our models.

S: They both use the same linker cubes as units. → They both have the same amount of blues and reds. → Both wholes have the same number of units, and the units are the same size.

T: The size of the units and the size of the whole didn't change. That means $\frac{1}{4}$ and $\frac{1}{4}$ are equal, or what we call equivalent fractions, even though the shapes our wholes make are different.

If necessary, do other examples to demonstrate the point made with Model 2.

Show Model 3:

T: Why isn't the fraction represented by the blue cubes equal to the other ones we made with cubes?

S: This fraction shows $\frac{2}{4}$ of the cubes are blue.

T: When we are finding equivalent fractions in area models, the shapes of the wholes can be different. However, equivalent fractions describe an equal amount of shaded and unshaded units.

Show Model 4:

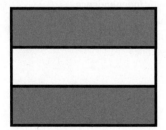

Equivalent Shapes Collage Activity

Materials: (S) copy of Model 4 (shown above), red crayon, scissors, glue stick, and blank paper

Lesson 20:   Recognize and show that equivalent fractions have the same size, though not necessarily the same shape.

Date: 11/19/13

5.E.5

Directions:

1. Color the white stripe red.
2. Cut out the rectangle. Cut it into 2-4 smaller shapes.
3. Reassemble the pieces into a new shape with no overlaps.
4. Glue the new shape onto a blank paper.

Each of the 6 shapes pictured to the right is an example of possible student work. Each of the new shapes is equivalent to Model 4. All show $\frac{2}{3}$ grey, although clearly in different shapes.

 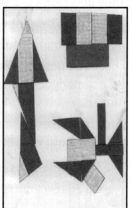

Problem Set (10 minutes)

Students should do their personal best to complete the Problem Set within the allotted 10 minutes. For some classes, it may be appropriate to modify the assignment by specifying which problems they work on first. Some problems do not specify a method for solving. Students solve these problems using the RDW approach used for Application Problems.

Student Debrief (10 minutes)

Lesson Objective: Recognize and show that equivalent fractions have the same size, though not necessarily the same shape.

The Student Debrief is intended to invite reflection and active processing of the total lesson experience.

Invite students to review their solutions for the Problem Set. They should check work by comparing answers with a partner before going over answers as a class. Look for misconceptions or misunderstandings that can be addressed in the Debrief. Guide students in a conversation to debrief the Problem Set and process the lesson.

You may choose to use any combination of the questions below to lead the discussion

MP.6

- Invite students to share their models for Problems 2A and 2B. Although answers will vary, students should consistently represent equivalent fractions for each question. Revisit the different work from the Equivalent Shapes Collage Activity.
- Problem Set Problem 3(c) presents seeing triangles as halves of squares. Some students might put $\frac{4}{8}$ as the answer since they see 8 units. You may want to pose the question, "Are all 8 parts equal

NOTES ON MULTIPLE MEANS OF ACTION AND EXPRESSION:

For students below grade level, break the task of labeling fractions on the Problem Set into steps with sentence frames:

- There are ____ equal parts.
- ____ parts are shaded.
- The fraction shaded is ____.

These open-ended responses are "just-right" for students above grade level who enjoy independence. Communicate high expectations for explaining their reasoning clearly and with evidence.

Lesson 20: Recognize and show that equivalent fractions have the same size, though not necessarily the same shape.
Date: 11/19/13

5.E.6

units?" Discuss how the answer can be $\frac{4}{12}$ if they choose to use the base unit of triangles or $\frac{2}{6}$ if they choose to use the base unit of squares. Lead them to see that the two fractions are equivalent.

- Problem 4 also presents an interesting discussion topic due to the use of containers that are different shapes with the same capacity. Without reading carefully, students are likely to make a mistake in their answer. This may provide you with an opportunity to further explore the difference between different sized wholes, and different looking wholes.

Exit Ticket (3 minutes)

After the Student Debrief, instruct students to complete the Exit Ticket. A review of their work will help you assess the students' understanding of the concepts that were presented in the lesson today and plan more effectively for future lessons. You may read the questions aloud to the students.

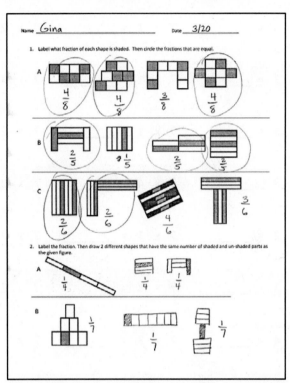

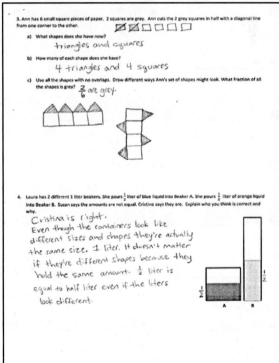

COMMON CORE

Lesson 20: Recognize and show that equivalent fractions have the same size, though not necessarily the same shape.

Date: 11/19/13

5.E.7

7 x 1 = _____   7 x 2 = _____   7 x 3 = _____   7 x 4 = _____

7 x 5 = _____   7 x 1 = _____   7 x 2 = _____   7 x 1 = _____

7 x 3 = _____   7 x 1 = _____   7 x 4 = _____   7 x 1 = _____

7 x 5 = _____   7 x 1 = _____   7 x 2 = _____   7 x 3 = _____

7 x 2 = _____   7 x 4 = _____   7 x 2 = _____   7 x 5 = _____

7 x 2 = _____   7 x 1 = _____   7 x 2 = _____   7 x 3 = _____

7 x 1 = _____   7 x 3 = _____   7 x 2 = _____   7 x 3 = _____

7 x 4 = _____   7 x 3 = _____   7 x 5 = _____   7 x 3 = _____

7 x 4 = _____   7 x 1 = _____   7 x 4 = _____   7 x 2 = _____

7 x 4 = _____   7 x 3 = _____   7 x 4 = _____   7 x 5 = _____

7 x 4 = _____   7 x 5 = _____   7 x 1 = _____   7 x 5 = _____

7 x 2 = _____   7 x 5 = _____   7 x 3 = _____   7 x 5 = _____

7 x 4 = _____   7 x 2 = _____   7 x 4 = _____   7 x 3 = _____

7 x 5 = _____   7 x 3 = _____   7 x 2 = _____   7 x 4 = _____

7 x 3 = _____   7 x 5 = _____   7 x 2 = _____   7 x 4 = _____

COMMON CORE Lesson 20: Recognize and show that equivalent fractions have the same size, though not necessarily the same shape.
Date: 11/19/13

5.E.

5.E.9

7 x 1 = _____   7 x 2 = _____   7 x 3 = _____   7 x 4 = _____

7 x 5 = _____   7 x 6 = _____   7 x 7 = _____   7 x 8 = _____

7 x 9 = _____   7 x 10 = _____   7 x 5 = _____   7 x 6 = _____

7 x 5 = _____   7 x 7 = _____   7 x 5 = _____   7 x 8 = _____

7 x 5 = _____   7 x 9 = _____   7 x 5 = _____   7 x 10 = _____

7 x 6 = _____   7 x 5 = _____   7 x 6 = _____   7 x 7 = _____

7 x 6 = _____   7 x 8 = _____   7 x 6 = _____   7 x 9 = _____

7 x 6 = _____   7 x 7 = _____   7 x 6 = _____   7 x 7 = _____

7 x 8 = _____   7 x 7 = _____   7 x 9 = _____   7 x 7 = _____

7 x 8 = _____   7 x 6 = _____   7 x 8 = _____   7 x 7 = _____

7 x 8 = _____   7 x 9 = _____   7 x 9 = _____   7 x 6 = _____

7 x 9 = _____   7 x 7 = _____   7 x 9 = _____   7 x 8 = _____

7 x 9 = _____   7 x 8 = _____   7 x 6 = _____   7 x 9 = _____

7 x 7 = _____   7 x 9 = _____   7 x 6 = _____   7 x 8 = _____

7 x 9 = _____   7 x 7 = _____   7 x 6 = _____   7 x 8 = _____

COMMON CORE

Lesson 20: Recognize and show that equivalent fractions have the same size, though not necessarily the same shape.

Date: 11/19/13

5.E.9

Name _____   Date _____

1. Label what fraction of each shape is shaded. Then circle the fractions that are equal.

    A.

    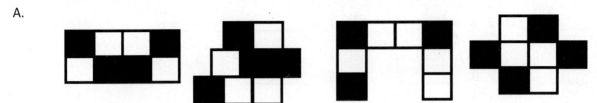

    _____

    B.

    _____

    C.

    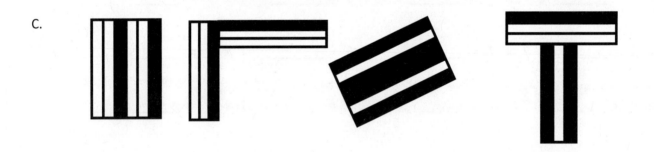

2. Label the fraction. Then draw 2 different shapes that have the same number of shaded and unshaded parts as the given figure.

    A.

    _____

    B.

    _____

5.E.1

3. Ann has 6 small square pieces of paper. 2 squares are grey. Ann cuts the 2 grey squares in half with a diagonal line from one corner to the other.

    a. What shapes does she have now?

    b. How many of each shape does she have?

    c. Use all the shapes with no overlaps. Draw different ways Ann's set of shapes might look. What fraction of the figure is grey?

4. Laura has 2 different beakers that hold exactly 1 liter. She pours $\frac{1}{2}$ liter of blue liquid into Beaker A. She pours $\frac{1}{2}$ liter of orange liquid into Beaker B. Susan says the amounts are not equal. Cristina says they are. Explain who you think is correct and why.

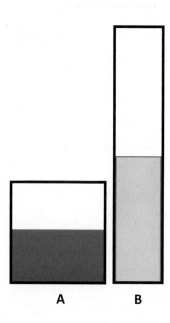

A   B

COMMON CORE

Lesson 20:   Recognize and show that equivalent fractions have the same size, though not necessarily the same shape.

Date: 11/19/13

5.E.11

Name _____   Date _____

1. Label what fraction of the figure is shaded. Then circle the fractions that are equal.

    A.

    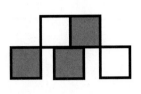   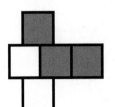   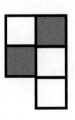   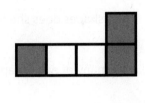

2. What fraction of the figures are shaded? Draw 2 different representations of the same fractional amount.

    A.

    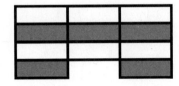

    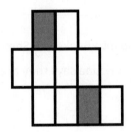

COMMON CORE | **Lesson 20:** Recognize and show that equivalent fractions have the same size, though not necessarily the same shape.   5.E.1

Date: 11/19/13

Name _____ Date _____

1. What fraction of the figure is shaded? Draw 2 different representations of the same fractional amount.

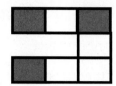

2.

   a. These two shapes both show $\frac{4}{5}$. Are they equivalent? Why or why not?

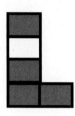 

   b. Draw two different representations of $\frac{4}{5}$ that are equivalent.

3. Diana ran a quarter mile straight down the street. Becky ran a quarter mile on a track. Who ran more? Explain your thinking.

      Diana   _____

      Becky

COMMON CORE

Lesson 20:   Recognize and show that equivalent fractions have the same size,
though not necessarily the same shape.

Date: 11/19/13

5.E.13

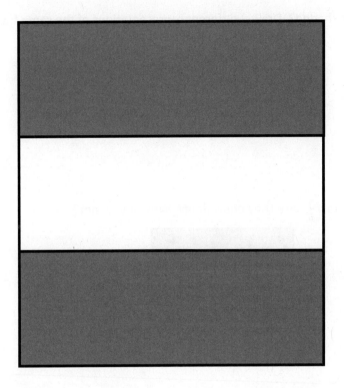

COMMON CORE

| **Lesson 20:** | Recognize and show that equivalent fractions have the same size, though not necessarily the same shape. |
| **Date:** | 11/19/13 |

5.E.

Lesson 21

Objective: Recognize and show that equivalent fractions refer to the same point on the number line.

Suggested Lesson Structure

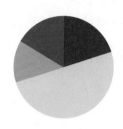

■ Fluency Practice   (12 minutes)
■ Application Problem   (8 minutes)
■ Concept Development   (30 minutes)
■ Student Debrief   (10 minutes)
   Total Time   **(60 minutes)**

Fluency Practice (12 minutes)

- Whole Number Division **3.OA.7**   (8 minutes)
- 1 Whole Expressed as Unit Fractions **3.NF.1**   (4 minutes)

Whole Number Division (8 minutes)

Timing Note: Steps 1 and 2 are timed for two minutes. Step 3 is timed for 1 minute of testing for each partner. Step 4 is timed for two minutes

Step 1:   Students self-select a number and write a set of multiples up to that number's multiple of 10 vertically down the left hand side of the page (e.g. 6, 12, 18, 24, 30, 36, 42, 48, 54, 60).

Step 2:   Divide the number by the multiple vertically down the page.

Step 3:   Change papers and test a partner out of order, e.g. "What is 24 divided by 6?"

Step 4:   Redo the process of steps 1 and 2 to see improvement.

Let the students know that the same activity will be done the next day so that they have a chance to practice and further improve, possibly advancing to the next number which might further challenge them.

1 Whole Expressed as Unit Fractions (4 minutes)

T: Show me a number bond which partitions a whole into 3 equal parts.

S: (Students show.)

T: What is the unit fraction?

S: 1 third.

Repeat with other examples.

 | Lesson 20: Recognize and show that equivalent fractions refer to the same point on the number line.
Date: 11/19/13

5.E.15

Application Problem (8 minutes)

Dorothea is training to run a 2 mile race. She marks off her starting point and the finish line. So that she can track her progress, she places a mark at 1 mile. She then places a mark halfway between her starting position and 1 mile, and another halfway between 1 mile and the finish line.

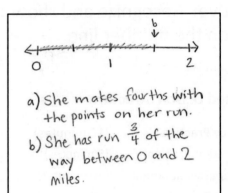

a) She makes fourths with the points on her run.

b) She has run $\frac{3}{4}$ of the way between 0 and 2 miles.

- Draw a number line to show what unit fraction she makes as she marks the points on her run.

- How far has she run when she gets to the third marker?

Concept Development (30 minutes)

Materials: (S) Fraction strips (4 ¼ inches by 1 inch), math journals, crayons, glue, tape, meter stick, number line on the floor

Each student has five fraction strips.

T: We're going to make copies of unit fractions with our fraction strips. Fold your first strip into halves.

S: (Students fold.)

T: Label each part with a unit fraction. Then use a crayon to shade in 1 half.

S: (Label and shade.)

T: Glue your fraction strip at the top of a new page in your math journal.

S: (Students glue.)

T: Fold another fraction strip to make copies of fourths. Label each part with a unit fraction. Then glue your fraction strip directly below the first one in your math journal. Make sure that the ends are lined up.

S: (Students fold, label, place, and glue fraction strips.)

T: Now shade the number of fourths that are equivalent to the shaded half. Whisper to your partner how many units you shaded.

S: (Students shade, whisper '2'.)

Guide students through the same sequence for a fraction strip folded into eighths.

T: Write the shaded fraction to the right of each fraction strip in your journal.

S: (Students write $\frac{1}{2}, \frac{2}{4}, \frac{4}{8}$.)

T: The unit fractions are different. Discuss with a partner whether or not the fractions are equal, or

NOTES ON MULTIPLE MEANS OF REPRESENTATION:

The vocabulary word 'equivalent' has the advantage of cognates in many languages. Build ELLs' understanding of 'equivalent fractions' through discussion, word webs, and questioning.

Ask:

- How are these equivalent fractions related?

- What particular property do they have in common?

- When might it be useful to interchange equivalent fractions?

Lesson 20: Recognize and show that equivalent fractions refer to the same point on the number line.

Date: 11/19/13

5.E.1

equivalent.

S: Since the unit fraction is different, then they are not equal. → They have a different number of shaded parts, so I'm not sure. → The same amount of the fraction strip is shaded for each one. That must mean they're equal.

T: I hear some uncertainty. Beside our fraction strips, what's another tool we can use to test their equivalence?

S: We can place them on a number line.

T: Let's do that. Place your personal board under the fraction strip folded into halves. Use the fraction strip to measure a number line from 0 to 1. Label 0 halves, rename the whole, and then label $\frac{1}{2}$.

S: (Measure, draw and label a number line.)

MP.7

T: Move your personal board down so that your number line is under your fourths fraction strip. On the same number line, label each unit fraction. See if any fractions are located at the same point on the number line.

S: Hey, $\frac{1}{2}$ and $\frac{2}{4}$ are on the same point! → So are $\frac{2}{2}$, $\frac{4}{4}$, and 1. → Zeros too, but we already knew that!

T: Discuss with your partner what it might mean when two fractions are at the same point on the number line.

S: I think it means they're the same. → It proves what we saw with the fraction strips. They had the same amount shaded before, and now they're in the same place on the number line. → The fractions must be equivalent because they are at the same point.

T: I can use the equal sign to show the fractions are equivalent when I write them. (Write $\frac{1}{2} = \frac{2}{4}$.) The equal sign is like a balance. It means 'the same as.' We might read this as $\frac{1}{2}$ is the same as $\frac{2}{4}$ because they have the same value. We just proved that with our number line! As long as the total values on both sides of the equal sign are the same, we can use it to show equivalence. (Write $\frac{2}{2} = \frac{4}{4} = 1$.) Turn and tell your partner, is this statement true?

S: The equal sign works when there are two things, not three. → But the total value of $\frac{2}{2}$ is 1, and $\frac{4}{4}$ is 1, and 1 is 1, so I think it's true. → Remember we can also say 'equals' as 'the same as'? $\frac{2}{2}$ is the same as $\frac{4}{4}$. Those are the same as 1. They are written differently, but they have the same value.

Direct students to follow the same process to label eighths independently.

T: Fold your last 2 fraction strips. One should be copies of thirds and the other should be copies of sixths. Label the parts with unit fractions and glue these strips

NOTES ON
MULTIPLE MEANS OF
ENGAGEMENT:

Slip the Problem Set into a clear plastic sheet protector. Using a dry erase marker, students below grade level can highlight the unit intervals, shade unit fractions as they count, and circle equivalent fractions.

Present an open-ended alternative for students above grade level who may enjoy finding unlimited equivalent fractions for a given point on the number line. Ask (for example), "How many equivalent fractions can you model for 3 halves?"

COMMON CORE   Lesson 20:   Recognize and show that equivalent fractions refer to the same point on the number line.   **5.E.17**

Date: 11/19/13

below the others in your math journal in order from greatest to least. Shade 1 third. Then shade the number of sixths equal to 1 third.

S: (Students follow the process for these 2 strips.)

T: Now work with your partner to measure and draw a new number line using your thirds and sixths. Then using your other strips, find and label all the fractions that are equivalent to thirds and sixths.

Note: If you do not use math journals in your classroom, have your students store these fraction strips in a safe place. They will used again in Lesson 22.

NOTES ON USING =:

It is worth spending a moment to make sure that students are clear on the meaning of the equal sign in this lesson, as it is an important symbol throughout the topic. Students get into the habit of associating its use with an operation and an answer, not fully understanding its application in a context like $\frac{1}{2} = \frac{2}{4}$.

Problem Set (10 minutes)

Students should do their personal best to complete the Problem Set within the allotted 10 minutes. For some classes, it may be appropriate to modify the assignment by specifying which problems they work on first. Some problems do not specify a method for solving. Students solve these problems using the RDW approach used for Application Problems.

Student Debrief (10 minutes)

Lesson Objective: Recognize and show that equivalent fractions refer to the same point on the number line.

The Student Debrief is intended to invite reflection and active processing of the total lesson experience.

Invite students to review their solutions for the Problem Set. They should check work by comparing answers with a partner before going over answers as a class. Look for misconceptions or misunderstandings that can be addressed in the Debrief. Guide students in a conversation to debrief the Problem Set and process the lesson.

You may choose to use any combination of the questions below to lead the discussion.

- The goal of discussion in the debrief is for students to articulate that equivalent fractions refer to the same point on the number line. You might stimulate their thinking by asking them to relate fractions strips to the number line. Make

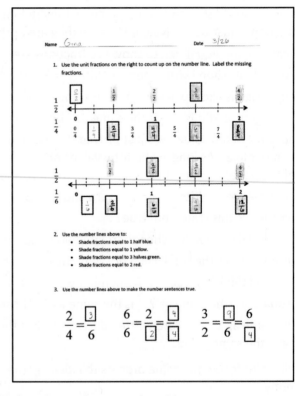

sure students are clear on what the word 'equivalent' means and are comfortable using it.

- After students have checked their work for Problems 4 and 5, ask them to use the fraction strips in their math journals to see if they can name another equivalent fraction. ($\frac{3}{6}$ is the only possibility.) Ask students to talk about how they know the fractions are equivalent and possibly plot them on the same number line to emphasize the lesson objective.

- In anticipation of Lesson 22, guide students to study the fractions in Problem Set Problem 4. Ask them to study the fractions equivalent to wholes. Get students to notice that the number of shaded parts is the same as the total number of parts (numerator and denominator are the same.) Have them use the pattern to name other wholes. Generate excitement by encouraging them to use extremely large numbers, as well as those that are more familiar.

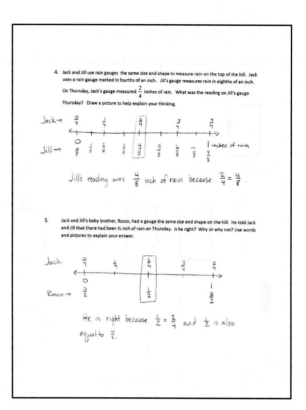

Exit Ticket (3 minutes)

After the Student Debrief, instruct students to complete the Exit Ticket. A review of their work will help you assess the students' understanding of the concepts that were presented in the lesson today and plan more effectively for future lessons. You may read the questions aloud to the students.

COMMON CORE

Lesson 20:   Recognize and show that equivalent fractions refer to the same point
             on the number line.
Date: 11/19/13

5.E.19

Name _____   Date _____

1. Use the unit fractions on the right to count up on the number line. Label the missing fractions.

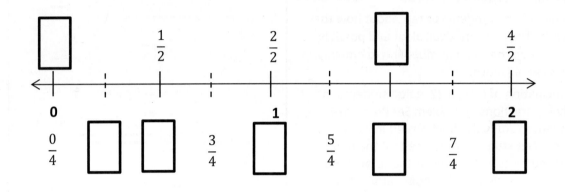

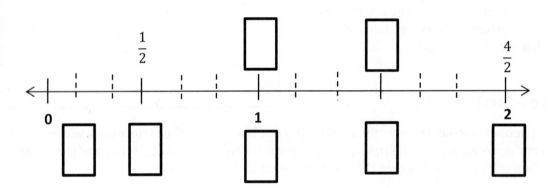

2. Use the number lines above to:

    ▪ Color fractions equal to 1 half blue.

    ▪ Color fractions equal to 1 yellow.

    ▪ Color fractions equal to 3 halves green.

    ▪ Color fractions equal to 2 red.

3. Use the number lines above to make the number sentences true.

$$\frac{2}{4} = \frac{\square}{6} \qquad \frac{6}{6} = \frac{2}{\square} = \frac{\square}{\square} \qquad \frac{3}{2} = \frac{\square}{6} = \frac{6}{\square}$$

COMMON CORE | **Lesson 20:** Recognize and show that equivalent fractions refer to the same point on the number line. | 5.E.2

Date: 11/19/13

4. Jack and Jill use rain gauges the same size and shape to measure rain on the top of a hill. Jack uses a rain gauge marked in fourths of an inch. Jill's gauge measures rain in eighths of an inch. On Thursday, Jack's gauge measured $\frac{2}{4}$ inches of rain. They both had the same amount of water, so what was the reading on Jill's gauge Thursday? Draw a number line to help explain your thinking.

5. Jack and Jill's baby brother Rosco also had a gauge the same size and shape on the same hill. He told Jack and Jill that there had been $\frac{1}{2}$ inch of rain on Thursday. Is he right? Why or why not? Use words and a number line to explain your answer.

COMMON CORE

Lesson 20:   Recognize and show that equivalent fractions refer to the same point on the number line.

Date: 11/19/13

5.E.21

Name _____   Date _____

1. Claire went home after school and shared with her mother that 1 whole is the same as $\frac{2}{2}$ and $\frac{6}{6}$. Her mother asked why, but she couldn't explain it. Use a number line and words to help Claire show and explain why $1 = \frac{2}{2} = \frac{6}{6}$.

Lesson 20:   Recognize and show that equivalent fractions refer to the same point
                   on the number line.

Date: 11/19/13

5.E.2

Name _____ Date _____

1. Use the unit fractions on the right to count up on the number line. Label the missing fractions.

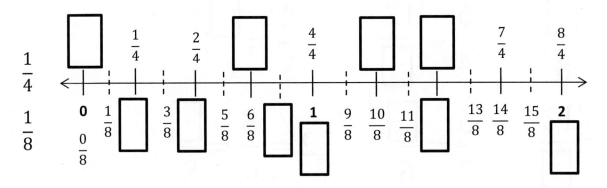

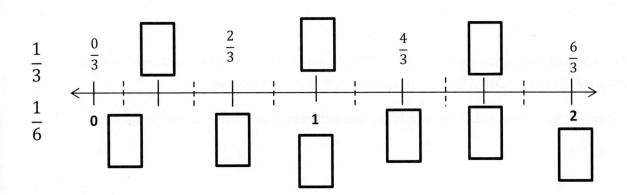

2. Use the number lines above to:
   - Color fractions equal to 1 purple.
   - Color fractions equal to 2 fourths yellow.
   - Color fractions equal to 2 blue.
   - Color fractions equal to 5 thirds green.
   - Write a pair of fractions that are equivalent.

   _____ = _____

3. Use the number lines on the previous page to make the number sentences true.

$$\frac{1}{4} = \frac{\square}{8}$$ $$\frac{6}{4} = \frac{12}{\square}$$ $$\frac{2}{3} = \frac{\square}{6}$$

$$\frac{6}{3} = \frac{12}{\square}$$ $$\frac{3}{3} = \frac{\square}{6}$$ $$2 = \frac{8}{4} = \frac{\square}{8}$$

4. Mr. Fairfax ordered 3 large pizzas for a class party. Group A ate $\frac{6}{6}$ of the first pizza, and Group B ate $\frac{8}{6}$ of the second pizza. During the party, the class discussed which group ate more pizzas.

   a. Did group A or B eat more pizza? Use words and and pictures to explain your answer to the class.

   b. Later Group C ate all remaining slices of pizza. What fraction of the pizza did group C eat? Use words and pictures to explain your answer.

COMMON CORE | **Lesson 20:**   Recognize and show that equivalent fractions refer to the same point on the number line.

Date: 11/19/13

5.E.2

Lesson 22

Objective: Generate simple equivalent fractions by using visual fraction models and the number line.

Suggested Lesson Structure

■ Fluency Practice   (12 minutes)
■ Application Problems   (8 minutes)
□ Concept Development   (30 minutes)
■ Student Debrief   (10 minutes)
  Total Time   **(60 minutes)**

Fluency Practice (12 minutes)

- Whole Number Division **3.OA.7**   (8 minutes)
- Counting by Fractions Equal to Whole Numbers on the Number Line **3.NF.3a**   (4 minutes)

Whole Number Division (8 minutes)

Timing Note: Steps 1 and 2 are timed for two minutes. Step 3 is timed for one minute of testing for each partner. Step 4 is timed for two minutes.

Step 1: Students self-select a number and write a set of multiples up to that number's multiple of 10 vertically down the left hand side of the page (E.g., 6, 12, 18. 24, 30, 36, 42, 48, 54, 60).

Step 2: Divide the number by the multiple vertically down the page.

Step 3: Change papers and test a partner out of order, e.g. "What is 24 divided by 6?".

Step 4: Redo the process of steps 1 and 2 to see improvement.

Counting by Fractions Equal to Whole Numbers on the Number Line (4 minutes)

Materials: (S) Personal white boards

T: (Project number line partitioned into 12 thirds.) Count by thirds.

S: (Write fractions as students count.) 1 third, 2 thirds, 3 thirds, 4 thirds, 5 thirds, 6 thirds, 7 thirds, 8 thirds, 9 thirds, 10 thirds 11 thirds, 12 thirds.

T: On your personal board, write the fractions equal to whole numbers in order from smallest to greatest. Continue beyond those shown on our number line if you finish early.

Repeating with halves and fourths are two possibilities.

	Lesson 22:	Generate simple equivalent fractions by using visual fraction models	
		and the number line.	5.E.25
	Date:	11/19/13	

Application Problem (8 minutes)

Mr. Ramos wants to nail the TV cord against the wall so no one trips. He puts 7 nails equally spaced along the cord. Draw a number line representing the cord. Label it from 0 at the start of the cord to 1 at the end. Mark where Mr. Ramos puts each nail with a fraction.

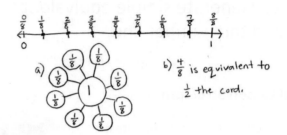

a. Build a number bond with unit fractions to 1 whole.

b. Write the fraction of the nail that is equivalent to $\frac{1}{2}$ the cord.

Concept Development (30 minutes)

Materials: (S) Math journal/fraction strips made in Lesson 21, new fraction strips, crayons, 8 inch x 8 inch paper squares, personal white boards, glue

T: Take out your math journal and turn to the page where you glued your fraction strips yesterday. Name the fraction that is equivalent to 1 third.

S: $\frac{2}{6}$.

T: Now name the fractions that are equivalent to 1 half.

S: $\frac{2}{4}, \frac{4}{8}, \frac{3}{6}$?

T: Good! Some of you remember that during our debrief yesterday I challenged you to find another fraction equivalent to 1 half even though it wasn't shaded. $\frac{3}{6}$ is the fraction you came up with.

T: Now I want you to work with a partner to look at your fraction strips again. See if you can find other equivalent fractions, shaded or unshaded. Draw and label them on your personal board. For example, using my fraction strips, I can see that $\frac{2}{2}$ and $\frac{4}{4}$ are equivalent. Fourths are just halves cut in half again. Be ready to explain how you know, just like I did.

MP.3

S: (Possible answers other than those already discussed: $\frac{2}{2}, \frac{4}{4}, \frac{8}{8}, \frac{3}{3}, \frac{6}{6}, \frac{3}{4}, \frac{2}{3}, \frac{4}{6}$.)

NOTES ON MULTIPLE MEANS OF ENGAGEMENT:

Students below grade level may alternatively use two fraction strips—one partitioned into sixths, the other partitioned into fourths—to compare 3 sixths and 2 fourths. Or, have students draw number lines on personal white boards, so that students may erase partitioned sixths before partitioning fourths.

NOTES ON MULTIPLE MEANS OF ENGAGEMENT:

Challenge students working above grade level to collect the data presented (e.g., sets of equivalencies) and organize it in a table or graph. Guide them to analyze the organized data and to draw conclusions. Ask (for example), "Which fraction has more equivalent fractions? Why?"

Lesson 22: Generate simple equivalent fractions by using visual fraction models and the number line.
Date: 11/19/13

5.E.2

T: (Have students share their work.) Let's look at $\frac{2}{3}$ and $\frac{4}{6}$. Talk with your partner. Do you notice a relationship between the numbers in these fractions?

MP.3

S: 3 is half of 6. And 2 is half of 4. → That's true. If you make 2 copies of $\frac{2}{3}$, then you get $\frac{4}{6}$. → I see what you mean about the numbers doubling, but it's not really 2 copies when you look at the fraction strips. Thirds are bigger than sixths. → The numbers double because you're cutting each third into 2 equal parts to get sixths. But that actually makes the pieces get smaller even though the number of pieces is doubled. It's still the same amount.

T: Now look at $\frac{3}{4}$ and $\frac{6}{8}$. Does the same pattern you just noticed apply to these fractions?

You may want to have students repeat the process with whole number fractions if they are unsure.

T: I'm hearing you say that the numbers in these equivalent fractions doubled. Look again at these equivalent fractions: $\frac{2}{3}$, $\frac{4}{6}$. What fraction would we get if we doubled the top and bottom numbers in $\frac{4}{6}$?

S: $\frac{8}{12}$.

T: (Pass out 3 fraction strips to each student.) Is it equivalent to $\frac{2}{3}$ and $\frac{4}{6}$? Fold your strips into thirds, sixths, and twelfths. Label the unit fractions. Then shade $\frac{2}{3}$, $\frac{4}{6}$ and $\frac{8}{12}$ to compare.

S: (After students work.) They are equivalent!

T: What did we do to the equal parts each time to make the top and bottom numbers double?

S: We cut them in 2! Thirds get cut in 2 to make sixths, and sixths get cut in 2 to make twelfths.

T: Did the whole change?

S: Nope, it just has more equal parts.

T: What happens to the shaded area?

S: It stays the same.

T: So the fractions are?

S: Equivalent!

Have students glue the equivalent fractions into their math journals and label them.

Show the pictorial models below.

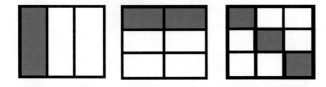

T: Let's look at a different model. These 3 wholes are the same. Name the shaded fraction as I point to the model.

Lesson 22:   Generate simple equivalent fractions by using visual fraction models and the number line.

Date: 11/19/13

5.E.27

As you point to each model, label with student responses:

$\frac{1}{3}, \frac{2}{6}, \frac{3}{9}$.

T: Are these fractions equivalent? Work with your partner to use the number line to prove your answer. Be ready to present your thinking.

After students work, have pairs share at tables or select partners to present different methods to the class. Provide other examples using pictorial models and the number line as necessary.

NOTES ON MULTIPLE MEANS OF REPRESENTATION:

Celebrate and encourage ELLs' use of math language in English. In the Problem Set encourage learners to whisper the unit fraction, whisper count the shaded units, and whisper the shaded fraction as they write.

Problem Set (10 minutes)

Students should do their personal best to complete the Problem Set within the allotted 10 minutes. For some classes, it may be appropriate to modify the assignment by specifying which problems they work on first. Some problems do not specify a method for solving. Students solve these problems using the RDW approach used for Application Problems.

Student Debrief (10 minutes)

Lesson Objective: Generate simple equivalent fractions by using visual fraction models and the number line.

The Student Debrief is intended to invite reflection and active processing of the total lesson experience.

Invite students to review their solutions for the Problem Set. They should check work by comparing answers with a partner before going over answers as a class. Look for misconceptions or misunderstandings that can be addressed in the Debrief. Guide students in a conversation to debrief the Problem Set and process the lesson.

You may choose to use any combination of the questions below to lead the discussion.

- What did you notice about the models in Problem 1?

- In Problem 1, which shapes were most difficult to match? Why?

- What might be another way to draw a fraction equivalent to $\frac{3}{4}$?

- Look at Problem 2. What pattern do you notice between the 3 sets of models?

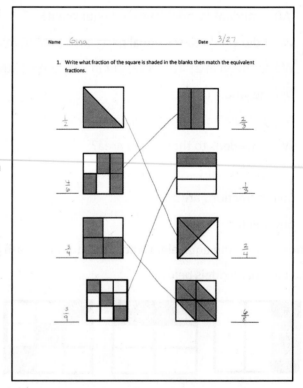

Lesson 22:   Generate simple equivalent fractions by using visual fraction models and the number line.
Date: 11/19/13

5.E.2

- How does the pattern you noticed in Problem 2 relate to other parts of today's lesson?

Exit Ticket (3 minutes)

After the Student Debrief, instruct students to complete the Exit Ticket. A review of their work will help you assess the students' understanding of the concepts that were presented in the lesson today and plan more effectively for future lessons. You may read the questions aloud to the students..

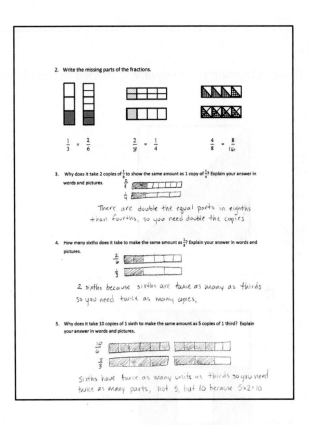

COMMON CORE

Lesson 22: Generate simple equivalent fractions by using visual fraction models and the number line.

Date: 11/19/13

5.E.29

© 2013 Common Core, Inc. All rights reserved. commoncore.org

Name _____ Date _____

1. Write what fraction of the square is shaded in the blanks then match the equivalent fractions.

_____ 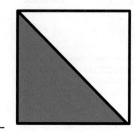   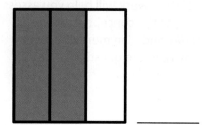 _____

_____ 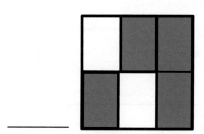   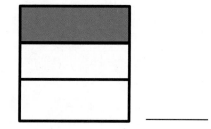 _____

_____ 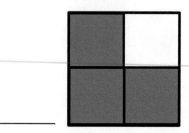   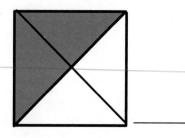 _____

_____ 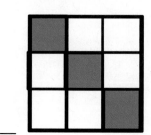   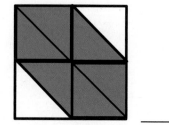 _____

COMMON CORE   Lesson 22:   Generate simple equivalent fractions by using visual fraction models and the number line.
Date: 11/19/13

5.E.3

2. Write the missing parts of the fractions.

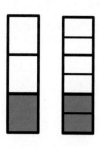   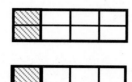   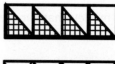

$\dfrac{1}{3} = \dfrac{}{6}$ $\dfrac{2}{} = \dfrac{1}{4}$ $\dfrac{4}{8} = \dfrac{8}{}$

3. Why does it take 2 copies of $\frac{1}{8}$ to show the same amount as 1 copy of $\frac{1}{4}$? Explain your answer in words and pictures.

4. How many sixths does it take to make the same amount as $\frac{1}{3}$? Explain your answer in words and pictures.

5. Why does it take 10 copies of 1 sixth to make the same amount as 5 copies of 1 third? Explain your answer in words and pictures.

COMMON CORE

Lesson 22: Generate simple equivalent fractions by using visual fraction models and the number line.

Date: 11/19/13

5.E.31

Name _____   Date _____

1. Draw and label two models that show equivalent fractions.

2. Draw a number line that proves your thinking about Problem 1.

Lesson 22:   Generate simple equivalent fractions by using visual fraction models
and the number line.

Date: 11/19/13

5.E.3

Name _____   Date _____

1. Write what fraction of the figure is shaded in the blanks then match the equivalent fractions.

_____   _____

_____   _____

_____   _____

_____   _____

Lesson 22:   Generate simple equivalent fractions by using visual fraction models
              and the number line.
Date: 11/19/13

5.E.33

2. Complete the fractions to make true statements.

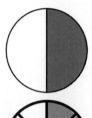

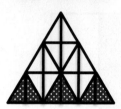

$$\frac{1}{2} = \frac{4}{\underline{}}$$ $$\frac{3}{5} = \frac{\underline{}}{10}$$ $$\frac{3}{9} = \frac{6}{\underline{}}$$

3. Why does it take 3 copies of $\frac{1}{6}$ to show the same amount as 1 copy of $\frac{1}{2}$? Explain your answer in words and pictures.

4. How many ninths does it take to make the same amount as $\frac{1}{3}$? Explain your answer in words and pictures.

5. A pie was cut into 8 slices equally. If Ruben ate $\frac{3}{4}$ of the pie, how many slices did he eat? Write the answer in eighths. Explain your answer using a number line and words.

COMMON CORE   Lesson 22:   Generate simple equivalent fractions by using visual fraction models and the number line.
Date: 11/19/13

5.E.34

Lesson 23

Objective: Generate simple equivalent fractions by using visual fraction models and the number line.

Suggested Lesson Structure

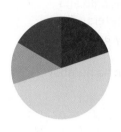

■ Fluency Practice　　　　　(12 minutes)
Concept Development　　(30 minutes)
Application Problem　　　(8 minutes)
■ Student Debrief　　　　　(10 minutes)
　Total Time　　　　　　**(60 minutes)**

Fluency Practice (12 minutes)

- Adding by 6 Sprint **2.NBT.5**　　　　(8 minutes)
- Find the Equivalent Fraction **3.NF.3d**　(4 minutes)

Adding by 6 Sprint (8 minutes)

Materials: (S) Adding by 6 Sprint

Find the Equivalent Fraction (4 minutes)

Materials: (T) Prepared fraction images (S) Personal white
　　　　　boards

NOTES ON
MULTIPLE MEANS OF
ENGAGEMENT:

Students below grade level may enjoy counting fractions more than once. First, with the addition of models (e.g.,. shading fourths), then without, gradually increasing speed with each repetition.

T: (Project a square partitioned into 2 parts with 1 part shaded in.) Say the fraction.

S: 1 half.

T: (Write $\frac{1}{2}$ underneath the square.) Copy my picture and fraction on your boards.

S: (Copy image and fraction on their boards.)

T: (Project an identical square to the right of the first.) On your board, draw a second identical square.

S: (Draw a second identical square.)

T: (Below the squares write $\frac{1}{2} = \frac{}{4}$.) On your board, make your second square into parts of 4 and fill-in the number sentence.

S: (Draw a horizontal line to show 2 parts of 4 shaded. Under pictures they write $\frac{1}{2} = \frac{2}{4}$.)

Continue with possible sequence: $\frac{1}{2} = \frac{}{6}$, $\frac{2}{8} = \frac{}{4}$, $\frac{5}{10} = \frac{}{20}$.

Application Problem (8 minutes)

The soccer player stood at the corner of a 100 meter field and kicked the ball to her teammate. She kicked it 20 meters. The commentator said she kicked it a quarter of the way across the field. Is that true? If not, what fraction should the commentator have said? Prove your answer by using a number line.

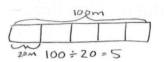

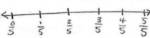

She did not kick it a quarter of the way. A quarter is $\frac{1}{4}$. She only kicked it $\frac{1}{5}$. They should have said $\frac{1}{5}$ of the way.

Concept Development (30 minutes)

Materials: (S) Index cards (1 per pair, described below), sentence strips, chart paper, markers, glue, math journals

Students are seated in pairs. Each pair gets one sentence strip and an index card. The index card designates endpoints on a number line and a unit with which to partition, example to the right.

Divide your class so each group is composed of pairs (each group contains more than 1 pair). Create the following index cards and distribute one card to each pair per group:

> Intervals 2-4
>
> Fifths
>
> Group A

Group A: Intervals 3-5, thirds and sixths

Group B: Intervals 1-3, sixths and twelfths

Group C: Intervals 3-5, halves and fourths

Group D: Intervals 1-3, fourths and eighths

Group E: Intervals 4-6, sixths and twelfths

Group F: Intervals 6-8, halves and fourths

T: With your partner use your sentence strip to make a number line with your given intervals. Then estimate to partition into your given unit by folding your sentence strip. Label the endpoints and the unit fractions. Rename the wholes.

S: (Work in pairs.)

T: (Give one piece of chart paper to a member of each letter group.) Now stand up and find your other letter group members. Once you've found them, glue your number lines in a column so that ends match up on your chart paper. Compare number lines to find equivalent fractions. Record all possible equivalent fractions in your math journals.

NOTES ON MULTIPLE MEANS OF ACTION AND EXPRESSION:

Differentiate the activity by strategically assigning "just right" intervals and units to pairs of students.

S: (Find letter group members, glue fraction strips onto chart paper. Letter group members discuss and record equivalent fractions.)

T: (Hang each chart paper around the room.) Now we're going to do a "gallery walk". As a letter group you will visit the other groups' chart papers. One person in each group will be the recorder. You can switch recorders each time you visit a new chart paper. Your job will be to find and list all of the equivalent fractions you see at each chart paper.

S: (Go to another letter group's chart paper and begin.)

T: (Rotate groups briskly so that at the beginning students don't finish finding all fractions at 1 station. As letter groups rotate and chart papers fill up, challenge groups to check others' work to make sure no fractions are missing.)

T: (After rotation is complete.) Go back to your own chart paper with your letter group. Take your math journals and check your friends' work. Did they name the same equivalent fractions you found?

NOTES ON MULTIPLE MEANS OF ENGAGEMENT:

Challenge above grade level students to write more than two equivalent fractions on the Problem Set. As they begin to generate equivalencies mentally and rapidly, guide students to articulate the pattern and its rule.

Problem Set (10 minutes)

Students should do their personal best to complete the Problem Set within the allotted 10 minutes. For some classes, it may be appropriate to modify the assignment by specifying which problems they work on first. Some problems do not specify a method for solving. Students solve these problems using the RDW approach used for Application Problems.

Student Debrief (10 minutes)

Lesson Objective: Generate simple equivalent fractions by using visual fraction models and the number line. [Day 2 of L23]

The Student Debrief is intended to invite reflection and active processing of the total lesson experience.

Invite students to review their solutions for the Problem Set. They should check work by comparing answers with a partner before going over answers as a class. Look for misconceptions or misunderstandings that can be addressed in the Debrief. Guide students in a conversation to debrief the Problem Set and process the lesson.

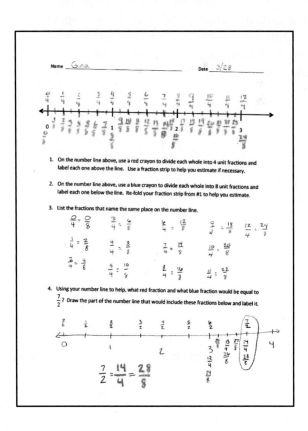

Lesson 23: Generate simple equivalent fractions by using visual fraction models and the number line.
Date: 11/19/13

5.E.37

You may choose to use any combination of the questions below to lead the discussion.

- Could you have compared with another number line? What would the result be?
- How did it change your work when the interval on your number line was no longer from 0 to 1?
- Could we sequentially connect the number lines we made by interval even though they are partitioned into different units? What would happen then?
- Compare all of the answers for Problem Set Problem 5. (Use this comparison to advance the idea that the world of fractions is endless. There are many different fractions that label a single point.)

Exit Ticket (3 minutes)

After the Student Debrief, instruct students to complete the Exit Ticket. A review of their work will help you assess the students' understanding of the concepts that were presented in the lesson today and plan more effectively for future lessons. You may read the questions aloud to the students.

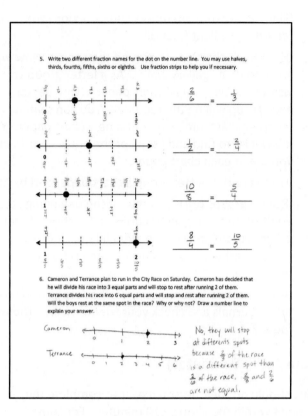

NOTES ON MULTIPLE MEANS OF REPRESENTATION:

To assist comprehension, develop multiples way to ask the same question. For example, you might change the question, "Could we sequentially…?" to "What if we put all the number lines together in numerical order?" or "What do you think of a number line whose unit intervals are partitioned into different unit fractions?"

Lesson 23: Generate simple equivalent fractions by using visual fraction models and the number line.

Date: 11/19/13

5.E.38

A

Correct _____

Add.

1	0 + 6 =		23	7 + 6 =	
2	1 + 6 =		24	17 + 6 =	
3	2 + 6 =		25	27 + 6 =	
4	3 + 6 =		26	37 + 6 =	
5	4 + 6 =		27	47 + 6 =	
6	6 + 4 =		28	77 + 6 =	
7	6 + 3 =		29	8 + 6 =	
8	6 + 2 =		30	18 + 6 =	
9	6 + 1 =		31	28 + 6 =	
10	6 + 0 =		32	38 + 6 =	
11	15 + 6 =		33	48 + 6 =	
12	25 + 6 =		34	78 + 6 =	
13	35 + 6 =		35	9 + 6 =	
14	45 + 6 =		36	19 + 6 =	
15	55 + 6 =		37	29 + 6 =	
16	85 + 6 =		38	39 + 6 =	
17	6 + 6 =		39	89 + 6 =	
18	16 + 6 =		40	6 + 75 =	
19	26 + 6 =		41	6 + 56 =	
20	36 + 6 =		42	6 + 77 =	
21	46 + 6 =		43	6 + 88 =	
22	76 + 6 =		44	6 + 99 =	

Lesson 23: Generate simple equivalent fractions by using visual fraction models and the number line.

Date: 11/19/13

5.E.39

B

Add.

Improvement _____   # Correct _____

1	6 + 0 =		23	7 + 6 =	
2	6 + 1 =		24	17 + 6 =	
3	6 + 2 =		25	27 + 6 =	
4	6 + 3 =		26	37 + 6 =	
5	6 + 4 =		27	47 + 6 =	
6	4 + 6 =		28	67 + 6 =	
7	3 + 6 =		29	8 + 6 =	
8	2 + 6 =		30	18 + 6 =	
9	1 + 6 =		31	28 + 6 =	
10	0 + 6 =		32	38 + 6 =	
11	5 + 6 =		33	48 + 6 =	
12	15 + 6 =		34	88 + 6 =	
13	25 + 6 =		35	9 + 6 =	
14	35 + 6 =		36	19 + 6 =	
15	45 + 6 =		37	29 + 6 =	
16	75 + 6 =		38	39 + 6 =	
17	6 + 6 =		39	79 + 6 =	
18	16 + 6 =		40	6 + 55 =	
19	26 + 6 =		41	6 + 76 =	
20	36 + 6 =		42	6 + 57 =	
21	46 + 6 =		43	6 + 98 =	
22	86 + 6 =		44	6 + 89 =	

Lesson 23: Generate simple equivalent fractions by using visual fraction models and the number line.
Date: 11/19/13

5.E.4

Name _____   Date _____

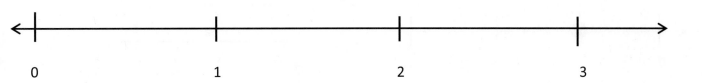

1. On the number line above, use a red colored pencil to divide each whole into 4 unit fractions and label each one above the line. Use a fraction strip to help you estimate if necessary.

2. On the number line above, use a blue colored pencil to divide each whole into 8 unit fractions and label each one below the line. Re-fold your fraction strip from #1 to help you estimate.

3. List the fractions that name the same place on the number line.

4. Using your number line to help, what red fraction and what blue fraction would be equal to $\frac{7}{2}$? Draw the part of the number line that would include these fractions below and label it.

COMMON CORE   Lesson 23:   Generate simple equivalent fractions by using visual fraction models   5.E.41
                   and the number line.
                   Date: 11/19/13

5. Write two different fraction names for the dot on the number line. You may use halves, thirds, fourths, fifths, sixths or eighths. Use fraction strips to help you if necessary.

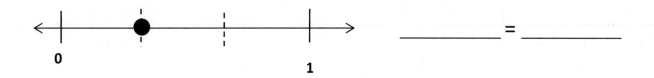

_____ = _____

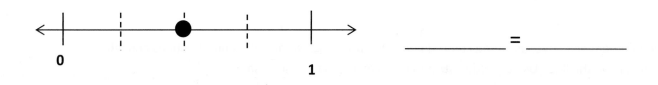

_____ = _____

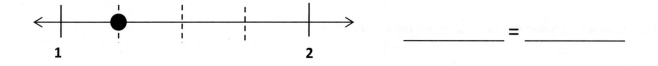

_____ = _____

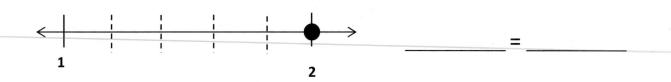

_____ = _____

6. Cameron and Terrance plan to run in the City Race on Saturday. Cameron has decided that he will divide his race into 3 equal parts and will stop to rest after running 2 of them. Terrance divides his race into 6 equal parts and will stop and rest after running 2 of them. Will the boys rest at the same spot in the race? Why or why not? Draw a number line to explain your answer.

COMMON CORE | **Lesson 23:** Generate simple equivalent fractions by using visual fraction models
                    and the number line.   5.E.4
                | **Date:**   11/19/13

© 2013 Common Core, Inc. All rights reserved. **commoncore.org**

Name _____   Date _____

1. Henry and Maddie were in a pie eating contest. The pies were cut either into thirds or sixths. Henry picked up a pie cut into sixths, and ate $\frac{4}{6}$ of it in 1 minute. Maddie picked up a pie cut into thirds. What fraction of pie does Maddie have to eat in 1 minute to tie with Henry? Draw a number line and use words to explain your answer.

Lesson 23:   Generate simple equivalent fractions by using visual fraction models
              and the number line.

Date: 11/19/13

5.E.43

Name _____ Date _____

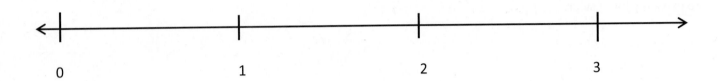

0   1   2   3

1. On the number line above, use a colored pencil to divide each whole into 3 unit fractions and label each one above the line.

2. On the number line above, use a different colored pencil to divide each whole into 6 unit fractions and label each one.

3. Write the fractions that name the same place on the number line below.

4. Using your number line to help, name the fraction equivalent to $\frac{20}{6}$. Name the fraction equivalent to $\frac{12}{3}$. Draw the part of the number line that would include these fractions below and label it.

$$\frac{20}{6} = \frac{}{3}$$ $$\frac{12}{3} = \frac{}{6}$$

COMMON CORE

Lesson 23: Generate simple equivalent fractions by using visual fraction models and the number line.

Date: 11/19/13

5.E.4

5. Write two different fraction names for the dot on the number line. You may use halves, thirds, fourths, fifths, sixths, eighths, or tenths.

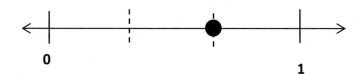

_____ = _____

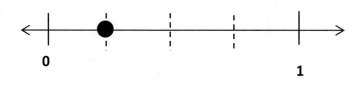

_____ = _____

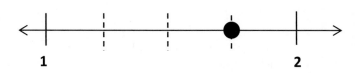

_____ = _____

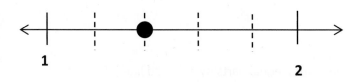

_____ = _____

6. Danielle and Mandy each ordered a large pizza for dinner. Danielle's pizza was cut into sixths, and Mandy's pizza was cut into twelfths. Danielle ate 2 sixths of her pizza. If Mandy wants to eat the same amount of pizza as Danielle, how many slices of pizza will she have to eat? Write the answer as a fraction. Draw a number line to explain your answer.

COMMON CORE

Lesson 23:   Generate simple equivalent fractions by using visual fraction models and the number line.

Date: 11/19/13

5.E.45

Lesson 24

Objective: Express whole numbers as fractions and recognize equivalence with different units.

Suggested Lesson Structure

■ Fluency Practice   (12 minutes)
■ Application Problem   (5 minutes)
□ Concept Development   (33 minutes)
■ Student Debrief   (10 minutes)
    Total Time   **(60 minutes)**

Fluency Practice (12 minutes)

▪ Sprint: Adding by 7 **2.NBT.5**   (8 minutes)
▪ Write Equal Fractions **3.NF.3d**   (4 minutes)

Sprint: Adding by 7 (8 minutes)

Materials: (S) Adding by 7 Sprint

Write Equal Fractions (4 minutes)

Materials: (S) Personal white boards

T: (Project number line with endpoints 0 and 1 partitioned into 2 equal parts by a dotted line.) Say the unit fraction represented by the dotted line.

S: 1 half. (Write $\frac{1}{2}$ below the dotted line.)

T: (To the right of the number line, write $\frac{1}{2} = \frac{}{4}$.) On your personal white boards, write the number sentence and fill in the blank.

S: (Write $\frac{1}{2} = \frac{2}{4}$.)

T: (Write $\frac{2}{4}$ below $\frac{1}{2}$ on the number line.)

Continue the process for new number lines: $\frac{1}{3} = \frac{2}{}$ and $\frac{1}{4} = \frac{}{8}$.

Lesson 24:   Express whole numbers as fractions and recognize equivalence with
               different units.
Date: 11/19/13

5.E.4

Application Problem (5 minutes)

The zipper on Robert's jacket is 1 foot long. It breaks on the first day of winter. He can only zip it $\frac{8}{12}$ of the way before it gets stuck. Draw and label a number line to show how far Robert can zip his jacket.

   a. Divide and label the number line in thirds. What fraction of the way can he zip his jacket in thirds?

   b. What fraction of Robert's jacket is not zipped? Write your answer in twelfths and in thirds.

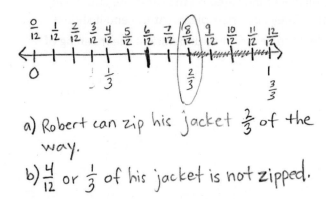

NOTES ON MULTIPLE MEANS OF ENGAGEMENT:

Partitioning the unit interval into two different unit fractions is a stimulating challenge for students above grade level.

Students below grade level can draw two separate number lines or use fraction strips to solve.

Concept Development (33 minutes)

Materials: (S) Fraction piece template (pictured below), scissors, envelopes, personal white boards, sentence strips, crayons

Each student starts with a fraction piece template, an envelope, and scissors.

   T: Cut out each of the boxes on your fraction piece template and initial each box so you know which ones are yours.

   S: (Students cut and initial.)

   T: Place the box that says '1 whole' on your personal white board. Take another box. How many halves make 1 whole? Show by folding and labeling each unit fraction.

   S: (Students fold the second box in half and label $\frac{1}{2}$ on

Fraction piece template

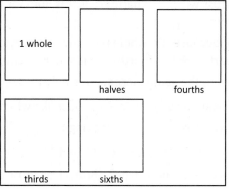

each of the 2 parts.)

T: Now cut on the fold. Draw circles around your whole and your parts to make a number bond.

S: (Students draw a number bond using their shapes to represent wholes and parts.)

T: In your whole, write an equality that shows how many halves are equal to 1 whole. Remember, the equal sign is like a balance. Both sides have the same value.

S: (The '1 whole' box now reads: 1 whole = $\frac{2}{2}$.)

T: Put your halves inside your envelope.

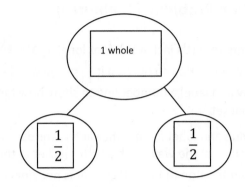

Follow the same sequence for each box so that children have all pieces indicated on the template cut. Have students update the equality on their '1 whole' square each time they cut a new piece. At the end it should read: 1 whole = $\frac{2}{2} = \frac{3}{3} = \frac{4}{4} = \frac{6}{6}$. Discuss the equality with students to ensure they understand the meaning of the equal sign and the role it plays in this number sentence.

T: (Project or show the following.)

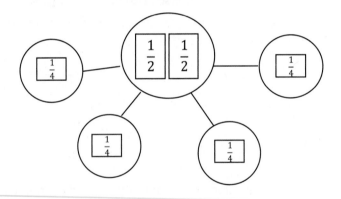

T: Use your pieces to make this number bond on your personal board.

S: (Copy the number bond.)

T: Discuss with your partner: Is this number bond true? Why or why not?

S: No, because the whole has only 2 pieces, but there are 4 parts! → But fourths are just halves cut in 2. So they're the same pieces, but smaller now. → $\frac{2}{4}$ is equivalent to $\frac{1}{2}$. → So $\frac{2}{2} = \frac{4}{4}$, just like what we wrote down on our '1 whole' rectangle.

T: I hear students saying that $\frac{2}{2}$ and $\frac{4}{4}$ both equal 1 whole. So can we say that this is true? (Project or show the following.)

MP.7

NOTES ON MULTIPLE MEANS OF ENGAGEMENT:

Students below grade level may appreciate tangibly proving that 2 halves is the same as 4 fourths. They or you can place the (paper) fourths on top of the halves to show equivalency.

COMMON CORE

Lesson 24:   Express whole numbers as fractions and recognize equivalence with different units.

Date: 11/19/13

5.E.4

S: No, because thirds aren't halves cut in 2. They look completely different. → But when we put our thirds together and our halves together, they make the same whole. → And before we found with our pieces that 1 whole = $\frac{2}{2} = \frac{3}{3} = \frac{4}{4}$. → Then it must be true!

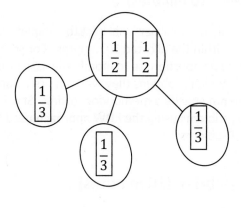

Follow the same sequence with a variety of 'wholes' and 'parts' until students are comfortable with this representation of equivalence.

T: Now let's place our different units on the same number line. Use your sentence strip to represent the interval from 0 to 1 on a number line. Mark the end points in with your pencil now.

S: (Mark end points 0 and 1 below the number line with pencil.)

T: Go ahead and fold your sentence strip to partition one unit at a time into halves, fourths, thirds, and then sixths. Label each fraction above the number line. As you count, be sure to rename 0 and the whole. Use a different color crayon to mark and label the fraction for each unit.

S: (Students fold sentence strips and label first halves, then fourths, then thirds, then sixths in different colors. They rename 0 and 1 in terms of each new unit.)

T: You should have a crowded number line! Compare it with your partner's.

S: (Students compare.)

T: Before today, we've been noticing lots of equivalent fractions between wholes on the number line. Today notice the fractions you wrote at 0 and 1. Look first at the fractions for 0. What pattern do you notice?

S: They all have a 0 on the top! → That's because there are 0 parts. → The bottom number changes. It shows you what unit you're going to count by. → Since our number line starts at 0, there are 0 of that unit in all of the fractions.

T: Even though the unit is different in each of our fractions at 0, are they equivalent? Think back to our work with shapes earlier.

S: We saw before that fractions with different units can still make the same whole. This time the whole is just 0!

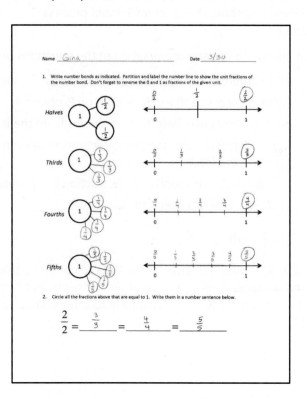

Follow the sequence to study the fractions written at 1. For both 0 and 1 students should see that every color they used is present.

Lesson 24:   Express whole numbers as fractions and recognize equivalence with
               different units.
Date: 11/19/13

5.E.49

© 2013 Common Core, Inc. All rights reserved. commoncore.org

Problem Set (10 minutes)

Students should do their personal best to complete the Problem Set within the allotted 10 minutes. For some classes, it may be appropriate to modify the assignment by specifying which problems they work on first. Some problems do not specify a method for solving. Students solve these problems using the RDW approach used for Application Problems.

Student Debrief (10 minutes)

Lesson Objective: Express whole numbers as fractions and recognize equivalence with different units.

The Student Debrief is intended to invite reflection and active processing of the total lesson experience.

Invite students to review their solutions for the Problem Set. They should check work by comparing answers with a partner before going over answers as a class. Look for misconceptions or misunderstandings that can be addressed in the Debrief. Guide students in a conversation to debrief the Problem Set and process the lesson.

You may choose to use any combination of the questions below to lead the discussion.

- Invite students to share their thinking about Problem 3.
- Invite students to share their work on Problem 4.
- Have students use their fraction shapes from the lesson to model the number bonds in Problem 1.
- Ask students to generate other fractions equivalent to wholes. Provide the unit, and ask them to generate the fraction. For example:
  - T: The unit is 1 millionth. What fraction is equivalent to the whole?
  - S: Wow! 1 million over 1 million!

Exit Ticket (3 minutes)

After the Student Debrief, instruct students to complete the Exit Ticket. A review of their work will help you assess the students' understanding of the concepts that were presented in the lesson today and plan more effectively for future lessons. You may read the questions aloud to the students.

Lesson 24: Express whole numbers as fractions and recognize equivalence with different units.
Date: 11/19/13

5.E.5

A

Correct _____

Add.

1	0 + 7 =		23	6 + 7 =	
2	1 + 7 =		24	16 + 7 =	
3	2 + 7 =		25	26 + 7 =	
4	3 + 7 =		26	36 + 7 =	
5	7 + 3 =		27	46 + 7 =	
6	7 + 2 =		28	66 + 7 =	
7	7 + 1 =		29	7 + 7 =	
8	7 + 0 =		30	17 + 7 =	
9	4 + 7 =		31	27 + 7 =	
10	14 + 7 =		32	37 + 7 =	
11	24 + 7 =		33	87 + 7 =	
12	34 + 7 =		34	8 + 7 =	
13	44 + 7 =		35	18 + 7 =	
14	84 + 7 =		36	28 + 7 =	
15	64 + 7 =		37	38 + 7 =	
16	5 + 7 =		38	78 + 7 =	
17	15 + 7 =		39	9 + 7 =	
18	25 + 7 =		40	19 + 7 =	
19	35 + 7 =		41	29 + 7 =	
20	45 + 7 =		42	39 + 7 =	
21	75 + 7 =		43	49 + 7 =	
22	55 + 7 =		44	79 + 7 =	

Lesson 24: Express whole numbers as fractions and recognize equivalence with different units.
Date: 11/19/13

5.E.51

B

Improvement _____   # Correct _____

Add.

1	7 + 0 =		23	6 + 7 =	
2	7 + 1 =		24	16 + 7 =	
3	7 + 2 =		25	26 + 7 =	
4	7 + 3 =		26	36 + 7 =	
5	3 + 7 =		27	46 + 7 =	
6	2 + 7 =		28	76 + 7 =	
7	1 + 7 =		29	7 + 7 =	
8	0 + 7 =		30	17 + 7 =	
9	4 + 7 =		31	27 + 7 =	
10	14 + 7 =		32	37 + 7 =	
11	24 + 7 =		33	67 + 7 =	
12	34 + 7 =		34	8 + 7 =	
13	44 + 7 =		35	18 + 7 =	
14	74 + 7 =		36	28 + 7 =	
15	54 + 7 =		37	38 + 7 =	
16	5 + 7 =		38	88 + 7 =	
17	15 + 7 =		39	9 + 7 =	
18	25 + 7 =		40	19 + 7 =	
19	35 + 7 =		41	29 + 7 =	
20	45 + 7 =		42	39 + 7 =	
21	85 + 7 =		43	49 + 7 =	
22	65 + 7 =		44	89 + 7 =	

COMMON CORE

Lesson 24:   Express whole numbers as fractions and recognize equivalence with
different units.

Date: 11/19/13

5.E.5

Name _____   Date _____

1. Write number bonds as indicated. Partition and label the number line to show the unit fractions of the number bond. Don't forget to rename the 0 and 1 as fractions of the given unit.

Halves

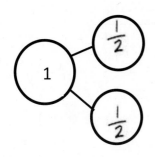

Thirds

Fourths

Fifths

COMMON CORE

Lesson 24:   Express whole numbers as fractions and recognize equivalence with different units.

Date: 11/19/13

5.E.53

2. Circle all the fractions above that are equal to 1. Write them in a number sentence below.

$$\frac{2}{2} = \underline{\hspace{2cm}} = \underline{\hspace{2cm}} = \underline{\hspace{2cm}}$$

3. What pattern do you notice in the fractions that are equivalent to 1?

4. Taylor took his little brother to get pizza. Each boy ordered a small pizza. Taylor's pizza was cut in fourths, and his brother's was cut in thirds. After they had both eaten all of their pizza, Taylor's little brother said, "Hey that was no fair! You got more than me! You got 4 pieces, I only got 3!"

    Should Taylor's little brother be mad? What could you say to explain the situation to him? Use words, pictures, or a number line.

COMMON CORE   Lesson 24:   Express whole numbers as fractions and recognize equivalence with different units.
Date: 11/19/13

5.E.5

Name _____   Date _____

1. Write number bonds as indicated. Partition and label the number line to show the unit fractions of the number bond. Don't forget to rename the 0 and 1 as fractions of the given unit.

Fourths (1)

2. How many copies of $\frac{1}{4}$ does it take to make 1 whole? What's the fraction for 1 whole in this case? Use the number line and/or the number bonds to help you explain.

COMMON CORE   Lesson 24:   Express whole numbers as fractions and recognize equivalence with
                                        different units.   5.E.55
                       Date: 11/19/13

Name _____   Date _____

1. Write number bonds as indicated. Partition and label the number line to show the unit fractions of the number bond. Don't forget to rename the 0 and 1 as fractions of the given unit.

Fifths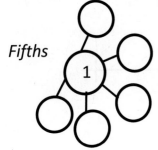

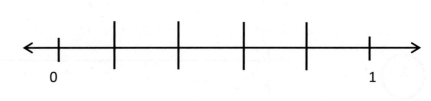

Sixths ①

Sevenths ①

Eighths ①

2. Circle all the fractions above that are equal to 1. Write them in a number sentence below.

$\dfrac{5}{5}$ = _____ = _____ = _____

3. What pattern do you notice in the fractions that are equivalent to 1? Following this pattern, how would you write the next whole as a fraction?

4. In an Art class, Mr. Joselyn gave everyone a 1 foot skewer to measure and cut. Vivian broke hers into 5 equal pieces, and Scott broke his into 7 equal pieces. Scott said to Vivian, "The total length of my stick must be longer than yours because I have 7 pieces and you only have 5." Is Scott correct? Use words, pictures, or a number line to help you explain.

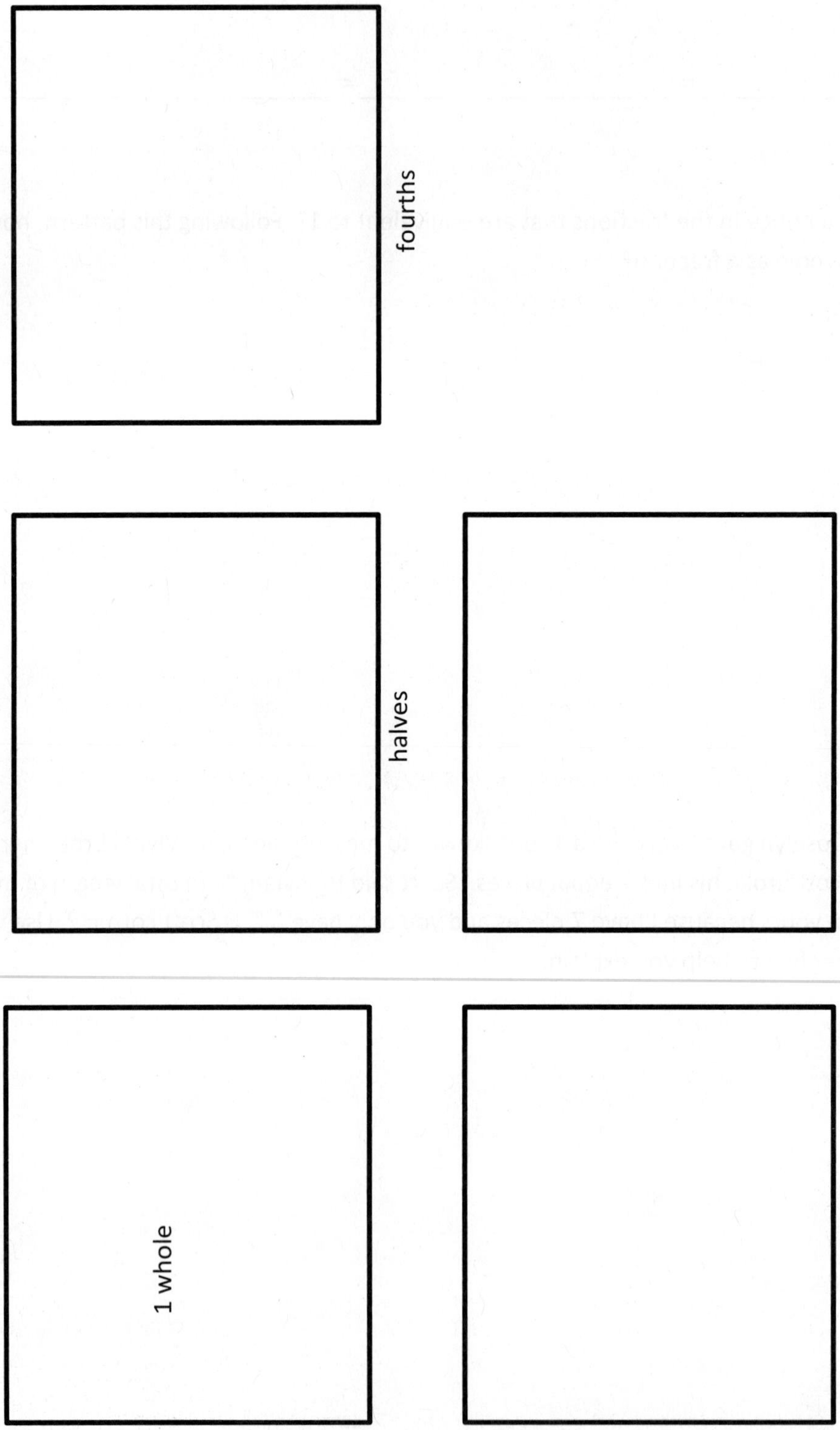

fourths

halves

sixths

1 whole

thirds

Lesson 24: Express whole numbers as fractions and recognize equivalence with different units.

Date: 11/19/13

5.E.

Lesson 25

Objective: Express whole number fractions on the number line when the unit interval is 1.

Suggested Lesson Structure

- ■ Fluency Practice   (12 minutes)
- ▨ Application Problem   (8 minutes)
- ▢ Concept Development   (30 minutes)
- ■ Student Debrief   (10 minutes)
  - **Total Time**   **(60 minutes)**

Fluency Practice (12 minutes)

- ▪ Sprint: Subtract by 6 **2.NBT.5**   (8 minutes)
- ▪ Express Whole Numbers as Different Fractions **3.NF.3c**   (4 minutes)

Sprint: Subtract by 6 (8 minutes)

Materials: (S) Subtract by 6 Sprint

Express Whole Numbers as Different Fractions (4 minutes)

Materials: (S) Personal white boards

T: (Project number line from 0-4. Below the 0 write $0 = \frac{}{5}$.) 0 is how many fifths?

S: 0 fifths. (Write $\frac{0}{5}$ below the 0 on the number line.)

T: Below the 1 write $1 = \frac{}{5}$.) 1 is how many fifths?

S: 5 fifths. (Write $\frac{5}{5}$ below the 1 on the number line.)

T: (Below the 2, write $2 = \frac{}{5}$.) On your boards, fill-in the number sentence.

S: (Write $2 = \frac{10}{5}$.)

T: (Write $\frac{10}{5}$ below the 2 on the number line.)

T: (Write $3 = \frac{}{5}$.) On your boards, fill in the number sentence.

Lesson 25:	Express whole number fractions on the number line when the unit interval is 1.
Date:	11/19/13

5.E.59

S: (Write $3 = \frac{15}{5}$.)

T: (Write $\frac{15}{5}$ below the 3 on the number line.)

T: (Write $4 = \frac{}{5}$.) On your boards, fill in the number sentence.

S: (Write $4 = \frac{20}{5}$.)

T: (Write $\frac{20}{5}$ below the 4 on the number line.)

Continue the process for fourths.

Application Problem (8 minutes)

Linc drinks 1 eighth gallon of milk every morning.

    a.   How many days would it take for him to drink 1 gallon of milk? Use a number line and words to explain your answer.

    b.   How many days would it take him to drink 2 gallons? Extend your number line to show 2 gallons and use words to explain your answer.

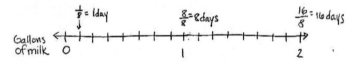

a) It will take 8 days to drink 1 gallon of milk because he drinks $\frac{1}{8}$ gallons of milk a day, and there are 8 eighths in a gallon.

b) 16 days because there are 16 eighths in 2 gallons.

**NOTES ON
MULTIPLE MEANS OF
ENGAGEMENT:**

Scaffold the Application Problem for students below grade level with step-by-step questioning. Ask (for example),

- What is the unit fraction?
- Name the unit that we are partitioning.
- Count by eighths to reach 1 whole, labeling the number line as you count.
- How many eighths in 1 gallon?
- How many days will it take to drink 1 gallon?
- Count by eighths to reach 2 wholes labeling the number line as you count.
- How many days will it take to drink 2 gallons?

Concept Development (30 minutes)

Materials: (S) Lesson 25 template, personal white boards

(Students slip the double-sided template into personal white boards and begin on Side A.)

    T: Each rectangle represents 1 whole. Partition the first rectangle into thirds. Write the whole as a fraction below it.

    S: (Partition and label with $\frac{3}{3}$.)

Lesson 25:   Express whole number fractions on the number line when the unit
                interval is 1.

Date: 11/19/13

5.E.

T: $\frac{3}{3}$ is equivalent to?

S: 1 whole!

T: Add that to your paper.

S: (Write: $\frac{3}{3} = 1$ whole.)

T: Now partition the second rectangle into halves. Label the whole as a fraction below it.

S: (Partition and label with $\frac{2}{2}$.)

T: $\frac{2}{2}$ is equivalent to?

S: 1 whole!

T: Add that to your paper.

S: (Write: $\frac{2}{2} = 1$ whole.)

T: Now partition the third rectangle into wholes.

S: What do you mean? It is already a whole. → That means 0 partitions!

T: Talk with your partner about how we label this whole as a fraction.

S: 1. → That's not a fraction! It's $\frac{0}{1}$ because there are no

parts. → No, it's $\frac{1}{0}$ because we didn't partition. →
There's a pattern of the same number on the top and
bottom for whole number fractions. So maybe this is
$\frac{1}{1}$?

**NOTES ON
MULTIPLE MEANS OF
ENGAGEMENT:**

Students above grade level will love
this discussion towards discovery.
Guide students to respectfully respond
to peers with sentence starters, such
as, "That's an idea. I have a different
way of seeing it. I think ….because…."
or "I see what you're saying
however…."

T: I hear some students noticing the pattern that whole
number fractions have the same values on the top and
bottom; therefore, an equivalent way of writing 1
whole as a fraction is to write it as $\frac{1}{1}$. We started with 1
whole. We didn't split it into more parts, so the whole
is still in 1 piece, and we're counting that 1 piece.

T: Let's look at the equivalent fractions we've written for 1 on the number line. At the bottom of your
template, mark each of the 3 number lines with end points 0 and 1 above the line.

S: (Students mark end points.)

T: Show each rectangle on a different number line. Be sure to partition, label, and rename the wholes
below the line.

S: (Students partition and label number lines. Teacher circulates to observe.)

T: What do you notice about the relationship between the partitioning on the rectangles and the number
lines?

S: It's the same. → It goes 2 partitions, 1 partition, no partitions on the last number line!

T: Right, and since we didn't partition because the unit is 1 whole, on the last number line we renamed
the whole?

	Lesson 25:	Express whole number fractions on the number line when the unit interval is 1.
	Date:	11/19/13

5.E.61

S: $\frac{1}{1}$!

T: Flip your personal board over to Side B. Each rectangle represents 1 whole. How many wholes are in each model?

S: 2 wholes.

T: Let's partition Model 1 into thirds, Model 2 into halves, and Model 3 into wholes. Use Side A to help you if you need it.

S: (Students partition.)

T: Now work with your partner to label each model.

S: (Label Model 1: $\frac{6}{3}$ = 2. Model 2: $\frac{4}{2}$ = 2. Students may or may not label model 3 correctly: $\frac{2}{1}$ = 2.)

T: Let's take a look at how you labeled Model 3. How did you partition the model?

S: There are no partitions because they're both wholes.

T: How many copies of 1 whole does the model have?

S: 2 copies of 1 whole.

T: The top number shows us the amount of copies, and the bottom number tells us the unit. So for model 3 we write the whole as $\frac{2}{1}$.

T: Let's use our number lines again with these models. Label the endpoints on each number line 0 and 2.

> NOTES ON
> MULTIPLE MEANS OF
> REPRESENTATION:
>
> For ELLs, increase wait time, speak clearly, use gestures, and make eye-contact. When giving instructions for partitioning the 3 Models, pause more frequently and check for understanding.

Guide students through a similar sequence to the number line work they did on Side A.

T: I'd like you to circle $\frac{2}{2}$ on your second number line. Now compare it to where you labeled $\frac{2}{1}$ on your third number line. Tell your partner the difference between $\frac{2}{1}$ and $\frac{2}{2}$.

S: $\frac{2}{2}$ means it's only 1 whole. There are 2 copies, and the unit is halves. → $\frac{2}{1}$ means there are 2 wholes, and the unit of each is 1 whole. → $\frac{2}{1}$ is much larger than $\frac{2}{2}$. It's another whole! You can see that right there on the number line.

If necessary, have students do a similar sequence with fourths.

Note: This template is used again in Lesson 27 and Lesson 29. You may want to collect these templates or have your students store it in a safe place for later use.

Lesson 25: Express whole number fractions on the number line when the unit interval is 1.

Date: 11/19/13

5.E.

Problem Set (10 minutes)

Students should do their personal best to complete the Problem Set within the allotted 10 minutes. For some classes, it may be appropriate to modify the assignment by specifying which problems they work on first. Some problems do not specify a method for solving. Students solve these problems using the RDW approach used for Application Problems.

Student Debrief (10 minutes)

Lesson Objective: Express whole number fractions on the number line when the unit interval is 1.

The Student Debrief is intended to invite reflection and active processing of the total lesson experience.

Invite students to review their solutions for the Problem Set. They should check work by comparing answers with a partner before going over answers as a class. Look for misconceptions or misunderstandings that can be addressed in the Debrief. Guide students in a conversation to debrief the Problem Set and process the lesson.

You may choose to use any combination of the questions below to lead the discussion.

- Problem Set Problem 1 presents a slightly different sequence than the lesson. Invite students to share what they notice about the relationship between the models in Problem 1. You might ask them to relate their work on that question to the guided practice in the lesson.

- Engage students in a conversation that gets them to articulate the difference between $\frac{2}{1}$ and $\frac{2}{2}$. To solidify their understanding, ask them to apply their thinking to different fractions like $\frac{3}{1}$ and $\frac{3}{3}$. You may want to use a number line during this portion of the discussion to help students notice that the difference between these fractions is even greater and continues to grow as the numbers go higher.

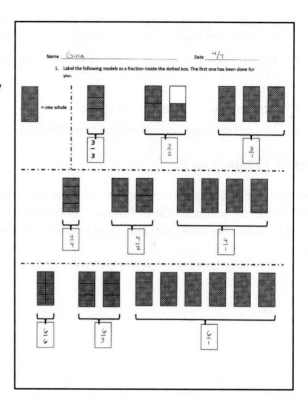

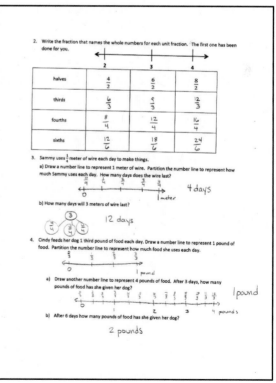

- Have students practice and articulate the lesson objective by closing with a series of pictures you quickly draw on the board. For example, you might make 10 circles. Then say:

  T: If each circle is 1 whole, how might you write the fraction for my total number of wholes?

  S: $\frac{10}{1}$!

  T: Explain to your partner how you know.

  S: (Articulate their understanding from the lesson.)

Exit Ticket (3 minutes)

After the Student Debrief, instruct students to complete the Exit Ticket. A review of their work will help you assess the students' understanding of the concepts that were presented in the lesson today and plan more effectively for future lessons. You may read the questions aloud to the students.

COMMON CORE   Lesson 25:   Express whole number fractions on the number line when the unit interval is 1.

Date: 11/19/13   5.E.

A

Subtract.

Correct _____

1	16 - 6 =		23	23 - 6 =	
2	6 - 6 =		24	33 - 6 =	
3	26 - 6 =		25	63 - 6 =	
4	7 - 6 =		26	83 - 6 =	
5	17 - 6 =		27	14 - 6 =	
6	37 - 6 =		28	24 - 6 =	
7	8 - 6 =		29	34 - 6 =	
8	18 - 6 =		30	74 - 6 =	
9	48 - 6 =		31	54 - 6 =	
10	9 - 6 =		32	15 - 6 =	
11	19 - 6 =		33	25 - 6 =	
12	59 - 6 =		34	35 - 6 =	
13	10 - 6 =		35	85 - 6 =	
14	20 - 6 =		36	65 - 6 =	
15	70 - 6 =		37	90 - 6 =	
16	11 - 6 =		38	53 - 6 =	
17	21 - 6 =		39	42 - 6 =	
18	81 - 6 =		40	71 - 6 =	
19	12 - 6 =		41	74 - 6 =	
20	22 - 6 =		42	95 - 6 =	
21	82 - 6 =		43	51 - 6 =	
22	13 - 6 =		44	92 - 6 =	

Lesson 25:	Express whole number fractions on the number line when the unit interval is 1.
Date:	11/19/13

5.E.65

B   Improvement _____   # Correct _____

Subtract.

1	6 - 6 =		23	23 - 6 =	
2	16 - 6 =		24	33 - 6 =	
3	26 - 6 =		25	53 - 6 =	
4	7 - 6 =		26	73 - 6 =	
5	17 - 6 =		27	14 - 6 =	
6	67 - 6 =		28	24 - 6 =	
7	8 - 6 =		29	34 - 6 =	
8	18 - 6 =		30	64 - 6 =	
9	78 - 6 =		31	44 - 6 =	
10	9 - 6 =		32	15 - 6 =	
11	19 - 6 =		33	25 - 6 =	
12	89 - 6 =		34	35 - 6 =	
13	10 - 6 =		35	75 - 6 =	
14	20 - 6 =		36	55 - 6 =	
15	90 - 6 =		37	70 - 6 =	
16	11 - 6 =		38	63 - 6 =	
17	21 - 6 =		39	52 - 6 =	
18	41 - 6 =		40	81 - 6 =	
19	12 - 6 =		41	64 - 6 =	
20	22 - 6 =		42	85 - 6 =	
21	42 - 6 =		43	91 - 6 =	
22	13 - 6 =		44	52 - 6 =	

Lesson 25: Express whole number fractions on the number line when the unit interval is 1.

Date: 11/19/13

5.E.6

Name _____ Date _____

1. Label the following models as a fraction inside the dotted box. The first one has been done for you.

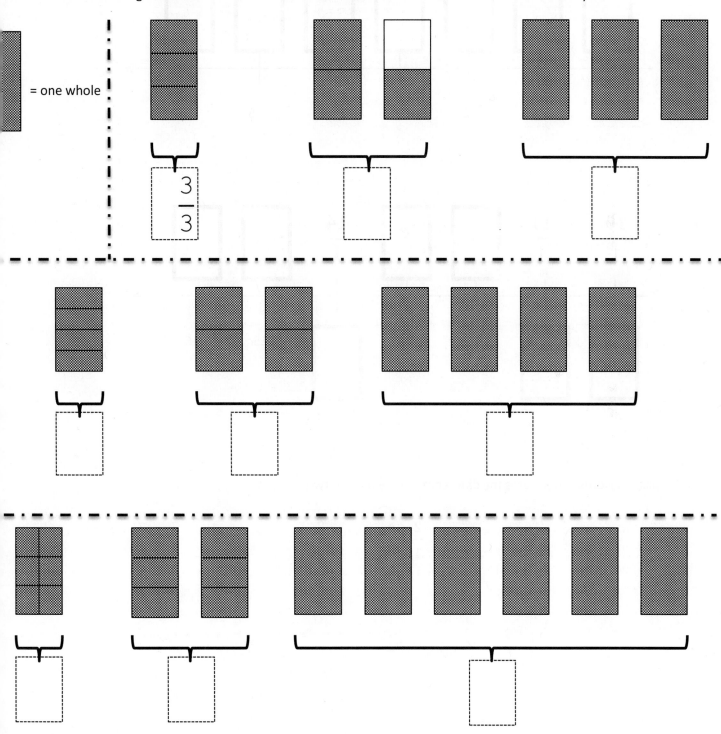

COMMON CORE | Lesson 25:   Express whole number fractions on the number line when the unit interval is 1.
Date: 11/19/13

5.E.67

2. Label the number lines with fractions representing whole numbers on top, and whole numbers beneath.

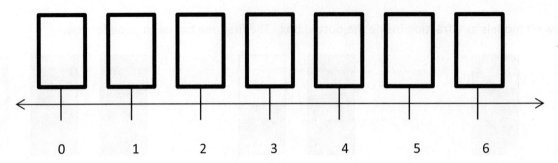

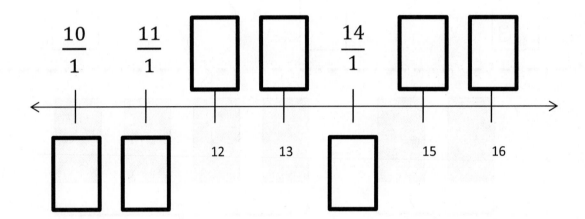

3. Explain in words and pictures the difference between these two fractions.

$$\frac{2}{1} \qquad\qquad \frac{2}{2}$$

COMMON CORE   **Lesson 25:**   Express whole number fractions on the number line when the unit interval is 1.

Date: 11/19/13

5.E.

Name _____   Date _____

1. Label the following models as fractions inside the boxes.

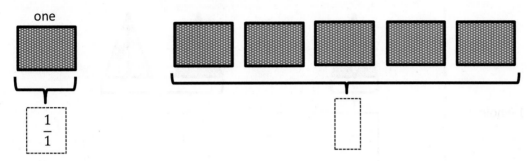

2. Parition the number line into thirds. Rename the fraction for 3 wholes. Use the number line and words to explain your answer.

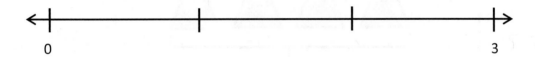

Name _____ Date _____

1. Label the following models as a fraction inside the boxes.

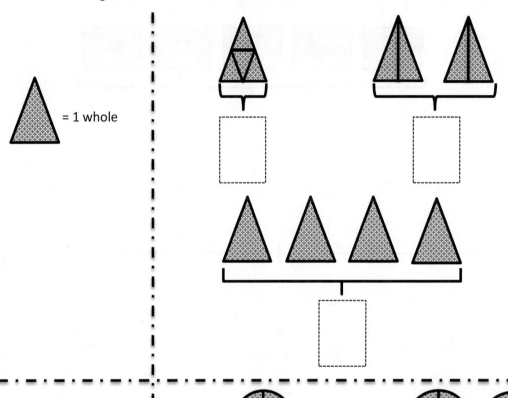

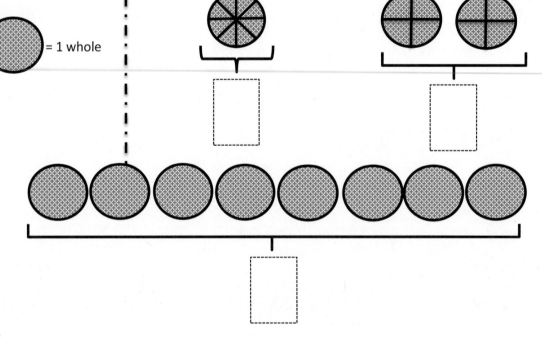

COMMON CORE

Lesson 25: Express whole number fractions on the number line when the unit interval is 1.

Date: 11/19/13

5.E.7

2. Fill in missing whole numbers. Then rename the wholes in the boxes.

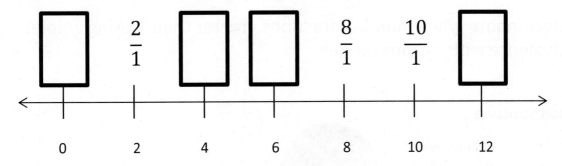

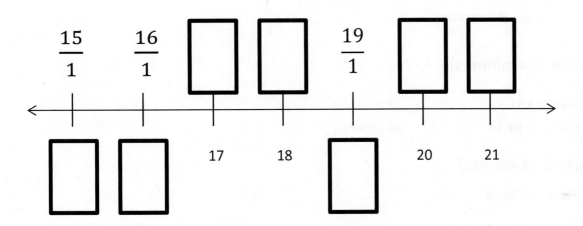

3. Explain the difference between these fractions using a number line, pictorial model, or words.

$$\frac{5}{1} \qquad \frac{5}{5}$$

Lesson 26

Objective: Decompose whole number fractions greater than 1 using whole number equivalence with various models.

Suggested Lesson Structure

■ Fluency Practice   (14 minutes)
■ Application Problem   (6 minutes)
■ Concept Development   (30 minutes)
■ Student Debrief   (10 minutes)
  Total Time   **(60 minutes)**

Fluency Practice (14 minutes)

- Sprint: Adding by 8 **2.NBT.5**   (8 minutes)
- Write Equal Fractions **3.NF.3d**   (6 minutes)

Sprint: Adding by 8 (8 minutes)

Materials: (S) Adding by 8 Sprint

Write Equal Fractions (6 minutes)

Materials: (S) Personal white boards

T: (Project $\frac{1}{2}$.) Say the fraction.

S: 1 half.

T: Draw a picture of 1 half and write the fraction below it.

S: (Draw a picture of 2 equal parts with one part shaded. Write $\frac{1}{2}$ below the picture.)

T: (Write $\frac{1}{2} = \frac{}{4}$.) Draw a second picture to show an equal number of fourths. Then complete the number sentence.

S: (Draw 4 equal parts with 2 parts shaded. Write $\frac{1}{2} = \frac{2}{4}$ below the picture.)

Repeat the process for $\frac{1}{3} = \frac{}{6}$, $\frac{1}{4} = \frac{}{8}$, and $\frac{1}{5} = \frac{2}{}$.

Lesson 26:	Decompose whole number fractions greater than 1 using whole number equivalence with various models.
Date:	11/19/13

5.E.7

Application Problem (6 minutes)

Antonio works on his project for 4 thirds of an hour. His mom tells him that he must spend another 2 thirds hour on it. Draw number bonds and a number line with copies of thirds to show how long Antonio worked altogether.

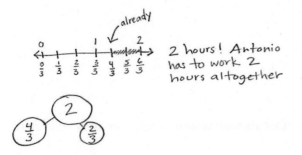

Concept Development (30 minutes)

Materials: (S) Personal white boards

(Draw or project the following number bond, also used in Lesson 24.)

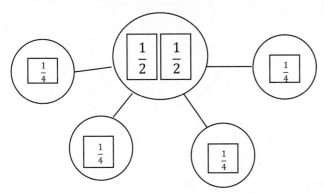

T: Turn and tell your partner why the number bond is true.

S: Because fourths come from cutting halves in 2 equal pieces. → Yeah, so $\frac{2}{2}$ and $\frac{4}{4}$ both equal 1 whole.

T: How do the parts change if we change the whole to look like this (Add 2 more halves to the whole.)?

T: Work with a partner to draw the new model on your personal board and change the parts so that the number bond is true.

S: (Students draw.)

Lesson 26:   Decompose whole number fractions greater than 1 using whole number equivalence with various models.

Date: 11/19/13

5.E.73

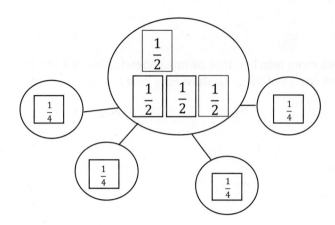

T: As I look around the room I see these two models. Discuss with your partner.   Are they equivalent?

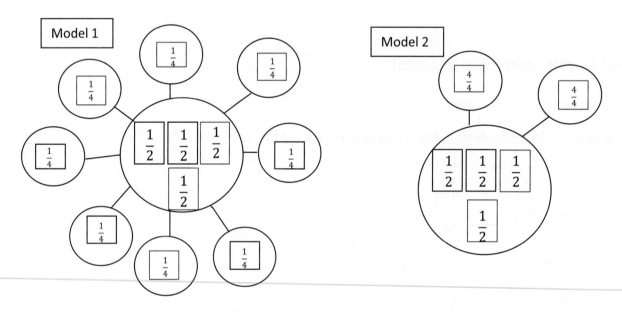

S: There are many more parts in the first model, so they aren't equal. → There are 8 total parts in both models. → 4 copies of $\frac{1}{4}$ makes $\frac{4}{4}$ and another 4 copies of $\frac{1}{4}$ makes another $\frac{4}{4}$. So they are equivalent. → In the second model they just made copies of 1 whole to show the total as 2 wholes.

T: Yes, Model 2 does show a different way of writing the copies in Model 1. Instead of showing copies of unit fractions, the second model shows copies of 1 whole.

NOTES ON MULTIPLE MEANS OF ACTION AND EXPRESSION:

Partner talk is a valuable opportunity for ELLs to speak about their math ideas in English confidently and comfortably. Support limited English speakers with a sentence frame such as, "They are equivalent because Model 1 shows _____ fourths and Model 2 shows _____ fourths."

COMMON CORE

Lesson 26:   Decompose whole number fractions greater than 1 using whole number equivalence with various models.

Date: 11/19/13

5.E.7

T: Let's see if we can show the equivalence of the number bonds on the number line. Draw a number line with end points 0 and 2. Label the wholes on top of the number line. Partition the number line into fourths and rename the wholes on the bottom.

S: (Draw.)

T: How many fourths in 0?

S: (Respond chorally.) 0 fourths!

T: How many fourths in 1?

S: (Respond chorally.) 4 fourths!

T: How many fourths in 2?

S: (Respond chorally.) 8 fourths!

T: Below each whole number on your number line work with a partner to draw a number bond. As you draw number bonds, show copies of 1 whole instead of unit fractions if you can.

S: (Draw.)

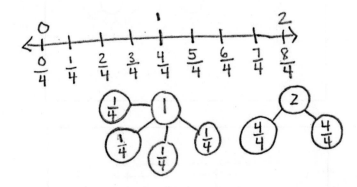

NOTES ON MULTIPLE MEANS OF ENGAGEMENT:

Use the chart on the Problem Set to help students below grade level build understanding. After students have completed the halves and thirds ask, "How is the number of unit intervals related to the number of unit fractions?" Discuss and verify predictions for sixths.

T: What is the relationship between Models 1 and 2 and the number line and number bonds you just drew?

S: Our number bond for 2 on the number line looks just like Model 2! → But Model 2 has halves as the whole. → 4 halves make 2, so they're the same.

T: What about Model 1?

S: There are 8 fourths on the number line, just like Model 1 shows.

T: What is the difference between these 2 ways of showing the number bond?

S: One's way faster to write. → It's also easier to read because you can see the number of wholes inside of 2.

Lesson 26:   Decompose whole number fractions greater than 1 using whole number equivalence with various models.

Date: 11/19/13

5.E.75

Problem Set (10 minutes)

Students should do their personal best to complete the Problem Set within the allotted 10 minutes. For some classes, it may be appropriate to modify the assignment by specifying which problems they work on first. Some problems do not specify a method for solving. Students solve these problems using the RDW approach used for Application Problems.

Student Debrief (10 minutes)

Lesson Objective: Decompose whole number fractions greater than 1 using whole number equivalence with various models.

The Student Debrief is intended to invite reflection and active processing of the total lesson experience.

Invite students to review their solutions for the Problem Set. They should check work by comparing answers with a partner before going over answers as a class. Look for misconceptions or misunderstandings that can be addressed in the Debrief. Guide students in a conversation to debrief the Problem Set and process the lesson.

You may choose to use any combination of the questions below to lead the discussion.

- Compare the number line and number bonds. What does each representation help you see?
- On Problem Set Problem 2 what strategy did you use to find the unit wholes without having to partition a number line again?
- Draw number bonds to demonstrate your answers on Problems 3 and 4 using copies of wholes.
- How is the way that we expressed whole number fractions today different from the way we've been doing it?
- Why is it helpful to know how to rename wholes to make number bonds with larger whole numbers?

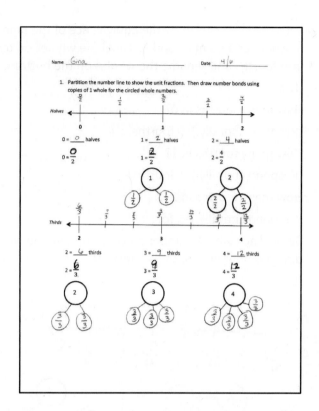

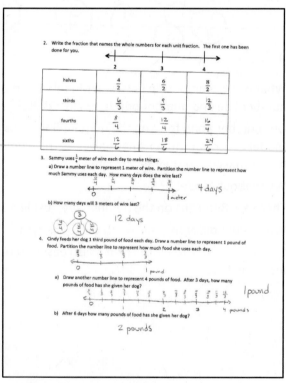

Lesson 26: Decompose whole number fractions greater than 1 using whole number equivalence with various models.
Date: 11/19/13

5.E.7

Exit Ticket (3 minutes)

After the Student Debrief, instruct students to complete the Exit Ticket. A review of their work will help you assess the students' understanding of the concepts that were presented in the lesson today and plan more effectively for future lessons. You may read the questions aloud to the students.

NOTES ON MULTIPLE MEANS OF ENGAGEMENT:

As an alternative for the Problem Set, offer students above grade level the option of drawing their own number lines with larger unit intervals (e.g., 6, 7, and 8) and their choice of unit fraction for partitioning (e.g., fifths).

Lesson 26:	Decompose whole number fractions greater than 1 using whole number equivalence with various models.
Date:	11/19/13

5.E.77

A

Correct _____

Add.

1	0 + 8 =		23	65 + 8 =	
2	1 + 8 =		24	6 + 8 =	
3	2 + 8 =		25	16 + 8 =	
4	8 + 2 =		26	26 + 8 =	
5	1 + 8 =		27	36 + 8 =	
6	0 + 8 =		28	86 + 8 =	
7	3 + 8 =		29	46 + 8 =	
8	13 + 8 =		30	7 + 8 =	
9	23 + 8 =		31	17 + 8 =	
10	33 + 8 =		32	27 + 8 =	
11	43 + 8 =		33	37 + 8 =	
12	83 + 8 =		34	77 + 8 =	
13	4 + 8 =		35	8 + 8 =	
14	14 + 8 =		36	18 + 8 =	
15	24 + 8 =		37	28 + 8 =	
16	34 + 8 =		38	38 + 8 =	
17	44 + 8 =		39	68 + 8 =	
18	74 + 8 =		40	9 + 8 =	
19	5 + 8 =		41	19 + 8 =	
20	15 + 8 =		42	29 + 8 =	
21	25 + 8 =		43	39 + 8 =	
22	35 + 8 =		44	89 + 8 =	

COMMON CORE

Lesson 26:   Decompose whole number fractions greater than 1 using whole
number equivalence with various models.

Date: 11/19/13

5.E.7

B

Add.

Improvement _____   # Correct _____

1	8 + 0 =		23	55 + 8 =	
2	8 + 1 =		24	6 + 8 =	
3	8 + 2 =		25	16 + 8 =	
4	2 + 8 =		26	26 + 8 =	
5	1 + 8 =		27	36 + 8 =	
6	0 + 8 =		28	66 + 8 =	
7	3 + 8 =		29	56 + 8 =	
8	13 + 8 =		30	7 + 8 =	
9	23 + 8 =		31	17 + 8 =	
10	33 + 8 =		32	27 + 8 =	
11	43 + 8 =		33	37 + 8 =	
12	73 + 8 =		34	67 + 8 =	
13	4 + 8 =		35	8 + 8 =	
14	14 + 8 =		36	18 + 8 =	
15	24 + 8 =		37	28 + 8 =	
16	34 + 8 =		38	38 + 8 =	
17	44 + 8 =		39	78 + 8 =	
18	84 + 8 =		40	9 + 8 =	
19	5 + 8 =		41	19 + 8 =	
20	15 + 8 =		42	29 + 8 =	
21	25 + 8 =		43	39 + 8 =	
22	35 + 8 =		44	89 + 8 =	

Lesson 26: Decompose whole number fractions greater than 1 using whole number equivalence with various models.

Date: 11/19/13

5.E.79

Name _____   Date _____

1. Partition the number line to show the unit fractions. Then draw number bonds using copies of 1 whole for the circled whole numbers.

Halves

0   1   2

0 = _____ halves   1 = _____ halves   2 = _____ halves

$0 = \dfrac{\square}{2}$ $1 = \dfrac{\square}{2}$ $2 = \dfrac{4}{2}$

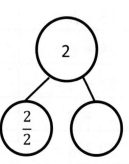

Thirds

2   3   4

2 = _____ thirds   3 = _____ thirds   4 = _____ thirds

$2 = \dfrac{\square}{3}$ $3 = \dfrac{\square}{3}$ $4 = \dfrac{\square}{3}$

(2)   (3)   (4)

COMMON CORE   **Lesson 26:**   Decompose whole number fractions greater than 1 using whole
                                              number equivalence with various models.   5.E.8
                         Date: 11/19/13

2. Write the fraction that names the whole numbers for each unit fraction. The first one has been done.

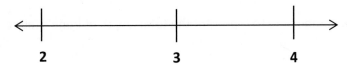

	2	3	4
halves	$\dfrac{4}{2}$	$\dfrac{6}{2}$	$\dfrac{8}{2}$
thirds			
fourths			
sixths			

3. Sammy uses $\dfrac{1}{4}$ meter of wire each day to make things.

   a. Draw a number line to represent 1 meter of wire. Partition the number line to represent how much Sammy uses each day. How many days does the wire last?

   b. How many days will 3 meters of wire last?

4. Cindy feeds her dog 1 third pound of food each day. Draw a number line to represent 1 pound of food. Partition the number line to represent how much food she uses each day.

   a. Draw another number line to represent 4 pounds of food. After 3 days, how many pounds of food has she given her dog?

   b. After 6 days how many pounds of food has she given her dog?

Lesson 26:   Decompose whole number fractions greater than 1 using whole number equivalence with various models.

Date: 11/19/13

5.E.81

Name _____   Date _____

1. Irene has 2 yards of fabric. Draw a number line to represent the total length of Irene's fabric.

    a. Irene cuts her fabric into pieces $\frac{1}{5}$ yard in length. Partition the number line to show her cuts.

    b. How many $\frac{1}{5}$ yard pieces does she cut altogether? Use number bonds with copies of wholes to help you explain.

Lesson 26:   Decompose whole number fractions greater than 1 using whole
number equivalence with various models.

Date: 11/19/13

5.E.82

Name _____ Date _____

1. Partition the number line to show the unit fractions. Then draw number bonds with copies of 1 whole for the circled whole numbers.

Sixths

0 .... 1 2

0 = _____ sixths   1 = _____ sixths   2 = _____ sixths

$0 = \dfrac{\square}{6}$ $1 = \dfrac{\square}{6}$ $2 = \dfrac{12}{6}$

(1)

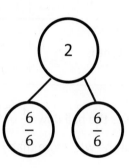

Fifths

2 .... 3 4

2 = _____ fifths   3 = _____ fifths   4 = _____ fifths

$2 = \dfrac{\square}{5}$ $3 = \dfrac{\square}{5}$ $4 = \dfrac{\square}{5}$

        (3)   (4)

COMMON CORE

Lesson 26: Decompose whole number fractions greater than 1 using whole number equivalence with various models.

Date: 11/19/13

5.E.83

2. Write the fraction that names the whole numbers for each unit fraction. The first one has been done for you.

	2	**3**	**4**
thirds	$\dfrac{6}{3}$	$\dfrac{9}{3}$	$\dfrac{12}{3}$
sevenths			
eighths			
tenths			

3. Rider dribbles the ball down $\frac{1}{3}$ of the basketball court on the first day of practice. Each day after that he dribbles $\frac{1}{3}$ of the way more than he did the day before.

    a. Draw a number line to represent the court. Partition the number line to represent how far Rider dribbles on Day 1, Day 2, and Day 3 of practice. What fraction of the way does he dribble on Day 3?

Lesson 27

Objective: Explain equivalence by manipulating units and reasoning about their size.

Suggested Lesson Structure

■ Fluency Practice   (12 minutes)
■ Application Problem   (8 minutes)
■ Concept Development   (30 minutes)
■ Student Debrief   (10 minutes)
   Total Time   **(60 minutes)**

Fluency Practice (12 minutes)

▪ Sprint: Subtract by 7 **2.NBT.5**   (8 minutes)
▪ Recognize the Fraction **3.G.2**   (4 minutes)

Sprint: Subtract by 7 (8 minutes)

Materials: (S) Subtract by 7 Sprint

Recognize the Fraction (4 minutes)

Materials: (S) Personal white boards

  T: (Project a shaded rectangular model.) This equals 1 whole. (Project 1 whole partitioned into 3 equal shaded units.) On your boards, write the fraction.

  S: (Write $\frac{3}{3}$.)

  T: (Project 2 wholes, each partitioned into 3 equal shaded units.) On your boards, write the fraction.

  S: (Write $\frac{6}{3}$.)

  T: (Project 3 wholes, each partitioned into 3 shaded parts.) On your boards, write the fraction.

  S: (Write $\frac{9}{3}$.)

  T: (Project 3 wholes, each partitioned into 3 parts. 3 parts in the first 2 wholes are shaded. 1 part of the third whole is shaded.) On your boards, write the fraction.

NOTES ON MULTIPLE MEANS OF REPRESENTATION:

Have ELLs "Recognize the Fraction" orally in order to practice speaking math language in English with the support of a model.

	Lesson 27:	Explain equivalence by manipulating units and reasoning about their size.	
	Date:	11/19/13	

                                                                        5.E.85

S: (Write $\frac{7}{3}$.)

Continue with possible sequence: $\frac{4}{4}, \frac{8}{4}, \frac{12}{4}, \frac{9}{4}, \frac{6}{5}, \frac{9}{8}$.

Application Problem (8 minutes)

The branch of a tree is 2 meters long. Monica chops the branch
for firewood. She cuts pieces that are $\frac{1}{6}$ meter long. Draw a
number line to show the total length of the branch. Partition
and label each of Monica's cuts.

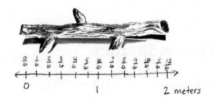

a.   How many pieces does Monica have altogether?

b.   Write 2 equivalent fractions to describe the total length
of Monica's branch.

Concept Development (30 minutes)

Materials: (S) Template from Lesson 25, personal white
boards, fraction strips

Pass out the template from Lesson 25 and have students slip it
into their personal white boards.

T: Start on Side A of the template. Each rectangle
represents 1 whole. Estimate to partition and label the
rectangles. Divide each rectangle into thirds.

S: (Partition.)

T: How can we double the number of units in the second
rectangle?

S: We cut each third in 2.

T: Go ahead and partition.

S: (Students partition.)

T: What's our new unit?

S: Sixths!

> **NOTES ON
> MULTIPLE MEANS OF
> ENGAGEMENT:**
>
> For ELLs, demonstrate that words can
> have multiple meanings. Here, 'cut'
> means to draw a line (or lines) that
> divides the unit into smaller equal
> parts.
>
> Students below grade level may benefit
> from revisiting the discussion of
> 'doubling', 'tripling,' halving, and
> cutting unit fractions as presented in
> Lesson 22.

Repeat this process for the third rectangle. Instead of having students double, have them triple the original
thirds.

T: Label the fractions in each model.

S: (Label.)

MP.3 T: What is different about these models?

S: They all started as thirds, but then we cut them into different parts. → The parts are different sizes.
→ Yes, they're different units.

Lesson 27:   Explain equivalence by manipulating units and reasoning about their
size.

Date: 11/19/13

5.E.8

T: What is the same about these models?

S: The whole.

MP.3

T: Talk to your partner about the relationship between the number of parts and the size of parts in each model.

S: 3 is the smallest number but thirds have the biggest size. → As I drew more lines to partition, the size of the parts got smaller. → That's because the whole is cut into more pieces when there are ninths than when there are thirds.

T: (Each student has 3 fraction strips.) Fold all 3 fraction strips into halves.

S: (Students fold.)

T: Fold your second fraction strip to double the number of units.

S: We have to fold it again! (Students fold.)

T: What's the new unit on your second fraction strip?

S: Fourths!

T: Fold your third fraction strip to double the number of units again.

S: (Students fold.)

T: Compare the number of parts and the size of the parts with the number of times you folded the strip. What happens to the size of the parts when you fold the strip more times?

S: The more I folded the smaller the parts got. → Yeah, that's because you folded the whole to make more units.

T: Open your math journal to a new page and glue your strips in a column, making sure the ends line up. Glue them from the largest unit to the smallest.

S: (Students glue.)

T: Using your fraction strips find the fractions equivalent to $\frac{4}{8}$. Shade them.

S: (Students shade: $\frac{4}{8}, \frac{2}{4}, \frac{1}{2}$.)

T: Turn and talk with your partner. What do you notice about the size of parts and the number of parts in equivalent fractions?

S: You can see that there are more eighths than halves or fourths shaded to cover the same amount of the strip. → It's the same as before then. As the number of parts gets bigger, the size of them gets smaller. → That's because the shaded area in equivalent fractions doesn't change even though the number of parts gets larger.

If necessary reinforce the concept with other examples using these fraction strips.

T: Let's practice this idea a bit more on our personal white boards. Draw my shape on your board. The entire figure represents 1 whole. (Show the image below.)

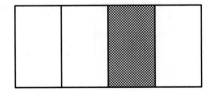

Lesson 27:   Explain equivalence by manipulating units and reasoning about their size.

Date: 11/19/13

5.E.87

S: (Students draw.)

T: Write the shaded fraction.

S: (Write $\frac{1}{4}$.)

T: Talk to your partner. How can you partition this shape to make an equivalent fraction with smaller units?

S: We can cut each small rectangle in 2 pieces from top to bottom to make eighths. → Or we can make 2 horizontal cuts to make twelfths.

T: Use one of these strategies now. (Circulate as students work to select a few different examples to share with the class.)

S: (Students partition.)

T: Let's look at our classmates' work. (Show examples in $\frac{2}{8}, \frac{3}{12}, \frac{4}{16}$ etc.) As we partitioned with more parts, what happens to the shaded area and the number of parts needed to make them equivalent?

S: The size of the parts gets smaller, but the number of them gets larger.

T: Even though the parts changed, did the area covered by the shaded region change?

S: No.

NOTES ON
MULTIPLE MEANS OF
ENGAGEMENT:

Extend number 5 on the Problem Set for students above grade level. Instead of "doubling," have students "triple" or "quadruple." Let students choose the unit fraction into which the rectangle is partitioned.

You may want to have students practice independently. The following shape is more challenging because triangles are more difficult to make into equal parts.

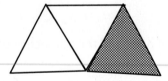

Problem Set (10 minutes)

Students should do their personal best to complete the Problem Set within the allotted 10 minutes. For some classes, it may be appropriate to modify the assignment by specifying which problems they work on first. Some problems do not specify a method for solving. Students solve these problems using the RDW approach used for Application Problems.

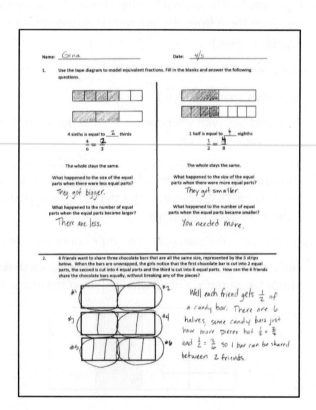

Lesson 27:   Explain equivalence by manipulating units and reasoning about their
               size.
Date: 11/19/13

5.E.8

Student Debrief (10 minutes)

Lesson Objective: Explain equivalence by manipulating units and reasoning about their size.

The Student Debrief is intended to invite reflection and active processing of the total lesson experience.

Invite students to review their solutions for the Problem Set. They should check work by comparing answers with a partner before going over answers as a class. Look for misconceptions or misunderstandings that can be addressed in the Debrief. Guide students in a conversation to debrief the Problem Set and process the lesson.

You may choose to use any combination of the questions below to lead the discussion.

- How did using the fraction strips help you with Problem 2? Talk about the relationship between them.

- What was your strategy for Problems 3 and 4? How did it change or stay the same?

- Why is it important that the magic wand in Problem 5 keeps the whole the same?

- How does the magic wand in Problem 5 make it easy to create equivalent fractions?

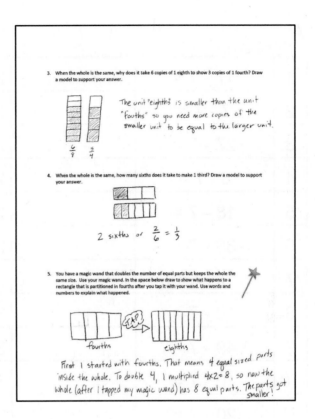

Exit Ticket (3 minutes)

After the Student Debrief, instruct students to complete the Exit Ticket. A review of their work will help you assess the students' understanding of the concepts that were presented in the lesson today and plan more effectively for future lessons. You may read the questions aloud to the students.

Lesson 27:	Explain equivalence by manipulating units and reasoning about their size.	5.E.89
Date:	11/19/13	

A

Correct _____

Subtract.

1	$17 - 7 =$		23	$24 - 7 =$	
2	$7 - 7 =$		24	$34 - 7 =$	
3	$27 - 7 =$		25	$64 - 7 =$	
4	$8 - 7 =$		26	$84 - 7 =$	
5	$18 - 7 =$		27	$15 - 7 =$	
6	$38 - 7 =$		28	$25 - 7 =$	
7	$9 - 7 =$		29	$35 - 7 =$	
8	$19 - 7 =$		30	$75 - 7 =$	
9	$49 - 7 =$		31	$55 - 7 =$	
10	$10 - 7 =$		32	$16 - 7 =$	
11	$20 - 7 =$		33	$26 - 7 =$	
12	$60 - 7 =$		34	$36 - 7 =$	
13	$11 - 7 =$		35	$86 - 7 =$	
14	$21 - 7 =$		36	$66 - 7 =$	
15	$71 - 7 =$		37	$90 - 7 =$	
16	$12 - 7 =$		38	$53 - 7 =$	
17	$22 - 7 =$		39	$42 - 7 =$	
18	$82 - 7 =$		40	$71 - 7 =$	
19	$13 - 7 =$		41	$74 - 7 =$	
20	$23 - 7 =$		42	$56 - 7 =$	
21	$83 - 7 =$		43	$95 - 7 =$	
22	$14 - 7 =$		44	$92 - 7 =$	

COMMON CORE

Lesson 27:   Explain equivalence by manipulating units and reasoning about their
size.

Date: 11/19/13

5.E.9

B

Subtract.

Improvement _____   # Correct _____

1	7 - 7 =		23	24 - 7 =	
2	17 - 7 =		24	34 - 7 =	
3	27 - 7 =		25	54 - 7 =	
4	8 - 7 =		26	74 - 7 =	
5	18 - 7 =		27	15 - 7 =	
6	68 - 7 =		28	25 - 7 =	
7	9 - 7 =		29	35 - 7 =	
8	19 - 7 =		30	65 - 7 =	
9	79 - 7 =		31	45 - 7 =	
10	10 - 7 =		32	16 - 7 =	
11	20 - 7 =		33	26 - 7 =	
12	90 - 7 =		34	36 - 7 =	
13	11 - 7 =		35	76 - 7 =	
14	21 - 7 =		36	56 - 7 =	
15	91 - 7 =		37	70 - 7 =	
16	12 - 7 =		38	63 - 7 =	
17	22 - 7 =		39	52 - 7 =	
18	42 - 7 =		40	81 - 7 =	
19	13 - 7 =		41	74 - 7 =	
20	23 - 7 =		42	66 - 7 =	
21	43 - 7 =		43	85 - 7 =	
22	14 - 7 =		44	52 - 7 =	

Lesson 27:   Explain equivalence by manipulating units and reasoning about their
size.

Date: 11/19/13

5.E.91

Name _____　Date _____

1. Use the tape diagram to model equivalent fractions. Fill in the blanks and answer the following questions.

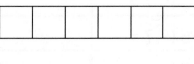

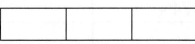

<table>
<tr><td>

4 sixths is equal to _____ thirds.

$$\frac{4}{6} = \frac{\square}{3}$$

The whole stays the same.

What happened to the size of the equal parts when there were less equal parts?

What happened to the number of equal parts when the equal parts became larger?

</td><td>

1 half is equal to _____ eighths.

$$\frac{1}{2} = \frac{\square}{8}$$

The whole stays the same.

What happened to the size of the equal parts when there were more equal parts?

What happened to the number of equal parts when the equal parts became smaller?

</td></tr>
</table>

2. 6 friends want to share three chocolate bars that are all the same size, represented by the 3 strips below. When the bars are unwrapped, the girls notice that the first chocolate bar is cut into 2 equal parts, the second is cut into 4 equal parts, and the third is cut into 6 equal parts. How can the 6 friends share the chocolate bars equally, without breaking any of the pieces?

COMMON CORE　│　**Lesson 27:**　Explain equivalence by manipulating units and reasoning about their size.

Date:　11/19/13

5.E.9

3. When the whole is the same, why does it take 6 copies of 1 eighth to show 3 copies of 1 fourth? Draw a model to support your answer.

4. When the whole is the same, how many sixths does it take to make 1 third? Draw a model to support your answer.

5. You have a magic wand that doubles the number of equal parts but keeps the whole the same size. Use your magic wand. In the space below draw to show what happens to a rectangle that is partitioned in fourths after you tap it with your wand. Use words and numbers to explain what happened.

Name _____   Date _____

1. Solve.

    2 thirds is equal to _____ twelfths.

    $$\frac{2}{3} = \frac{}{12}$$

2. Draw and label two models that show fractions equivalent to those in Problem 1.

3. Use words to explain why the two fractions in Problem 1 are equal.

Name _____   Date _____

1. Use the tape diagram to model equivalent fractions. Fill in the blanks and answer the following questions.

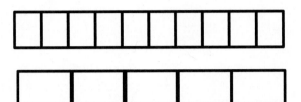   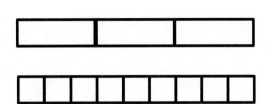

2 tenths is equal to _____ fifths.

$$\frac{2}{10} = \frac{}{5}$$

The whole stays the same.

What happened to the size of the equal parts when there were less equal parts?

1 third is equal to _____ ninths.

$$\frac{1}{3} = \frac{}{9}$$

The whole stays the same.

What happened to the size of the equal parts when there were more equal parts?

2. 8 students want to share 2 pizzas that are the same size, represented by the 2 circles below. They notice that the first pizza is cut into 4 equal slices, and the second is cut into 8 equal slices. How can the 8 students share the pizzas equally, without breaking any of the pieces?

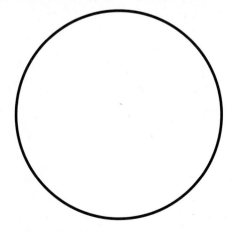   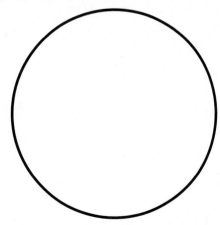

COMMON CORE

Lesson 27:	Explain equivalence by manipulating units and reasoning about their size.
Date:	11/19/13

5.E.95

3. When the whole is the same, why does it take 4 copies of 1 tenth to show 2 copies of 1 fifth? Draw a model to support your answer.

4. When the whole is the same, how many eighths does it take to make 1 fourth? Draw a model to support your answer.

5. Mr. Pham cuts a cake into 8 equal slices. Then he cuts every slice in half. How many of the small slices does he have? Use words and numbers to explain your answer.

Topic F

Comparison, Order, and Size of Fractions

3.NF.3d

Focus Standards:	3.NF.3	Explain equivalence of fractions in special cases, and compare fractions by reasoning about their size.
		d. Compare two fractions with the same numerator or the same denominator by reasoning about their size. Recognize that comparisons are valid only when the two fractions refer to the same whole. Record the results of comparisons with the symbols >, =, or <, and justify the conclusions, e.g., by using a visual fraction model.
Instructional Days:	3	
Coherence -Links from:	G2–M7	Time, Shapes, and Fractions as Equal Parts of Shapes
-Links to:	G4–M5	Fraction Equivalence, Ordering, and Operations

Fraction strips and the number line carry into Topic F as students compare fractions with the same numerator. As they study and compare different fractions, students continue to reason about their size. They develop understanding that the numerator or number of copies of the fractional unit (shaded parts) does not necessarily determine the size of the fraction. The module closes with an exploration in which students are guided to develop a method for precisely partitioning various wholes into any fractional unit using the number line as a measurement tool.

A Teaching Sequence Towards Mastery of Comparison, Order, and Size of Fractions
Objective 1: Compare fractions with the same numerator pictorially. (Lesson 28)
Objective 2: Compare fractions with the same numerator using <,>, or = and use a model to reason about their size. (Lesson 29)
Objective 3: Partition various wholes precisely into equal parts using a number line method. (Lesson 30)

Lesson 28

Objective: Compare fractions with the same numerator pictorially.

Suggested Lesson Structure

- ■ Fluency Practice   (12 minutes)
- ■ Application Problems   (8 minutes)
- ■ Concept Development   (30 minutes)
- ■ Student Debrief   (10 minutes)
  - **Total Time**   **(60 minutes)**

Fluency Practice (12 minutes)

- Sprint: Subtract by 8 **2.NBT.5**   (8 minutes)
- Recognize Equal Fractions **3.NF.3b**   (4 minutes)

Sprint: Subtract by 8 (8 minutes)

Materials: (S) Subtract by 8 Sprint

Recognize Equal Fractions (4 minutes)

Materials: (S) Personal white board

T: (Project a tape diagram partitioned into 2 equal units with the first unit shaded.) Say the fraction that's shaded.

S: 1 half.

T: (Write $\frac{1}{2}$ to the side of the tape diagram. Project a tape diagram partitioned into 4 equal, unshaded units directly below the first tape diagram.) Say the unit of this fraction.

S: Fourths.

T: I'm going to start shading in fourths. Tell me to stop when I've shaded enough fourths to make 1 half. (Shade 2 fourths.)

S: Stop!

T: (Write $\frac{1}{2} = \frac{}{4}$ to the side of the tape diagram.) 1 half is the same as how many fourths?

S: 2 fourths.

T: (Write $\frac{1}{2} = \frac{2}{4}$.)

Continue process for $\frac{1}{3} = \frac{}{9}$ and $\frac{6}{8} = \frac{}{4}$.

Application Problem (8 minutes)

LaTonya has 2 equal sized hotdogs. She cut the first one into thirds at lunch. Later she cut the second hotdog to make double the number of pieces. Draw a model of LaTonya's hotdogs.

     a.   How many pieces is the second hotdog cut into?

     b.   If she wants to eat $\frac{2}{3}$ of the second hotdog, how many pieces should she eat?

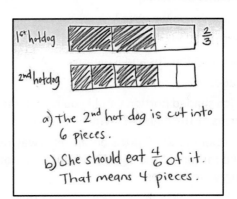

Concept Development (30 minutes)

Materials: (S) Work from application problem, personal white boards

T: Look again at your models of LaTonya's hotdogs. Let's change the problem slightly. What if LaTonya eats 2 pieces of each hotdog? Figure out what fraction of each hotdog she eats.

S: (Students work.) She eats $\frac{2}{3}$ of the first one and $\frac{2}{6}$ of the second one.

T: Did LaTonya eat the same amount of the first hotdog and the second hotdog?

S: (Use models for help.) No.

T: But she ate 2 pieces of each hotdog. Why is the amount she ate different?

S: The number of pieces is the same, but the size of each piece is different. → Just like we saw yesterday, the more you cut up a whole, the smaller the pieces get. → So eating 2 pieces of thirds is more hotdog than 2 pieces of sixths.

(Project or draw the image below.)

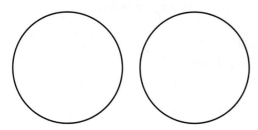

NOTES ON MULTIPLE MEANS OF ENGAGEMENT:

Give students below grade level the option of rectangular pizzas (rather than circles) to ease the task of partitioning.

T: Draw my pizzas on your personal white board.

S: (Draw shapes.)

MP.2   T: Estimate to partition both pizzas into fourths.

S: (Students partition.)

T: Partition the second pizza to double the number of

Lesson 28:   Compare fractions with the same numerator pictorially.
Date: 11/19/13

5.F.3

units.

S: (Students partition.)

T: What units do we have?

S: Fourths and eighths.

T: Shade in 3 fourths and 3 eighths.

S: (Shade.)

MP.2

T: Which shaded portion would you rather eat? The fourths or the eighths? Why?

S: I'd rather eat the fourths because it's way more pizza. → I'd rather eat the eighths because I'm not that hungry, and it's less.

T: But both choices are 3 pieces. Aren't they equivalent?

S: No. You can see fourths are bigger. → We know because the more times you cut the whole the smaller the pieces get. → So eighths are tiny compared to fourths! → The number of pieces is the same but the sizes of the pieces are different, so the shaded amounts are not equivalent.

If necessary, continue with other examples varying the pictorial models.

T: Let's work in pairs to play a comparison game. Partner A, draw a whole and shade a fraction of the whole. Label the shaded part.

S: (Partner A draws.)

T: Partner B, draw a fraction that is less. Use the same whole, and the same number of shaded parts. Label the shaded parts.

S: (Draws.)

T: Partner A, check your friend's work.

S: (Partner A checks and helps make any corrections necessary.)

T: Now switch who draws first. I will say 'greater than' or 'less than.'

(Play several rounds.)

Problem Set (10 minutes)

Students should do their personal best to complete the Problem Set within the allotted 10 minutes. For some classes, it may be appropriate to modify the assignment by specifying which problems they work on first. Some problems do not specify a method for solving. Students solve these problems using the RDW approach used for Application Problems.

NOTES ON MULTIPLE MEANS OF ACTION AND EXPRESSION:

As students play a comparison game, facilitate peer-to-peer talk for ELLs with sentence frames, such as:

- "I partitioned _____ (unit fractions). I shaded _____ (number of) _____ (unit fraction)."
- "I drew _____ (unit fraction), too. I shaded _____ (number of) _____ (unit fractions.) _____ is less than _____."

NOTES ON MULTIPLE MEANS OF ENGAGEMENT:

Extend page one of the Problem Set for students above grade level, using their knowledge of equivalencies. Ask, "If 2 thirds is greater than 2 fifths, use equivalent fractions to name the same comparison. For example, 4 sixths is greater than 2 fifths."

| Lesson 28: | Compare fractions with the same numerator pictorially. |
| Date: | 11/19/13 |

5.F.

Student Debrief (10 minutes)

Lesson Objective: Compare fractions with the same numerator pictorially.

The Student Debrief is intended to invite reflection and active processing of the total lesson experience.

Invite students to review their solutions for the Problem Set. They should check work by comparing answers with a partner before going over answers as a class. Look for misconceptions or misunderstandings that can be addressed in the Debrief. Guide students in a conversation to debrief the Problem Set and process the lesson.

You may choose to use any combination of the questions below to lead the discussion.

- Look at your answers for Problems 7 and 8 on the Problem Set. Is 2 parts always equal to 2 parts? Why or why not?

- If you only know the number of shaded parts, can you tell if fractions are equivalent? Why or why not?

Exit Ticket (3 minutes)

After the Student Debrief, instruct students to complete the Exit Ticket. A review of their work will help you assess the students' understanding of the concepts that were presented in the lesson today and plan more effectively for future lessons. You may read the questions aloud to the students.

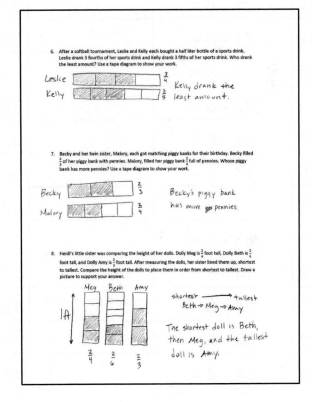

A

Correct _____

Subtract.

1	18 - 8 =		23	74 - 8 =	
2	8 - 8 =		24	15 - 8 =	
3	28 - 8 =		25	25 - 8 =	
4	9 - 8 =		26	35 - 8 =	
5	19 - 8 =		27	85 - 8 =	
6	39 - 8 =		28	65 - 8 =	
7	10 - 8 =		29	16 - 8 =	
8	20 - 8 =		30	26 - 8 =	
9	50 - 8 =		31	36 - 8 =	
10	11 - 8 =		32	96 - 8 =	
11	21 - 8 =		33	76 - 8 =	
12	71 - 8 =		34	17 - 8 =	
13	12 - 8 =		35	27 - 8 =	
14	22 - 8 =		36	37 - 8 =	
15	82 - 8 =		37	87 - 8 =	
16	13 - 8 =		38	67 - 8 =	
17	23 - 8 =		39	70 - 8 =	
18	83 - 8 =		40	62 - 8 =	
19	14 - 8 =		41	84 - 8 =	
20	24 - 8 =		42	66 - 8 =	
21	34 - 8 =		43	91 - 8 =	
22	54 - 8 =		44	75 - 8 =	

B

Subtract.

Improvement _____　　　# Correct _____

1	8 - 8 =		23	94 - 8 =	
2	18 - 8 =		24	15 - 8 =	
3	28 - 8 =		25	25 - 8 =	
4	9 - 8 =		26	35 - 8 =	
5	19 - 8 =		27	95 - 8 =	
6	69 - 8 =		28	75 - 8 =	
7	10 - 8 =		29	16 - 8 =	
8	20 - 8 =		30	26 - 8 =	
9	60 - 8 =		31	36 - 8 =	
10	11 - 8 =		32	66 - 8 =	
11	21 - 8 =		33	46 - 8 =	
12	81 - 8 =		34	17 - 8 =	
13	12 - 8 =		35	27 - 8 =	
14	22 - 8 =		36	37 - 8 =	
15	52 - 8 =		37	97 - 8 =	
16	13 - 8 =		38	77 - 8 =	
17	23 - 8 =		39	80 - 8 =	
18	93 - 8 =		40	71 - 8 =	
19	14 - 8 =		41	53 - 8 =	
20	24 - 8 =		42	45 - 8 =	
21	34 - 8 =		43	87 - 8 =	
22	74 - 8 =		44	54 - 8 =	

COMMON CORE　　Lesson 28:　　Compare fractions with the same numerator pictorially.　　　　5.F.7

Date:　　11/19/13

Name _____   Date _____

Directions: Shade the models to compare the following fractions. Circle the larger fraction for each problem.

1.   2 fifths

     2 thirds

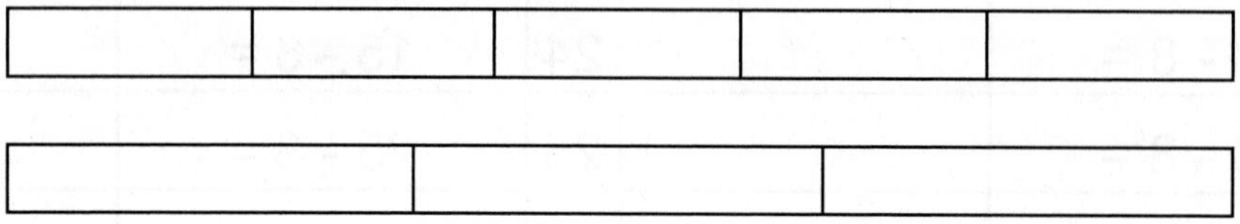

2.   2 tenths

     2 eighths

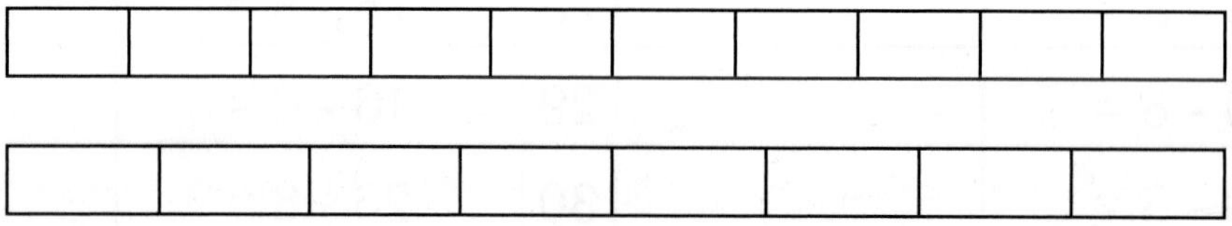

3.   3 fourths

     3 eighths

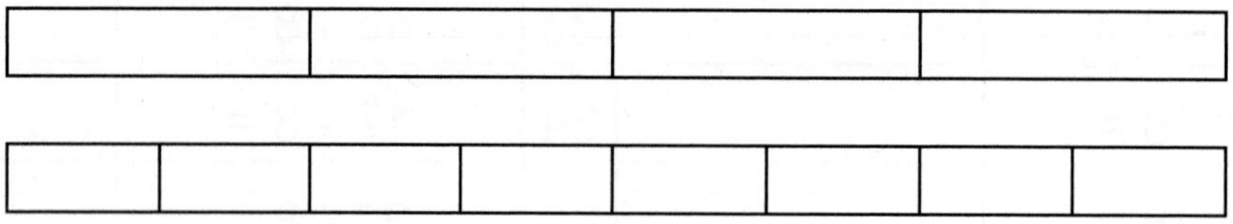

4.   4 eighths

     4 sixths

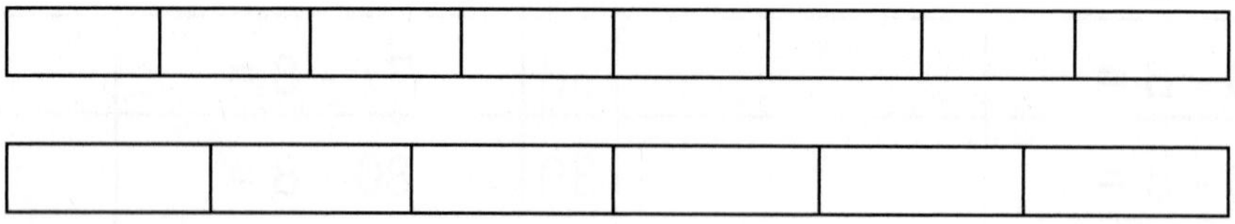

5.   3 thirds

     3 sixths

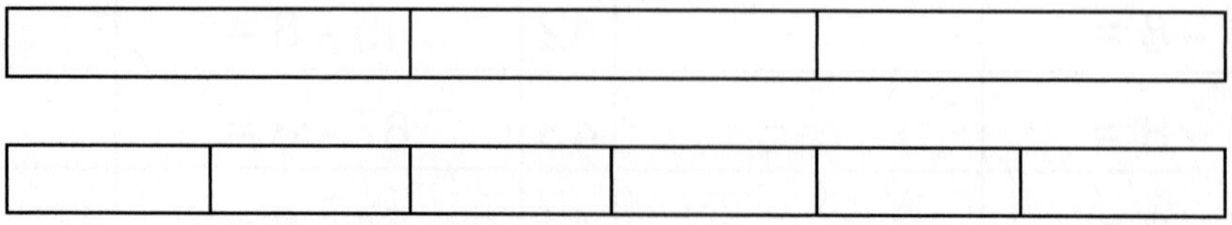

6. After a softball tournament, Leslie and Kelly each bought a half liter bottle of a sports drink. Leslie drank 3 fourths of her sports drink, and Kelly drank 3 fifths of her sports drink. Who drank the least amount? Use a tape diagram to show your work.

7. Becky and her twin sister, Malory, each got matching piggy banks for their birthday. Becky filled $\frac{2}{3}$ of her piggy bank with pennies. Malory filled $\frac{2}{4}$ of her piggy bank with pennies. Whose piggy bank has more pennies? Use a tape diagram to show your work.

8. Heidi's little sister was comparing the height of her dolls. Dolly Meg is $\frac{2}{4}$ foot tall, Dolly Beth is $\frac{2}{6}$ foot tall, and Dolly Amy is $\frac{2}{3}$ foot tall. After measuring the dolls, her sister lined them up, shortest to tallest. Compare the height of the dolls to place them in order from shortest to tallest. Draw a picture to support your answer.

Name _____   Date _____

1. Directions: Shade the models to compare the following fractions.

2 thirds

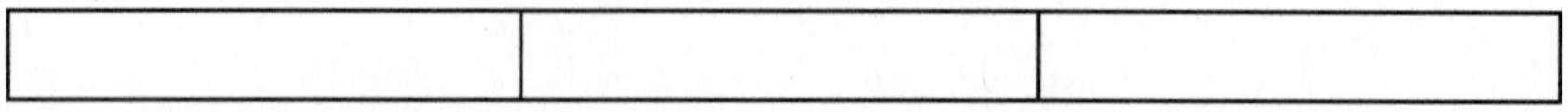

2 eighths

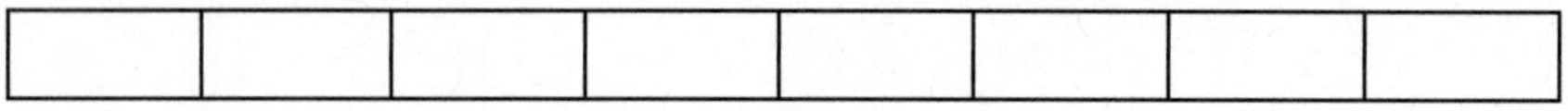

a. Which is larger, 2 thirds or 2 eighths? Why? Use words to explain.

2. Draw a model for each fraction and circle the smaller fraction.

   3 sevenths

   3 fourths

COMMON CORE Lesson 28: Compare fractions with the same numerator pictorially.
Date: 11/19/13

5.F.

Name _____   Date _____

Directions: Shade the models to compare the following fractions. Circle the larger fraction for each problem.

1.   1 half

       1 fifth

2.   2 sevenths

       2 fourths

3.   4 fifths

       4 ninths

4.   5 sevenths

       5 tenths

5.   4 sixths

       4 fourths

Lesson 28:   Compare fractions with the same numerator pictorially.
Date: 11/19/13

5.F.11

6. In science Saleem and Edwin used an inch ruler to measure the length of each of their small caterpillars. Saleem's caterpillar measured 3 fourths of an inch, and Edwin's caterpillar measured 3 eighths of an inch. Whose caterpillar is longer? Use a tape diagram to show your work.

7. Lily and Jasmine are baking the same size chocolate cake. Lily put $\frac{5}{10}$ of a cup of sugar into her cake, and Jasmine put $\frac{5}{6}$ of a cup of sugar into her cake. Who used less sugar? Use a tape diagram to show your work.

Lesson 29

Objective: Compare fractions with the same numerator using <, >, or = and use a model to reason about their size.

Suggested Lesson Structure

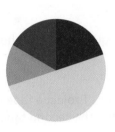

■ Fluency Practice	(12 minutes)	
■ Application Problems	(8 minutes)	
■ Concept Development	(30 minutes)	
■ Student Debrief	(10 minutes)	
Total Time	**(60 minutes)**	

Fluency Practice (12 minutes)

- Multiply by 8 **3.OA.4**   (8 minutes)
- Compare Fractions with the Same Numerator **3.NF.3d**   (4 minutes)

Multiply by 8 (8 minutes)

Materials: (S) Double-sided Multiply by 8 Problem Sets

T: Skip-count by eights. (Write multiples horizontally as students count.)

S: 8, 16, 24, 32, 40, 48, 56, 64, 72, 80.

T: (Write 8 x 5 = _____.) Let's skip-count by eights to find the answer. (Count with fingers to 5 as students count.)

S: 8, 16, 24, 32, 40.

T: (Circle 40 and write 8 x 5 = 40 above it. Write 8 x 3 = _____.) Let's skip-count up by eights again. (Count with fingers to 3 as students count.)

S: 8, 16, 24.

T: Let's see how we can skip-count down to find the answer, too. Start at 40. (Count down with your fingers as students say numbers.)

S: 40, 32, 24.

T: (Write 8 x 7 = _____.) Let's skip-count up by eights. (Count with fingers to 7 as students count.)

S: 8, 16, 24, 32, 40, 48, 56.

T: (Write 8 x 9 = _____.) Let's skip-count up by eights. (Count with fingers to 8 as students count.)

S: 8, 16, 24, 32, 40, 48, 56, 64, 72.

T: Let's see how we can skip-count down to find the answer, too. Start at 80. (Count down with your

COMMON CORE	Lesson 29:	Compare fractions with the same numerator using <, >, or = and use a model to reason about their size.
	Date:	11/19/13

5.F.13

fingers as student say numbers.)

S: 80, 72.

T: Let's get some practice multiplying by 8. Be sure to work left to right across the page. (Distribute Multiply by 8 Problem Set.)

Compare Fractions with the Same Numerator (4 minutes)

Materials: (S) Personal white boards

T: (Project a tape diagram partitioned into 3 equal units with the first 2 units shaded.) Say the fraction that is shaded.

S: 2 thirds.

T: (Write 2 thirds to the left of the tape diagram. Project a tape diagram of 6 equal, unshaded units directly below the first tape diagram. Next to the second tape diagram, write 2 sixths.) How many units should I shade to show 2 sixths?

S: 2.

T: (Shade the first 2 units in the second tape diagram). On your personal white board, write the larger fraction.

S: (Write $\frac{1}{2}$.)

Continue process for 3 tenths and 3 fourths, 5 sixths and 5 eighths, and 7 eighths and 7 tenths.

Application Problem (8 minutes)

Catherine and Diana bought matching scrapbooks. Catherine decorated $\frac{5}{9}$ of the pages in her book. Diana decorated $\frac{5}{6}$ of the pages in her book. Use a tape diagram to show who has decorated more pages of their scrapbooks.

NOTES ON
MULTIPLE MEANS OF
ENGAGEMENT:

Challenge students above grade level to model the comparison on a number line (or two), as well. Have students evaluate and compare the models. Ask (for example), "How might you decide when to use a tape diagram rather than a number line to solve?"

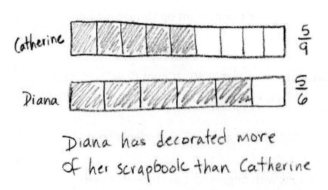

Diana has decorated more of her scrapbook than Catherine

	Lesson 29:	Compare fractions with the same numerator using <, >, or = and use a model to reason about their size.	5.F.
	Date:	11/19/13	

Concept Development (30 minutes)

Materials: (S) Personal white boards, Lesson 25 Template (pictured below)

Students begin in pairs facing each other, arranged in a large circle around the room. Students slip the template from Lesson 25 into personal white boards.

Lesson 25 Template, Side A

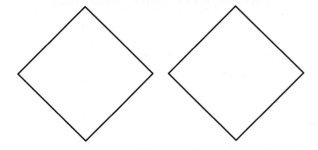

- T: Start on Side A of your template. Today we'll only use the first rectangle. On my signal, draw and shade a fraction less than $\frac{1}{2}$ and label it below the rectangle. (Signal.)
- S: (Draw and label.)
- T: Check your partner's work to make sure it's less than $\frac{1}{2}$.
- S: (Check.)
- T: This is how we're going to play a game today. For the next round, we'll see which partner is quicker but still accurate. As soon as you finish drawing raise your board. If you are quicker, then you are the winner of the round. You'll move to partner with the person on your right who stays. Ready? Erase your boards. On my signal draw and label a fraction that is greater than $\frac{1}{2}$. (Signal.)
- S: (Draw and label.)

The student who goes around the entire circle and arrives back at their original place faster than the other students wins the game. The winner can also just be the student who has moved the furthest if it takes too long to play all the way around. Move the game at a brisk pace. Use a variety of fractions and mix it up between greater than and less than so that students constantly need to update their drawings and feel challenged. You may even decide to mix it up by calling out 'equal to.'

- T: Draw my shapes on your personal white board. Make sure they match in size like mine. (Draw or show the image below.)

- S: (Draw.)
- T: Partition both squares into sixths.
- S: (Partition.)

Lesson 29:	Compare fractions with the same numerator using <, >, or = and use a model to reason about their size.	5.F.15
Date:	11/19/13	

T: Partition the second square to show double the number of units in the same whole.

S: (Partition.)

T: What units do we have?

S: Sixths and twelfths.

T: Shade in 4 units of each shape and label the shaded fraction below the square.

S: (Shade and label.)

T: Whispering to your partner, say a sentence comparing the fractions using the words 'greater than,' 'less than,' or 'equal to.'

S: $\frac{4}{6}$ is greater than $\frac{4}{12}$.

T: Now place the correct symbol between the fractions.

S: (Students show $\frac{4}{6} > \frac{4}{12}$.)

T: Draw my shapes on your personal board. Make sure they match in size like mine. (Draw or show the image below.)

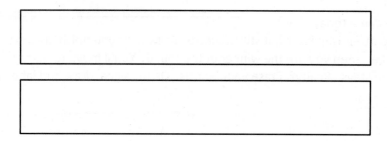

S: (Draw.)

T: Partition the first rectangle into sevenths and the second one into fifths.

S: (Partition.)

T: Shade in 3 units of each shape and label the shaded fraction below the square.

S: (Shade and label.)

T: Whispering to your partner, say a sentence comparing the fractions using the words 'greater than,' 'less than,' or 'equal to.'

S: $\frac{3}{7}$ is less than $\frac{3}{5}$.

T: Now place the correct symbol between the fractions.

S: (Students show $\frac{3}{7} < \frac{3}{5}$.)

Do other examples if necessary using a variety of shapes and units.

T: Draw 2 number lines on your personal white board. And label the endpoints 0 and 1.

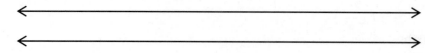

COMMON CORE

Lesson 29: Compare fractions with the same numerator using <, >, or = and use a model to reason about their size.

Date: 11/19/13

5.F.1

S: (Draw and label.)

T: Partition the first number line into eighths and the second one into tenths.

S: (Partition.)

T: On the first number line, make an arrow to label $\frac{8}{8}$ of the unit fraction.

S: (Label.)

T: On the second number line, make an arrow to label 2 copies of $\frac{5}{10}$.

S: (Label.)

T: Whispering to your partner, say a sentence comparing the fractions using the words 'greater than,' 'less than,' or 'equal to.'

S: Wait, they're the same! $\frac{8}{8}$ is equal to $\frac{10}{10}$.

T: How do you know?

S: Because they have the same point on the number line. That means they're equivalent.

T: Now write the comparison as a number sentence with the correct symbol between the fractions.

S: (Students show $\frac{8}{8} = \frac{10}{10}$.)

Do other examples with the number line. In subsequent examples that use smaller units or units that are farther apart, move to using a single number line.

Problem Set (10 minutes)

Students should do their personal best to complete the Problem Set within the allotted 10 minutes. For some classes, it may be appropriate to modify the assignment by specifying which problems they work on first. Some problems do not specify a method for solving. Students solve these problems using the RDW approach used for Application Problems.

Student Debrief (10 minutes)

Lesson Objective: Compare fractions with the same numerator using <, >, or = and use a model to reason about their size.

The Student Debrief is intended to invite reflection and active processing of the total lesson experience.

Invite students to review their solutions for the Problem Set. They should check work by comparing answers with a partner before going over answers as a class. Look for misconceptions or misunderstandings that can be addressed in the Debrief. Guide students in a

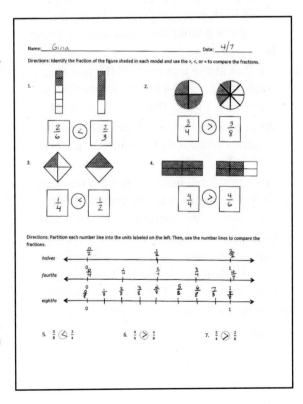

COMMON CORE

Lesson 29:   Compare fractions with the same numerator using <, >, or = and use a
              model to reason about their size.
Date: 11/19/13

5.F.17

conversation to debrief the Problem Set and process the lesson.

You may choose to use any combination of the questions below to lead the discussion.

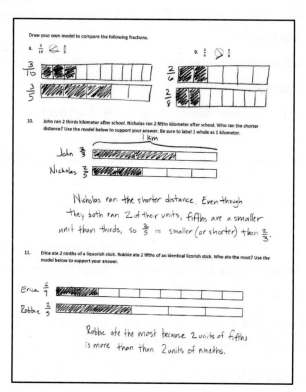

- Use the questions in the vignette below to guide a conversation in which students reflect on their learning and articulate the objective of the lesson.
  - T: Think back on our work from yesterday and today. What have we compared?
  - S: Fractions. → Number lines and pictorial models. → Fractions with the same amount of shaded parts and different units.
  - T: When comparing fractions, why is it so important that the wholes are the same size?
  - S: Because you have to compare the same wholes. → If the wholes are different sizes, then you can't really tell how big the pieces are. A ninth might actually be bigger than a sixth if the whole is way bigger.
  - T: If the wholes are the same, like the ones we've been practicing with, how do we determine greater than, less than, or equal to?
  - S: We look at the unit to see if the pieces are small or big. → The bigger the number of pieces, the smaller the actual pieces are.
  - T: What about when you're just looking at fractions without number lines or pictorial models?
  - S: You can still tell from the bottom number. → Bigger numbers on the bottom mean more pieces, but therefore smaller in size.
  - T: Let's try a few without models. (Write a handful of comparisons on the board and have students write the symbols that go between them on their personal boards.)

- To extend the lesson, draw fraction models greater than 1 and guide students to compare. For example, use $\frac{12}{9}$ and $\frac{12}{7}$.

NOTES ON MULTIPLE MEANS OF ACTION AND EXPRESSION:

ELLs and students below grade level may benefit from math (and English) fluency practice using the Problem Set. For Numbers 1 through 4, encourage learners to whisper the unit fraction, whisper count the shaded units (e.g., 1 sixth, 2 sixths), and whisper the shaded fraction as they write.

Exit Ticket (3 minutes)

After the Student Debrief, instruct students to complete the Exit Ticket. A review of their work will help you assess the students' understanding of the concepts that were presented in the lesson today and plan more effectively for future lessons. You may read the questions aloud to the students.

Lesson 29:   Compare fractions with the same numerator using <, >, or = and use a
model to reason about their size.

Date: 11/19/13

5.F.19

8 x 1 = _____   8 x 2 = _____   8 x 3 = _____   8 x 4 = _____

8 x 5 = _____   8 x 1 = _____   8 x 2 = _____   8 x 1 = _____

8 x 3 = _____   8 x 1 = _____   8 x 4 = _____   8 x 1 = _____

8 x 5 = _____   8 x 1 = _____   8 x 2 = _____   8 x 3 = _____

8 x 2 = _____   8 x 4 = _____   8 x 2 = _____   8 x 5 = _____

8 x 2 = _____   8 x 1 = _____   8 x 2 = _____   8 x 3 = _____

8 x 1 = _____   8 x 3 = _____   8 x 2 = _____   8 x 3 = _____

8 x 4 = _____   8 x 3 = _____   8 x 5 = _____   8 x 3 = _____

8 x 4 = _____   8 x 1 = _____   8 x 4 = _____   8 x 2 = _____

8 x 4 = _____   8 x 3 = _____   8 x 4 = _____   8 x 5 = _____

8 x 4 = _____   8 x 5 = _____   8 x 1 = _____   8 x 5 = _____

8 x 2 = _____   8 x 5 = _____   8 x 3 = _____   8 x 5 = _____

8 x 4 = _____   8 x 2 = _____   8 x 4 = _____   8 x 3 = _____

8 x 5 = _____   8 x 3 = _____   8 x 2 = _____   8 x 4 = _____

8 x 3 = _____   8 x 5 = _____   8 x 2 = _____   8 x 4 = _____

COMMON CORE

Lesson 29: Compare fractions with the same numerator using <, >, or = and use a model to reason about their size.

Date: 11/19/13

5.F.2

8 x 1 = _____   8 x 2 = _____   8 x 3 = _____   8 x 4 = _____

8 x 5 = _____   8 x 6 = _____   8 x 7 = _____   8 x 8 = _____

8 x 9 = _____   8 x 10 = _____   8 x 5 = _____   8 x 6 = _____

8 x 5 = _____   8 x 7 = _____   8 x 5 = _____   8 x 8 = _____

8 x 5 = _____   8 x 9 = _____   8 x 5 = _____   8 x 10 = _____

8 x 6 = _____   8 x 5 = _____   8 x 6 = _____   8 x 7 = _____

8 x 6 = _____   8 x 8 = _____   8 x 6 = _____   8 x 9 = _____

8 x 6 = _____   8 x 7 = _____   8 x 6 = _____   8 x 7 = _____

8 x 8 = _____   8 x 7 = _____   8 x 9 = _____   8 x 7 = _____

8 x 8 = _____   8 x 6 = _____   8 x 8 = _____   8 x 7 = _____

8 x 8 = _____   8 x 9 = _____   8 x 9 = _____   8 x 6 = _____

8 x 9 = _____   8 x 7 = _____   8 x 9 = _____   8 x 8 = _____

8 x 9 = _____   8 x 8 = _____   8 x 6 = _____   8 x 9 = _____

8 x 7 = _____   8 x 9 = _____   8 x 6 = _____   8 x 8 = _____

8 x 9 = _____   8 x 7 = _____   8 x 6 = _____   8 x 8 = _____

COMMON CORE

Lesson 29:   Compare fractions with the same numerator using <, >, or = and use a
             model to reason about their size.

Date: 11/19/13

5.F.21

Name _____   Date _____

Directions: Identify the fraction of the figure shaded in each model and use the >, <, or = to compare the fractions.

1.

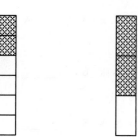

$\dfrac{2}{6}$ 〈 $\dfrac{2}{3}$

2.

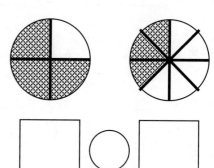

3.

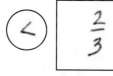

4.

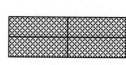

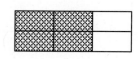

Directions: Partition each number line into the units labeled on the left. Then, use the number lines to compare the fractions.

halves   ←———————+———————————————————————+———→
                      0   1

fourths   ←———————+———————————————————————+———→
                      0   1

eighths   ←———————+———————————————————————+———→
                      0   1

5. $\dfrac{3}{8}$ ◯ $\dfrac{3}{4}$ 6. $\dfrac{4}{4}$ ◯ $\dfrac{4}{8}$ 7. $\dfrac{2}{4}$ ◯ $\dfrac{2}{8}$

COMMON CORE | **Lesson 29:**   Compare fractions with the same numerator using <, >, or = and use a
                            model to reason about their size.

Date: 11/19/13

5.F.2

Draw your own model to compare the following fractions.

8. $\dfrac{3}{10}$ ◯ $\dfrac{3}{5}$

9. $\dfrac{2}{6}$ ◯ $\dfrac{2}{8}$

10. John ran 2 thirds kilometer after school. Nicholas ran 2 fifths kilometer after school. Who ran the shorter distance? Use the model below to support your answer. Be sure to label 1 whole as 1 kilometer.

11. Erica ate 2 ninths of a licorice stick. Robbie ate 2 fifths of an identical licorice stick. Who ate the most? Use the model below to support your answer.

COMMON CORE | Lesson 29: | Compare fractions with the same numerator using <, >, or = and use a model to reason about their size. | 5.F.23

Date: 11/19/13

© 2013 Common Core, Inc. All rights reserved. commoncore.org

Name _____   Date _____

1. Complete the number sentence by writing >, <, or =.

$$\frac{3}{5} \underline{\hspace{2cm}} \frac{3}{9}$$

2. Draw 2 number lines with endpoints 0 and 1 to show each fraction in Problem 1. Use the models to explain how you know your comparison in Problem 1 is correct.

COMMON CORE

Lesson 29:   Compare fractions with the same numerator using <, >, or = and use a
model to reason about their size.

Date: 11/19/13

5.F.2

Name _____   Date _____

Directions: Label each shaded fraction. Use >, <, or = to compare.

1.
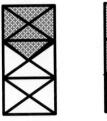 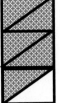

2.
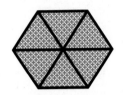

3.
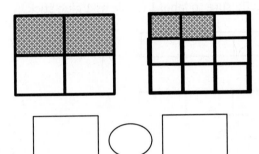

4.
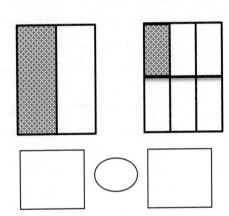

Directions: Partition each number line into the units labeled on the left. Then, use the number lines to compare the fractions.

thirds

0   1

sixths

0   1

ninths

0   1

5. $\dfrac{2}{6}$ ⬭ $\dfrac{2}{3}$ 6. $\dfrac{5}{9}$ ⬭ $\dfrac{5}{6}$ 7. $\dfrac{3}{3}$ ⬭ $\dfrac{3}{9}$

Lesson 29: Compare fractions with the same numerator using <, >, or = and use a model to reason about their size.

Date: 11/19/13

5.F.25

Draw your own models to compare the following fractions.

8. $\dfrac{7}{10}$ $\bigcirc$ $\dfrac{7}{8}$

9. $\dfrac{4}{6}$ $\bigcirc$ $\dfrac{4}{9}$

10. For an art project, Michello used $\dfrac{3}{4}$ of a glue stick. Yamin used $\dfrac{3}{6}$ of an identical glue stick. Who used more of the glue stick? Use the model below to support your answer. Be sure to label 1 whole as 1 glue stick.

11. After gym class, Jahsir drank 2 eighths of a bottle of water. Jade drank 2 fifths of an identical bottle of water. Who drank less water? Use the model below to support your answer.

COMMON CORE **Lesson 29:** Compare fractions with the same numerator using <, >, or = and use a model to reason about their size.
Date: 11/19/13

5.F.2

Lesson 30

Objective: Partition various wholes precisely into equal parts using a number line method.

Suggested Lesson Structure

■ Fluency Practice   (12 minutes)
□ Concept Development   (40 minutes)
■ Student Debrief   (8 minutes)
   Total Time   **(60 minutes)**

Fluency Practice (12 minutes)

■ Multiply by 9 **3.OA.4**   (8 minutes)
■ Compare Fractions with the Same Numerator **3.NF.3d**   (4 minutes)

Multiply by 9 (8 minutes)

Materials: (S) Multiplication by 9 Sprint

T: Skip-count by nines. (Write multiples horizontally as students count.)
S: 9, 18, 27, 36, 45, 54, 63, 72, 81, 90.
T: (Write 9 x 5 = to the side of the number line.) Let's skip-count by nines to find the answer. (Count with fingers to 5 as students count.)
S: 9, 18, 27, 36, 45.
T: (Circle 45 and write 9 x 5 = 45 above it. Write 9 x 4 = to the side of the number line.) Skip-count by nines. (Count with fingers to 4 as students count.)
S: 9, 18, 27, 36.
T: Let's arrive at the answer by skip-counting down starting at 45. (Hold up 5 fingers as students say 45 and take away 1 finger as students count.)
S: 45, 36.
T: (Write 9 x 7 = to the side of the number line.) Skip-count by nines. (Count with fingers to 7 as students count.)
S: 9, 18, 27, 36, 45, 54, 63.
T: Let's skip-count starting at 45. (Hold up 5 fingers as students say 45 and count up with fingers as students count.)
S: 45, 54, 63.
T: (Write 9 x 9 = to the side of the number line.) Skip-count by nines. (Count with fingers to 9 as

Lesson 30:	Partition various wholes precisely into equal parts using a number line method.
Date:	11/19/13

5.F.27

students count.)

S: 9, 18, 27, 36, 45, 54, 63, 72, 81.

T: Let's skip-count down starting at 90. (Hold up 10 fingers as students say 90 and remove 1 finger as students count.)

S: 90, 81.

T: Let's get some practice multiplying by 9. Be sure to work left to right across the page. (Distribute Multiply by 9 Problem Set.)

Compare Fractions with the Same Numerator (4 minutes)

Materials: (S) Personal white boards

T: (Project a figure showing 3 fourths.) Say the fraction of the figure that is shaded.

S: 3 fourths.

T: (Write $\frac{3}{4}$ directly below the figure. To the right of the first figure, project one that is the same size and shape.) Say the fraction of the figure that is shaded.

S: 3 eighths.

T: (Write $\frac{3}{8}$ directly below the second figure.) On your boards, write each fraction. Between the fractions, use the greater than or less than symbol (Write < and >.) to show which fraction is larger.

S: (Write $\frac{3}{4} > \frac{3}{8}$.)

Continue process for $\frac{5}{10}$ and $\frac{5}{8}$, $\frac{2}{5}$ and $\frac{2}{3}$, $\frac{4}{5}$ and $\frac{4}{6}$.

NOTES ON MULTIPLE MEANS OF ACTION AND EXPRESSION:

Students below grade level may benefit from naming the unit fraction (e.g., "eighths") before naming the shaded fraction. Solidify understanding of greater than/less than symbols by soliciting a simultaneous oral response, e.g., "3 fourths is greater than 3 eighths."

Provide sentence frames for ELLs, such as "____ is greater than ____."

Concept Development (40 minutes)

Materials: (S) At least 5- 9"x 1" strips of red construction paper per student, 1 copy of the Lined Paper Template or simple notebook paper, 12-inch ruler (Please see the notes about the Exit Ticket.)

T: Think back on our lessons. Talk to your partner about how to partition a number line into thirds.

S: Draw the line and then estimate 3 equal parts. → Use your folded fraction strip to measure. → Measure a 3-inch line with a ruler and then mark off each inch. → Or on a 6-inch line, 1 mark would be at each 2 inches. → And don't forget to mark 0. → Yes, you always have to start measuring from 0.

T: What if you want to mark off *any* fractional unit *precisely* without the use of a ruler, just with lined paper? Let's explore a method to do that.

MP.6

Lesson 30:   Partition various wholes precisely into equal parts using a number line method.
Date: 11/19/13   5.F.2

© 2013 Common Core, Inc. All rights reserved. commoncore.org

Step 1: Draw a number line and mark the 0 endpoint.

T: (Give students 1 sheet of lined notebook paper.) Turn your paper so the margin is horizontal. Draw a number line on top of the margin.

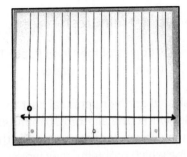

T: Mark 0 on the point where I did (Demonstrate.). How can we equally and precisely partition this number line into thirds? Talk to your partner.

S: We can use the vertical lines. → Each line can be an equal part. → We can count 2 lines for each third. → Or 3 spaces or 4 to make an equal part, just so long as each part has the same number. → Oh, I see, this is the answer. → But the teacher said any piece of paper. If we make thirds on this paper, it won't help us make thirds on every paper.

Step 2: Measure equal units using the paper's lines.

T: Use the paper's vertical lines to measure. Let's make each part 5 spaces long. Label the number line from 0 to 1 using 5 spaces for each third. Discuss in pairs how you know these are precise thirds.

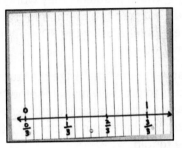

Step 3: Extend the equal parts to the top of the notebook paper with a line.

T: Draw vertical lines up from your number line to the top of the paper at each third. (Hold up 1 red strip of paper.) Talk to your partner about how we might use these lines to partition this red strip into thirds.

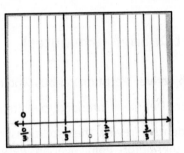

T: (Pass out 1 red strip to each student.) The challenge is to partition the red strip precisely into thirds. Let the left end of the strip be 0. The right end of the strip is 1.

S: The strip is too long. → We can't cut it? → No. The teacher said no. How can we do this? (Circulate and listen but don't give an answer.)

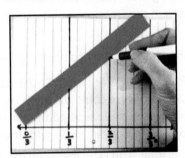

Step 4: Angle the red strip so that the left end touches the 0 endpoint on the original number line. The right end touches the line at 1.

Step 5: Mark off equal units, indicated by the vertical extensions of the points on the original number line.

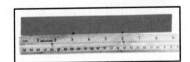

T: Do your units look equal?

T: Verify they are equal with your ruler. Measure the full length of the red strip in inches. Measure the equal parts.

T: I made this strip 9 inches long just so that you could verify that our method partitions precisely.

Lesson 30:	Partition various wholes precisely into equal parts using a number line method.	5.F.29
Date:	11/19/13	

Have the students think about why this method works. Have them review the process step by step.

Problem Set (10 minutes)

Materials: (S) Copies of the Lined Paper Template or
simple notebook paper

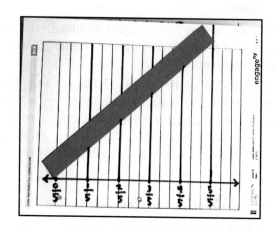

Students should do their personal best to complete the Problem Set within the allotted 10 minutes. For some classes, it may be appropriate to modify the assignment by specifying which problems they work on first. Some problems do not specify a method for solving. Students solve these problems using the RDW approach used for Application Problems.

In cooperative groups, challenge the students to use the same process to precisely mark off other red strips into halves, fourths, etc. It is particularly exciting to partition fifths, sevenths, ninths, and tenths since those are so challenging to fold.

Student Debrief (8 minutes)

Lesson Objective: Partition various wholes precisely into equal parts using a number line method.

The Student Debrief is intended to invite reflection and active processing of the total lesson experience.

Invite students to review their solutions for the Problem Set. They should check work by comparing answers with a partner before going over answers as a class. Look for misconceptions or misunderstandings that can be addressed in the Debrief. Guide students in a conversation to debrief the Problem Set and process the lesson.

You may choose to use any combination of the questions below to lead the discussion.

- (Present a meter strip.) Could we use this method to partition any length strip? Talk to your partner about how we could partition this longer strip. Model partitioning the meter strip by using the same method. Simply tape additional lined papers above the lined paper with the thirds. This allows you to make a sharper angle with the meter strip.
- This long strip (The meter length.), this shorter strip (The red length.), and this number line (The one at the base of the paper.) were all partitioned during our work. What is the same and different about them?
- Why do you think this method works? Why are the fractional units still equal when we angle the paper? Do you need to measure to check that they are?
- How might having this skill be helpful in your lives or math class?
- Explain to the students that this lesson will be very important in their high school mathematics and that a mathematician invented it in order to prepare them for success later in their math journey.

Lesson 30: Partition various wholes precisely into equal parts using a number line method.
Date: 11/19/13

5.F.3

Exit Ticket (3 minutes)

Since this is an exploratory lesson, rather than giving an Exit Ticket, circulate and take notes on each student's work during the lesson. Is the student able to generalize the method to partition into other fractional units? Make notes about the quality of the new efforts and what mistakes a student made either conceptually (not understanding the angling of the strip) or at a skill level (such as not using the paper's lines properly to partition equal units.) Make notes, too, on the role students take within cooperative groups. Which students articulate directions? Explanations? Which students execute well but silently?

	Lesson 30:	Partition various wholes precisely into equal parts using a number line method.	5.F.31
	Date:	11/19/13	

9 x 1 = _____   9 x 2 = _____   9 x 3 = _____   9 x 4 = _____

9 x 5 = _____   9 x 1 = _____   9 x 2 = _____   9 x 1 = _____

9 x 3 = _____   9 x 1 = _____   9 x 4 = _____   9 x 1 = _____

9 x 5 = _____   9 x 1 = _____   9 x 2 = _____   9 x 3 = _____

9 x 2 = _____   9 x 4 = _____   9 x 2 = _____   9 x 5 = _____

9 x 2 = _____   9 x 1 = _____   9 x 2 = _____   9 x 3 = _____

9 x 1 = _____   9 x 3 = _____   9 x 2 = _____   9 x 3 = _____

9 x 4 = _____   9 x 3 = _____   9 x 5 = _____   9 x 3 = _____

9 x 4 = _____   9 x 1 = _____   9 x 4 = _____   9 x 2 = _____

9 x 4 = _____   9 x 3 = _____   9 x 4 = _____   9 x 5 = _____

9 x 4 = _____   9 x 5 = _____   9 x 1 = _____   9 x 5 = _____

9 x 2 = _____   9 x 5 = _____   9 x 3 = _____   9 x 5 = _____

9 x 4 = _____   9 x 2 = _____   9 x 4 = _____   9 x 3 = _____

9 x 5 = _____   9 x 3 = _____   9 x 2 = _____   9 x 4 = _____

9 x 3 = _____   9 x 5 = _____   9 x 2 = _____   9 x 4 = _____

COMMON CORE

Lesson 30:   Partition various wholes precisely into equal parts using a number
             line method.
Date: 11/19/13

5.F.3

9 x 1 = _____   9 x 2 = _____   9 x 3 = _____   9 x 4 = _____

9 x 5 = _____   9 x 6 = _____   9 x 7 = _____   9 x 8 = _____

9 x 9 = _____   9 x 10 = _____   9 x 5 = _____   9 x 6 = _____

9 x 5 = _____   9 x 7 = _____   9 x 5 = _____   9 x 8 = _____

9 x 5 = _____   9 x 9 = _____   9 x 5 = _____   9 x 10 = _____

9 x 6 = _____   9 x 5 = _____   9 x 6 = _____   9 x 7 = _____

9 x 6 = _____   9 x 8 = _____   9 x 6 = _____   9 x 9 = _____

9 x 6 = _____   9 x 7 = _____   9 x 6 = _____   9 x 7 = _____

9 x 8 = _____   9 x 7 = _____   9 x 9 = _____   9 x 7 = _____

9 x 8 = _____   9 x 6 = _____   9 x 8 = _____   9 x 7 = _____

9 x 8 = _____   9 x 9 = _____   9 x 9 = _____   9 x 6 = _____

9 x 9 = _____   9 x 7 = _____   9 x 9 = _____   9 x 8 = _____

9 x 9 = _____   9 x 8 = _____   9 x 6 = _____   9 x 9 = _____

9 x 7 = _____   9 x 9 = _____   9 x 6 = _____   9 x 8 = _____

9 x 9 = _____   9 x 7 = _____   9 x 6 = _____   9 x 8 = _____

COMMON CORE   Lesson 30:   Partition various wholes precisely into equal parts using a number
                            line method.
              Date: 11/19/13

5.F.33

Lesson 30: Partition various wholes precisely into equal parts using a number
line method.

Date: 11/19/13

5.F.34

Name _____   Date _____

Instructions: Write a friendly letter to a friend or family member. Describe step-by-step the experience you had of partitioning a length into equal units simply using a piece of notebook paper and a straight edge. Illustrate the process. Your teacher will give you a lined paper and strip to take home.

Lesson 30:   Partition various wholes precisely into equal parts using a number
                line method.
Date: 11/19/13

5.F.35

Name _____   Date _____

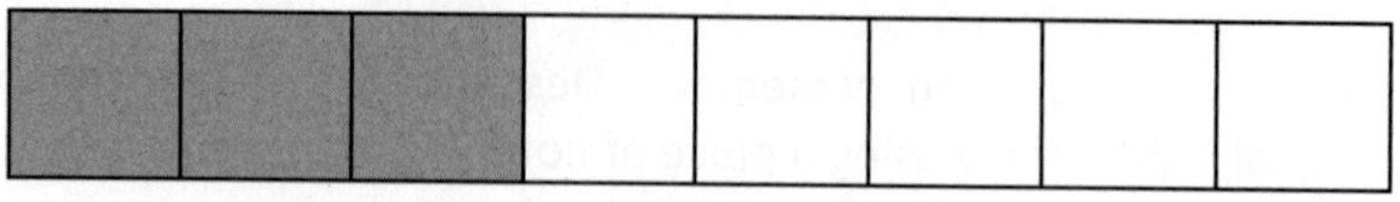

1. Natalie folded 1 whole fraction strip as pictured above.

    a. How many equal parts did she divide the whole into?

    b. Label each equal part with a unit fraction.

    c. Identify the fraction of the strip she shaded.

    d. Identify the fraction of the strip she did not shade.

2. Draw 2 rectangles the same size. Each rectangle represents 1 whole.

    a. Partition each rectangle into 3 equal parts. Shade and label a fraction greater than 1.

    b. Draw a number bond that shows 1 whole rectangle as 3 unit fractions.

3. The bakery had a chocolate cake and a vanilla cake that were exactly the same size. Mr. Chu bought 1 fourth of the chocolate cake. Mrs. Ramirez bought 1 sixth of the vanilla cake. Who bought a larger piece of cake? Explain your answer using words, pictures, and numbers.

4. Natalie explained, "My drawing shows a picture of $\frac{3}{2}$." Kosmo says, "It looks like a picture of $\frac{3}{4}$ to me."

    a. Show and explain how they could both be correct by choosing different wholes. Use words, pictures, and numbers.

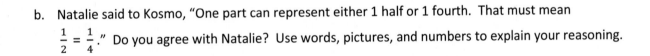

    b. Natalie said to Kosmo, "One part can represent either 1 half or 1 fourth. That must mean $\frac{1}{2} = \frac{1}{4}$." Do you agree with Natalie? Use words, pictures, and numbers to explain your reasoning.

Mid-Module Assessment Task	Topics A–C
Standards Addressed	

Develop understanding of fractions as numbers.

3.NF.1   Understand a fraction 1/b as the quantity formed by 1 part when a whole is partitioned into b equal parts; understand a fraction a/b as the quantity formed by a parts of size 1/b.

3.NF.3   Explain equivalence of fractions in special cases, and compare fractions by reasoning about their size.

     c.   Express whole numbers as fractions, and recognize fractions that are equivalent to whole numbers. *Examples: Express 3 in the form 3 = 3/1; recognize that 6/1 = 6; locate 4/4 and 1 at the same point of a number line.*

     d.   Compare two fractions with the same numerator or the same denominator by reasoning about their size. Recognize that comparisons are valid only when the two fractions refer to the same whole. Record the results of comparisons with the symbols >, =, or <, and justify the conclusions, e.g., by using a visual fraction model.

Reason with shapes and their attributes.

3.G.2   Partition shapes into parts with equal areas. Express the area of each part as a unit fraction of the whole. For example, partition a shape into 4 parts with equal area, and describe the area of each part as 1/4 of the area of the shape.

Evaluating Student Learning Outcomes

A Progression Toward Mastery is provided to describe steps that illuminate the gradually increasing understandings that students develop *on their way to proficiency.* In this chart, this progress is presented from left (Step 1) to right (Step 4). The learning goal for each student is to achieve Step 4 mastery. These steps are meant to help teachers and students identify and celebrate what the student CAN do now and what they need to work on next.

	Module 5:	Fractions as Numbers on the Number Line
	Date:	11/19/13

5.S.3

A Progression Toward Mastery

Assessment Task Item and Standards Assessed	STEP 1 Little evidence of reasoning without a correct answer. (1 Point)	STEP 2 Evidence of some reasoning without a correct answer. (2 Points)	STEP 3 Evidence of some reasoning with a correct answer or evidence of solid reasoning with an incorrect answer. (3 Points)	STEP 4 Evidence of solid reasoning with a correct answer. (4 Points)
1 3.NF.1	The student has one answer correct.	The student has two answers correct.	The student answers Parts (b) through (d) correctly, but answers Part (a) with a fractional answer, or has answered one of the four questions incorrectly or incompletely.	The student correctly: a. Identifies how many parts the whole is divided into, 8. b. Labels each unit fraction as 1/8. c. Identifies the fraction shaded, 3/8. d. Identifies the fraction un-shaded, 5/8.
2 3.NF.3c 3.G.2	The student is unable to answer either question correctly.	The student is not able to shade a fraction greater than 1, but answers Part (b) correctly.	The student answers Part (a) correctly, but does not seem to understand Part (b).	The student correctly: a. Shows two rectangles divided into thirds with a fraction greater than 3/3 shaded. b. Writes a number bond with the whole as 1 or 3/3, and 1/3, 1/3, and 1/3 as the parts.
3 3.NF.3d 3.G.2	The student's work shows no evidence of being able to partition the cakes into fractional units to make sense of the problem.	The student has poorly represented the cakes, making it difficult to compare the fractions. The student incorrectly states that Mr. Ramirez bought the larger piece.	The student draws two equivalent cakes and realizes Mr. Chu has the larger piece, but the explanation is not clear, perhaps poorly labeled, lacking a statement of the solution.	The student clearly: ▪ Explains that Mr. Chu bought the larger piece of cake using words, pictures, and numbers.

Module 5:   Fractions as Numbers on the Number Line
Date: 11/19/13

A Progression Toward Mastery				
4 **3.NF.1** **3.NF.3d** **3.G.2**	The student is not able to recognize or show that he recognizes either fraction in the model.	The student recognizes 3 fourths, but is not able to recognize 3 halves within the picture, or vice versa.	The student is able to recognize 3 fourths and 3 halves within the same picture, which is clear perhaps by markings on the strip, but the explanation lacks clarity.	The student clearly: a. Shows how the picture can be interpreted either as 4 halves with 3 halves shaded, the whole being defined by the middle line of the strip *or* as 3 fourths with the whole being defined by the whole strip. b. Illustrates that the whole units do not match in the comparison Natalie makes.

Name __Gina_____   Date _____

$\frac{1}{8}$	$\frac{1}{8}$	$\frac{1}{8}$	$\frac{1}{8}$	$\frac{1}{8}$	$\frac{1}{8}$	$\frac{1}{8}$	$\frac{1}{8}$

1. Natalie folded 1 whole fraction strip as pictured above.

   a. How many equal parts did she divide the whole into?   8 equal parts

   b. Label each equal part with a unit fraction.

   c. Identify the fraction of the strip she shaded. $\frac{3}{8}$

   d. Identify the fraction of the strip she did not shade. $\frac{5}{8}$

2. Draw 2 rectangles the same size. Each rectangle represents 1 whole.

   a. Partition each rectangle into 3 equal parts. Shade and label a fraction greater than 1.

   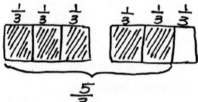

   b. Draw a number bond that shows 1 whole rectangle as 3 unit fractions.

   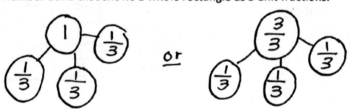

3. The bakery had a chocolate and a vanilla cake that were exactly the same size. Mr. Chu bought 1 fourth of the chocolate cake. Mrs. Ramirez bought 1 sixth of the vanilla cake. Who bought a larger piece of cake? Explain your answer using words, pictures, and numbers.

Mr. Chu bought a larger piece of cake because $\frac{1}{4} > \frac{1}{6}$. 1 fourth has less parts so each piece is bigger.

4. Natalie explained, "My drawing shows a picture of $\frac{3}{2}$." Kosmo says, "It looks like a picture of $\frac{3}{4}$ to me."

    a. Show and explain how they could both be correct by choosing different wholes. Use words, pictures, and numbers.

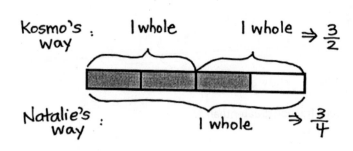

They can both be right. It depends on the whole, and they don't know what it is.

    b. Natalie said to Kosmo, "One part can represent either 1 half or 1 fourth. That must mean $\frac{1}{2} = \frac{1}{4}$." Do you agree with Natalie? Use words, pictures, and numbers to explain your reasoning.

Natalie is wrong because the wholes are not the same size. The wholes have to be the same size to compare fractions.

Kosmo's whole : | $\frac{1}{2}$ | $\frac{1}{2}$ |

Natalie's whole : | $\frac{1}{4}$ | $\frac{1}{4}$ | $\frac{1}{4}$ | $\frac{1}{4}$ |

Name _____   Date _____

1. Jerry put 7 equally spaced hooks on a straight wire so students could hang up their coats. The whole length is from the first hook to the last hook.

    a. On the illustration below, label the fraction of the wire's length where each hook is located.

    b. At what fraction is Betsy's coat if she hangs it at the halfway point?

    c. Write a fraction that is equivalent to your answer for (b).

2. Jerry used the diagram below to show his son how to find a fraction equal to $\frac{2}{3}$. Explain what Jerry might have said and done using words, pictures, and numbers.

3. Jerry and his son have the exact same granola bars. Jerry has eaten $\frac{3}{6}$ of his granola bar. His son has eaten $\frac{3}{8}$ of his. Who has eaten more? Explain your answer using words, pictures, and numbers.

4. Jerry has a fruit roll that is 4 feet long.

    a. Label the number line to show how Jerry might cut his fruit roll into pieces $\frac{1}{3}$ foot in length. Label every fraction on the number line, including renaming the wholes.

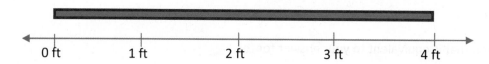

    b. Jerry cut his fruit roll into pieces that are $\frac{1}{3}$ feet in length. Jerry and his 2 sons each eat one piece. What fraction of the whole fruit roll is eaten? Draw and partition a tape diagram. Also explain using words or numbers.

    c. One of Jerry's sons cut his third of a fruit roll into 2 equal parts. His son says that 1 third is the same as 2 sixths. Do you agree? Why or why not? Use pictures, words, and numbers to explain your answer.

End-of-Module Assessment Task	Topics A–F
Standards Addressed	

Develop understanding of fractions as numbers.

3.NF.1   Understand a fraction $1/b$ as the quantity formed by 1 part when a whole is partitioned into b equal parts; understand a fraction a/b as the quantity formed by a parts of size $1/b$.

3.NF.2   Understand a fraction as a number on the number line; represent fractions on a number line diagram.

     a.   Represent a fraction $1/b$ on a number line diagram by defining the interval from 0 to 1 as the whole and partitioning it into b equal parts. Recognize that each part has size $1/b$ and that the endpoint of the part based at 0 locates the number $1/b$ on the number line.

     b.   Represent a fraction a/b on a number line diagram by marking off a lengths $1/b$ from 0. Recognize that the resulting interval has size a/b and that its endpoint locates the number a/b on the number line.

3.NF.3   Explain equivalence of fractions in special cases, and compare fractions by reasoning about their size.

     a.   Understand two fractions as equivalent (equal) if they are the same size, or the same point on a number line.

     b.   Recognize and generate simple equivalent fractions, e.g., 1/2 = 2/4, 4/6 = 2/3). Explain why the fractions are equivalent, e.g., by using a visual fraction model.

     c   Express whole numbers as fractions, and recognize fractions that are equivalent to whole numbers. *Examples: Express 3 in the form 3 = 3/1; recognize that 6/1 = 6; locate4/4 and 1 at the same point of a number line.*

     d   Compare two fractions with the same numerator or the same denominator by reasoning about their size. Recognize that comparisons are valid only when the two fractions refer to the same whole. Record the results of comparisons with the symbols >, =, or <, and justify the conclusions, e.g., by using a visual fraction model.

Reason with shapes and their attributes.

3.G.2   Partition shapes into parts with equal areas. Express the area of each part as a unit fraction of the whole. For example, partition a shape into 4 parts with equal area, and describe the area of each part as 1/4 of the area of the shape.

Evaluating Student Learning Outcomes

A Progression Toward Mastery is provided to describe steps that illuminate the gradually increasing understandings that students develop *on their way to proficiency*. In this chart, this progress is presented from left (Step 1) to right (Step 4). The learning goal for each student is to achieve Step 4 mastery. These steps are meant to help teachers and students identify and celebrate what the student CAN do now and what they need to work on next.

A Progression Toward Mastery				
Assessment Task Item and Standards Assessed	STEP 1 Little evidence of reasoning without a correct answer. (1 Point)	STEP 2 Evidence of some reasoning without a correct answer. (2 Points)	STEP 3 Evidence of some reasoning with a correct answer or evidence of solid reasoning with an incorrect answer. (3 Points)	STEP 4 Evidence of solid reasoning with a correct answer. (4 Points)
1 3.NF.2a 3.NF.3a	The student is unable to label the number line.	The student labels the number line but thinks 2 sixths is 1/2 because of the 2 in the numerator. Clear flaws in understanding are visible.	The student shows good reasoning and makes one small mistake such as failing to correctly label 0 sixths or failing to identify the fraction equal to 1/2.	The student correctly: ▪ Labels the number line with sixths. ▪ Identifies 3/6 as the halfway point for Betsy's coat. ▪ Writes any fraction equivalent to 3/6, such as 1/2.
2 3.NF.3b 3.G.2 3.NF.1	The student does not demonstrate understanding.	The student may partition the strip correctly, but gives no clear explanation.	The student's explanation lacks clarity, but the drawing shows understanding. The strip is labeled.	The student explains or shows both: ▪ Jerry would make smaller equal parts. ▪ A fraction equal to 2/3, such as 4/6, 6/9, or 8/12.

A Progression Toward Mastery

3 **3.NF.3d** **3.NF.1**	The student does not demonstrate understanding of the meaning of the question and produces nonsensical work.	The student may say that the son has eaten more, but does show some understanding. This is possibly evidenced by two fraction strips correctly partitioned but perhaps not the same size.	The student shows that Jerry has eaten more and compares 3/8 to 3/10 correctly; the explanation includes some reasoning.	The student clearly explains: • Jerry has eaten more of his granola bar. • 3/6 > 3/8. • 3/6 is greater than 3/8 because the units are larger.
4 **3.NF.2a, b** **3.NF.3a, b, c, d** **3.NF.1**	The student does not grasp what is asked and does not produce meaningful work.	The student completes part of the problem correctly, but may fail to draw accurate models or explain reasoning.	The student completes Parts (a), (b), and (c) correctly; the explanation includes some reasoning.	The student clearly: • Shows all the fractions from 0 thirds up to 12 thirds numerically. • Explains 1 whole or 3/3 of the roll was eaten with an accurate tape diagram and draws a number line to explain that 1/3 is equal to 2/6.

Module 5:   Fractions as Numbers on the Number Line
Date: 11/19/13

5.S.12

Name __Gina__   Date _____

1. Jerry put 7 equally spaced hooks on a straight wire so students could hang up their coats. The whole length is from the first hook to the last hook.

   a. On the illustration below, label the fraction of the wire's length where each hook is located.

   $$\frac{0}{6} \qquad \frac{1}{6} \qquad \frac{2}{6} \qquad \frac{3}{6} \qquad \frac{4}{6} \qquad \frac{5}{6} \qquad \frac{6}{6}$$

   b. At what fraction is Betsy's coat if she hangs it at the halfway point? $\frac{3}{6}$

   c. Write a fraction that is equivalent to your answer for 'b.' $\frac{1}{2}$

2. Jerry used the diagram below to show his son how to find a fraction equal to $\frac{2}{3}$. Explain what Jerry might have said and done using words, pictures, and numbers.

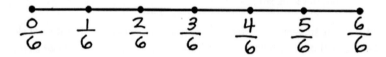

$$\frac{2}{3} = \frac{4}{6}$$

I made $\frac{1}{3}$ into 2 smaller equal parts. I did that 2 more times. So then it wasn't just thirds anymore, it was sixths too!

3. Jerry and his son have the exact same granola bars. Jerry has eaten $\frac{3}{6}$ of his granola bar. His son has eaten $\frac{3}{8}$ of his. Who has eaten more? Explain your answer using words, pictures, and numbers.

Jerry $\frac{3}{6}$

Son $\frac{3}{8}$

$\frac{3}{6} > \frac{3}{8}$

Jerry has eaten more because his pieces are bigger than his son's pieces.

4. Jerry has a fruit roll that is 4 feet long.

   a. Label the number line to show how Jerry might cut his fruit roll into pieces $\frac{1}{3}$ foot in length. Label every fraction on the number line, including renaming the wholes.

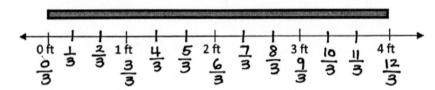

   b. Jerry cut his fruit roll into pieces that are $\frac{1}{3}$ foot in length. Jerry and his 2 sons each eat one piece. What fraction of the whole fruit roll is eaten? Draw and partition a tape diagram. Also explain using words or numbers.

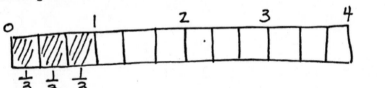

$\frac{3}{3}$ are eaten because 3 people ate $\frac{1}{3}$ each.

   c. One of Jerry's sons cut his third of a fruit roll into 2 equal parts. His son says that 1 third is the same as 2 sixths. Do you agree? Why or why not? Use pictures, words, and numbers to explain your answer.

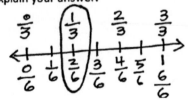

Yes, I agree. When I partition the thirds in half, it makes sixths. 2 sixths and 1 third are the same size.